RHOSNEIGR

~then & now~
series

volume two

The Rhosneigr Romanticist.

W.D.Owen and the stories of Elin Cadwaladr & Madam Wen

Compiled & Edited by
T.T.M. Hale

with

Translations from Welsh by
J.W. Hyatt

Copyright© 2009 T.T.M. Hale
All Rights Reserved. No part of this publication may be reproduced, stored in a retrieval system or utilised in any form or by any means, electronic or mechanical, including photocopying, recording, web publishing, or scanning, without the prior written permission from the copyright owner.

13579108642

Published by
www.rhosneigrpublishing.co.uk
2 Roman Ridge Rd.
Sheffield, S9 1XG

ISBN 978-0-9562962-0-7

Introduction

When I was a youngster in the 1960s, playing on the beach and among the sand dunes of Rhosneigr, I heard stories about 'Madam Wen' and the 'ghostly white horse' she rode. The tales of Smugglers and her fearful Band of Robbers were good reasons not to be out too late at night, and the thought of maybe one day finding her Treasure Cave in the rocks, was exciting stuff. It was a great disappointment to me to discover that the famous book about her exploits was only available in Welsh – a language that I didn't speak.

In my early thirties, as I began to take an interest in Local History and to accumulate a collection of Rhosneigr picture postcards and ephemera, I discovered more about the village and its connections for my first book. It became something of a revelation to realise that Madam Wen's author, William David Owen, actually lived in the village for many years, and through a cruel twist of fate died here, barely a fortnight after his novel was published in book form.

Researching and compiling this volume has been immensely challenging and frustrating at times. Often repeated 'facts' have sometimes proved completely unverifiable and on occasions, tracking down Owen and his family connections has proved as elusive and ethereal as 'Madam Wen' herself.

There have been a few articles written about W.D.Owen in the past, almost all of them in Welsh and justifiably so. However, that still leaves us non Welsh speakers in almost complete ignorance of one of Anglesey's unassuming but fascinating characters and I offer this book as a tribute to his work and to the interesting life and times of the period.

Mae braidd yn mynd yn groes i'r bwriad i ddarparu cyfieithiadau Cymraeg o rannau allweddol o'r llyfr hwn; wedi'r cwbl 'rydych chi'r Cymry Cymraeg yn ddigon ffodus i fedru darllen y fersiynau gwreiddiol yn llawn, petasech chi am wneud hynny. Gobeithiaf y byddwch yn fy maddau am hyn ac yn deall fy nymuniad i ddod â rhan o chwedloniaeth a llenyddiaeth Cymru o fewn gafael Saeson sydd ddim yn siarad Cymraeg.

T.T.M.Hale
September 2009

Acknowledgements

It would have been impossible to research & compile this book without the interest, skill & assistance of Jenni Wyn Hyatt, whose ability to read & translate a myriad of Welsh documents has been invaluable.

Over the course of several years research, many people have contributed to my search for information about W.D.Owen and his connections. All these sources have been recognised under the relevant references at the back of the book. I am grateful to you all for your help, and for permission to quote extracts from publications.

In particular though, I would like to thank the following for their continuing encouragement and assistance.

Anne Venables, Gaynor Nice & Amanda Sweet at Llangefni Archives who have been unfailingly supportive. Members of the Owen family including Haulwen Morgan, John Owen, Ida Owen, and Robert Owen. Fellow students of Local History including Vaughan Evans, Eflyn Owen-Jones, Tomos Roberts, Maldwyn Thomas, Dafydd Wyn Williams and William Williams. Also Cliff Williams, Janet Owen, Hugh Garnsworthy and Sue Baxter. And the assistance of Dwynwen Powell and Richard Williams of Bryngwran who have usually been able to answer most of my many questions over the last eighteen months.

Finally not forgetting my Rhosneigr stalwarts including Pauline Gasson, Dilys Moore, Charles (Tiffy) Owen, Sara Richards and Charles Stephenson, whose total memory would stretch back to the18th Century if it could be combined !

"He wrote a book in my spare time."
With special thanks to my wife, Jane, for indulging me.

Contents

Editorial Conventions

Throughout the text and translations, the following conventions have been adopted.

[ ] editor's alterations or notes in square brackets to improve clarity or meaning.

[name] In order to aid the flow of the narrative, Welsh names (personal, house or place) have only been translated into English, the first time they occur. It is useful to understand their meaning, but they are names, and are rarely critical to the story.

Italics or *handwriting* - translated verbatim from the Welsh text, or quoted verbatim from the English text, as may be appropriate. Italics have also been used to indicate proper names, and where relevant, English translations of Welsh names.

" " (inverted commas) have been used within the text as normal, to indicate speech, but are not verbatim in the translations unless also in italics.

(sic) signifying that the text is as originally written, but is recognised as being grammatically or orthographically incorrect.

*1a (asterisk with a number and/or letter), indicates a short reference at the end of the current section or chapter, [In a tinted panel.]

{101} blue numbers or letters {V1} in curly brackets or 'braces' indicate that a reference exists in the separate section at the back of the book.

WD, WDO, Owen, William etc have all been used to refer to the subject of this work – William David Owen – depending on the context of each sentence.

William David Owen

Biography

William David Owen, 1874 - 1925

1.0 W D Owen, The Rhosneigr Romanticist

William David Owen was born William Owen, on 21st October 1874, in 'Ty Franan', Bodedern, Anglesey, the only son of William Owen, a farmer and driver of thrashing engines, and his wife, Jane. His home, a cottage on the country lanes just outside Bryngwran, was within a stone's throw of the district of the lakes, about which he wrote in his only published novel - *Madam Wen*.

He had two older sisters, Elinor (also known as Ellen), born in 1867, and Sarah, born in 1871. It is thought that he probably 'adopted' the Christian name of his maternal grandfather, David Roberts, later in life - the adoption of a middle name being common practice amongst Welshmen in the early years of the twentieth century. {101}

His father died in 1884 when William was only ten and his mother and sister, Sarah, began to make their living as dressmakers. Ellen went into service from her middle teens, managing to secure employment with the wealthy Verney family at their holiday house in Rhoscolyn, before moving to London to take up a position as kitchen maid to Florence Nightingale – part of the Verney's extended family).

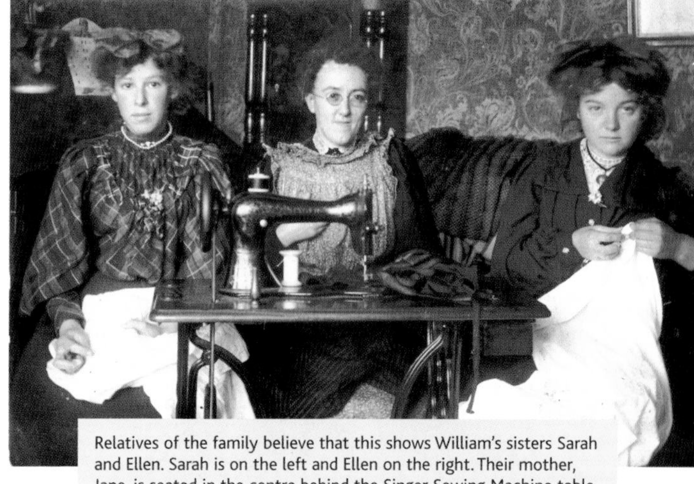

Relatives of the family believe that this shows William's sisters Sarah and Ellen. Sarah is on the left and Ellen on the right. Their mother, Jane, is seated in the centre behind the Singer Sewing Machine table. This early photo is believed to date from the mid-1880s.

William attended the Board School in Bryngwran Village where he later became a pupil teacher. He then also served as a pupil teacher under Lewis D. Jones, (who was well-known as the President of the National Eisteddfod), in the Garth, Bangor, before training at Bangor Normal College in 1894 - 95 to become a Science teacher. He was one of only 19 students who gained a first-class teaching certificate and was appointed to his first post at Joy's Green Board School, in the district of Lydbrook, Gloucestershire.

In Feb 1898, at the age of twenty-four, Owen left Joy's Green for Clay Lane National School, just south of Chesterfield, Derbyshire. Owen spent twelve years in the area, mainly teaching at Clay Cross Science School, part of the Clay Lane United District School Board.

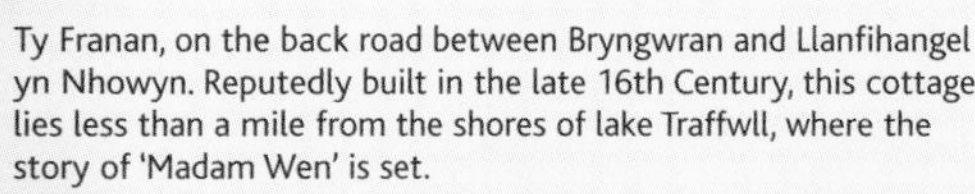

Ty Franan, on the back road between Bryngwran and Llanfihangel yn Nhowyn. Reputedly built in the late 16th Century, this cottage lies less than a mile from the shores of lake Traffwll, where the story of 'Madam Wen' is set.

Part of the Clay Lane United District Schools complex. Since the school closed in 2009 (transferring to the new Sharley Park Community Primary School) most of these buildings have remained empty behind security fencing, awaiting a new use.

According to Owen's obituary in Y Cloriannydd *(The Evaluator)*, it was at Clay Cross school where he met a fellow teacher, Edith Gwendolen Empsall, who was to become his wife and they were married on August 9th 1904 in the English Presbyterian Church in Newry Street, Holyhead.

W. D. Owen continued to teach for some time after their marriage and he and Gwen lived in a house in Pilsley, just south of Clay Cross. Owen gradually moved away from teaching into school administration, and he also began to take an interest in the Law.

He was admitted to the legal institution of the Middle Temple as an undergraduate of London University on 11th November 1905, and called to the bar on 17th November 1909. Sometime around that date William and Gwen moved to Muswell Hill, the Middlesex village North of London.

After graduation, the legal records indicate that Owen practised on the Chester and North Wales circuit, although detailed information about which chambers he was with and what cases he worked on have proved elusive. At some point before 1914, Owen also found time to write at least two long stories which were serialised in the Welsh newspaper 'Y Genedl Gymreig' *(The Welsh Nation)*. These were 'Strike a Chord and Change Key' (later retitled Elin Cadwaladr) and the better known 'Madam Wen' (White Lady).

W D Owen was said not to have a strong constitution, and it was probably in the hope of improving his health that he

The Presbyterian Chapel on Newry St. Holyhead became the English Presbyterian Church at around the turn of the 20th century, as a means of distinguishing it from Welsh Presbyterian Churches which were a lot 'stronger' than the English Churches. The Welsh Calvinistic Methodist Church was renamed the Welsh Presbyterian Church in 1920.

returned with his wife to Anglesey, at around the time of the First World War. They settled in Rhosneigr - by this time a popular and thriving holiday village. His mother and sisters were now living in 'Bronant', on the High Street, while he and Gwen first made their home at 'Seaforth' on Warren Road and some time later moved to 'Ashton' at 5 Station Road.

'Seaforth' on the far right of this photograph, is on Warren Road and has spectacular views over the sand dunes and the Crigyll estuary towards Crigyll and Cymyran beaches, Tywyn Trewan common and the sea.

Station Road, Rhosneigr.

This postcard, dating from about 1910, shows 'Ashton' and the other houses on Station Road, Morristown, Rhosneigr. 'Ashton' (No.5) was renamed 'Rhysann' – it is thought sometime during the 1960s - and was last sold in 2002. It no longer appears to bear a name.

Bronant (Brook Land) was built in c1903 by Thomas Rowlands on land purchased from Owen G. Owen in 1901, and was originally part of a farm called Tyn y Pant (Smallholding in the Hollow). It is a semi-detached property with its neighbour 'Ambleside'. The Owen sisters and their mother, Jane were probably tenants in the house for several years before they bought it in 1920 after several years of occupation by William and Ellen Roberts and prior to them, the alliteratively named Mr Pickering Pick. Bronant is the second house on the right in the picture.

Owen's obituary in Y Cloriannydd notes that he was, for a time, in charge of the "Soldiers' Pensions Office" in Llangefni – an office set up to administrate war pensions (see panel 1.1 opposite) - and had also set himself up in business as a solicitor in Rhosneigr and Llangefni *a. He was a Calvinistic Methodist and worshipped at Paran Chapel, Rhosneigr *b, and was a member of Rhosneigr Golf Club *c and of the Freemasons, where he attended the regular monthly meetings of the Cefni Lodge in Llangefni. (see panel 1.2 opposite)

He soon became well-known in public circles in Rhosneigr. The village had started promoting itself as a holiday resort and was already known, (perhaps more amongst the locals than the visitors), for the Madam Wen legend. She was described, in an early guidebook for visitors, as "The Famous Lady Robin Hood of North Wales" {102} and it has even been suggested (without any proof) that part of Owen's intention in writing the novel was to 'help put Rhosneigr on the map'.

During their time in Rhosneigr, Gwen gradually became unwell and, as her health deteriorated, she was looked after by her husband's mother and sisters in 'Bronant', which by this time had been bought by Ellen and Sarah who continued to work as dressmakers, and also regularly let out the house to summer visitors in the burgeoning resort of Rhosneigr.

Owen's diary for 1925 survives (see section 1.8) and reveals some interesting details about what became the last year of his life. For some reason – probably due to her illness – he was living apart from Gwen, and he notes that when they met – usually once or twice a week – he gave her money (probably housekeeping money). Whilst she stayed in 'Bronant', he usually spent the evenings at 'Morlais' No.7 Beach Rd, the home of Henry Jones the builder, who also took in lodgers. {103}

His own health deteriorated during the year, and whilst he was able to maintain a normal workload until the autumn, succesfully continuing to build up his client base, he writes very tellingly on 30th September - "a lovely day and I feel rotten".

Alongside his legal work, he also continued to work on adapting the original serialised version of Madam Wen for publication as a novel and was also in the process of having a new house built by Henry Jones. From the available evidence, this appears to be 'Laneton' on Sandy Lane. {104}

Soldiers Pension Office

Owen's Obituary indicated that he looked after the "Soldier's Pension Office"In Llangefni, but an office under that title has proved impossible to find. His cryptic entry under the Cefni Masonic Lodge – 'Sec War Pensions Cll' (Secretary of the War Pensions Council) has however given a vital clue.

"War Pensions Committees were first established in 1921, in the wake of World War I, to assist the Ministry of Pensions. Members undertook the adjudication and administration of grants to disabled ex-servicemen, the organisation of care for Widows and neglected children, and the monitoring of Ministry of Pensions administration of the War Disablement Pensions scheme." {105}

It is most likely therefore that WD was the Secretary of the local War Pensions Committee, set up under the 1916 Ministry of Pensions Act, (although even under this title, no records have survived through to the archives).

The Committees are still operating and are independent of the Ministry of Defence Service and the Service Personnel and Veterans Agency.

[Panel 1.1]

Cefni Masonic Lodge

Owen was admitted to the Cefni Lodge No. 4086 on the 3rd December 1920, at which time his recorded name on the Lodge entry book was William David Owen – the first written record of him starting to use the name 'David'.

The fact that he joined at the level of initiate, 'passing' in February 1921 and 'raising' in March indicates that he had not been a Mason before he returned to Anglesey.

His address is noted as 'Ashton', Rhosneigr and his profession at the time of entry was recorded as 'Barrister. Sec. War Pensions Cll.'

Owen was a member of the Lodge until his death, but unfortunately did not live long enough to occupy the chair of the lodge as 'Worshipful Master'.

[Panel 1.2]

The first houses on Beach Road were built in 1905. This partial section from a later postcard provides an excellent view of Henry Jones's workshop and land, where the 'Norman Court' houses and those on Glan y Mor road now stand.

His condition continued to worsen and it was in 'Bronant', his sisters' house, that Owen was nursed during his final days, and where he died, from Pulmonary Tuberculosis, on 4th November 1925. He was just fifty-one years old, and it was particularly ironic that tuberculosis, with which he had dealt in such depth, in his novel *Elin Cadwaladr,* would be the cause of his own death.

Madam Wen - dedicated to his wife, Gwen - was published in book form shortly before he died. His wife, whose health had caused him so much concern during their marriage, outlived him by thirty-seven years, dying in Llangefni Hospital on 16th November 1962, aged 86. They are buried together in the chapel graveyard at Jerusalem Chapel, Upper Gwalchmai. Also buried with them is W D Owen's sister, Ellen, who died in 1954.

Jerusalem Calvinistic Methodist Chapel, Upper Gwalchmai, built in 1849, is the second chapel to be built on the site (the first was built in 1780). It was extensively remodelled in 1925 in a simple Renaissance style, and is now listed grade II.

His father and mother (who survived him by two years), are also buried in Upper Gwalchmai chapel graveyard. However, the last resting place of his sister Sarah, who died in 1960, has proved a little more elusive.

W. D. Owen and Gwen did not have children and neither of his sisters married but a number of cousins attended his funeral. *d

It is a matter of record that Owen left an estate worth £891, 16 shillings and 8 pence to his widow, Gwen. The present-day value of this would be in the region of £162,000. {106}

According to his obituary in Y Cloriannydd, he had read many English classics and, in addition to his two novels, had written Welsh sonnets. He is said to have enjoyed studying the

REMEMBERING FONDLY
WILLIAM DAVID OWEN
SOLICITOR, RHOSNEIGR
BORN OCTOBER 21ST 1874
DIED NOVEMBER 4TH 1925
AUTHOR OF THE ROMANCE "MADAM WEN"
ALSO
EDITH GWENDOLINE OWEN
WIFE OF THE ABOVE
WHO DIED NOVEMBER 16TH 1962
AGED 86 YEARS
ALSO
ELLENOR OWEN
BRONANT, RHOSNEIGR
DIED JANUARY 6TH 1954
AGED 86 YEARS

characteristics of the Welsh language, was noted for his honesty and hated every form of falseness and insincerity.

Unfortunately, the contemporary obituary gives no clue as to where or when or how many of these sonnets may have been published, and despite considerable investigation, none of these have as yet come to light. Although unproven, it is likely that they were published in the same newspaper which published his novels in serial form.

In fact only one other piece of Owen's writing has surfaced during the research for this book – a short undated "paper sketch" on "Sports and their Advantages" which is shown in **panel 1.3** alongside (originally written in Welsh).

William David Owen had a varied career – schoolteacher, barrister, solicitor and author. He travelled from the backwaters of Anglesey, to rural parishes in Gloucestershire and Derbyshire, thence to study in London and back home again to Rhosneigr. His writings reveal a man of principle with an appreciation of religion and politics – and the humour within them both - at a period when great changes in society were taking place. His novels were essentially simple moral historical romances set partly in legend and partly in reality and even though here presented in abridged format, they reveal him to be a true Romanticist at heart.

The following ten sections explore certain aspects of Owen's life and experiences in more detail.

*a The record book of the Clerk to Anglesey Council indicates that Owen had a new office built in Rhosneigr in June 1923, but its location is not recorded. See also Section 1.6

*b Paran Chapel records have been examined in detail and do not mention WD by name at all, although his mother Jane and sisters Ellen and Sarah are mentioned. It is only by virtue of a note in Hugh Owen's book on the 'History of Calvinistic Methodism in Anglesey' that we can be sure of his membership of Paran. On P.178 he writes : "The same year that R.E.Jones [one of the Deacons] died, another prominent member of this church passed away - W.D.Owen, solicitor, and author of the popular novel "Madam Wen". See bibliography.

*c Unfortunately, although Owen's diary for 1925 records several instances of him playing the game, no written records of the Anglesey Golf Club survive from that date.

*d A report of the funeral is shown after his obituary, in section 1.9

Sports and their Advantages by W.D.Owen

(Foreword) Public sports for young people have become so common that they have attracted the attention of the country. Articles in which the subject is discussed are seen on a daily basis in newspapers and magazines: some praising and others condemning. But despite the condemnation, the games go on, gaining ground every day. What I aim to do in a few words is to show the advantages of sports, if used correctly, for young people.

The first advantage. All young things develop through exercise. Living, as we do, in the country, we are familiar with watching young creatures like foals and lambs in the fields. We have seen a little foal running around a field for no reason other than to give work to his legs. Some instinct in the foal tells him that is how he will grow and become strong. We have seen a group of lambs jumping to and from the top of a bank for half an hour without tiring. It is the desire for exercise which makes them behave thus. It is the same instinct which makes puppies and kittens so playful. Every young thing is full of the same desire, the desire to exercise its body. So it is with children and young people. Instinct calls for them to have enough play of the type which is likely to develop their limbs and give their bodies suitable exercise. Thus they become stronger and grow fit and healthy to their full size.

The second advantage. Suitable sports teach obedience and co-operation, two virtues which are of the greatest importance in life. Take football as an example. The game calls for the obedience of every team member to the captain. If there is a man on the field who is not ready to give his leader perfect obedience at all times, he will do more harm than good to his companions. And if there is a player who is selfish and insists on having his own way, refusing to co-operate, everyone on the field would prefer to be without his company. The selfish man is not welcome in sport and the sportsman gradually learns that it is through obedience and co-operation that he will win the respect and admiration of his companions. In time this will become a part of his nature and will come to the fore in every circle in which he moves – in his home, in school, with his work, in society, in every part of every circumstance. In an easy and pleasurable way he learns one of the biggest lessons of life.

The third advantage. The playing field is one of the best places in the world to discipline a man and make him genial of temper. There is no room in sport for someone short and rough of temper. The player has to endure many minor trials and he often has to suffer a little. But he is expected to smile through it all and keep his temper. If a man shows a petulant, impatient spirit, and if he is thin-skinned, he is condemned by everyone on the field, and he quickly learns that it does not pay to scowl. One must be genial and affable through everything on the playing-field, or stay away.

In that way also the young are disciplined in another virtue, a virtue which is highly valued in life. Who is more acceptable than the cheerful, even-tempered man, wherever he goes? He will be warmly welcomed everywhere and will get the best that his fellow-men have to give. But who has a nastier face than the man of surly, unpleasant temper, the man whose companions have to take great care not to anger? No-one wants the company of such a person and he will never be elevated to a position of honour by his fellow-men.

There are various other virtues which are taught on playing fields, the value of which can be shown in a man's character. One is gentlemanly conduct. It is true that this is not as evident in some sporting circles as it ought to be. But things are improving in this direction also. And certainly the tendency of proper sport is to nurture gentlemanliness and solicitude for the feelings of others, a virtue which, before long, will become much more evident and common than it is today.

The conclusion is that sports have a place in developing and nurturing the body and character of a young person and everyone who takes an interest in young people should support games. If there are, at present, weaknesses and failings, it is our place to rout out such weaknesses and failings rather than condemning games. Sports are beneficial, indeed, they are essential, but the things which bring them into disrepute are things which should be fought against in this sphere as in all other spheres. Our efforts should be directed at cleaning and purifying all sport and we should not make the mistake of condemning sport per se: because it has its part in the life of every young person.

[Panel 1.3]

1.1 *At School in Bryngwran*

A D M I S S I O N

The Entries in these Columns should be copied from the "Child's School Book," which, ... admission...is to be given to the Teacher, who will keep it, &c.".......

Admission Number.	Date of Admission and Deposit of "Child's School Book."			NAME OF CHILD.		RESIDING AT	WAS BORN				
	Day	Of (M'th.)	18 (Y'r.)	Surname.	Christian.	Enter Number of the House and Street (if any.)	At (Place.)	On the (Day)	Of (M'th.)	18 (Y'r.)	As Certified by the Registrar of the District of
181	7	June	80	Williams	Jane	Glimbŵch	Glimbwch	20	2	72	
182	"	"	"	Williams	Eliza	"	"	20	7	73	
183	8	"	"	Jones	Robert	Ty'n Gate	Ty'n Gate	27	7	72	
184	5	July	80	Thomas	Grace	Refail Ceirchiog	Refail Ceirch.	23	1	72	
185	5	"	"	Thomas	John	" "	"	20	4	74	
186	3	Aug	"	Hughes	Solomon	Bôth Bach	Bwth Bach	8	1	73	
187	14	Sept	"	Owen	William /	Ty Frannan	Ty Franan	21	May	74	
188	21	"	"	Hughes	Jane	Tai'r Cae	Tai'r Cae	21	4	76	

Section from the Admission Register showing William Owen entering the school on 14th September 1880. Note also that his date of birth has been entered as 21st May 1874, (it should have been entered as October).

Postcard showing Bryngwran High Street c.1905.

The Old Schoolroom, Bryngwran

William Owen started school on 14th September 1880 at the age of six. Like all schools, the Head-Master of Bryngwran Board School (Thomas Pritchard in 1880) was obliged to keep a school log book, for recording all significant matters, and fortunately, the log books for the period do survive, although not entirely intact.

Recorded events from his school days show little mention of his name – which is good, as most of the names which are mentioned are in respect of 'naughty boys' - from which we can conclude that Owen managed to keep out of trouble for much of the time.

There is only one mention of his name as follows :

January 4th 1882 (aged 8)

"Two cases of scarlet fever in the neighbourhood - both of them being among school children. One of them - William Owen - being seriously ill, through his having contracted a cold while convalescent. The other - Thomas Davies Jones - gets on well."

This small village school, (where the Head Master and one assistant teacher looked after between 80 and 100 children) suffered from many closures. This was not untypical of rural village schools, where the staff were few and the pupils were often kept away by their parents if something 'more important' was going on. In Bryngwran's case, recorded closures for half or full days included the following reasons:

Helping in the corn harvest.

Gleaning for the poor.

An 'excursion' to the seashore with Salem Sunday school.

Gathering blackberries and helping in the corn harvest.

The weeding season [is] in full swing.

Thanksgiving meeting for the harvest.

A heavy fall of snow.

Oddfellows anniversary with Procession and Cycle Races.

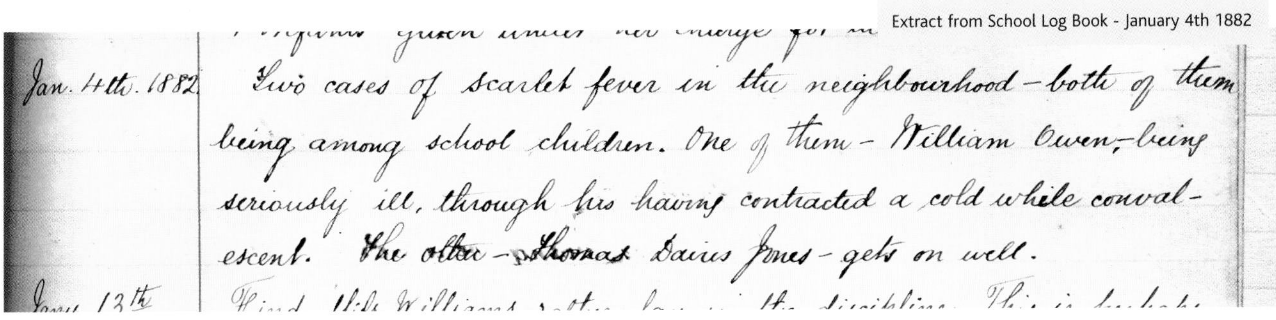

Jan. 4th. 1882 Two cases of scarlet fever in the neighbourhood – both of them being among school children. One of them – William Owen – being seriously ill, through his having contracted a cold while conval-escent. The other – Thomas Davies Jones – gets on well.

Extract from School Log Book - January 4th 1882

Measles (sometimes leading to the death of the pupil and the children also attending their funeral).

Preaching meeting in Hebron Chapel.

Gone to see a vessel which foundered on the coast last week.

A large 'fair' in Bodedern.

At home to weed the Turnips.

A large agricultural show held at Llangefni.

To put down the potatoes.

Stormy weather.

Chapel Excursions to South Stack, Holyhead & Menai Bridge.

And even when the school did not close, the Head master noted on many occasions that the school was 'weakly attended' when the Calvinistic Methodists were holding their monthly meetings, or when Measles or Scarlet fever or some other childhood disease was active.

Bryngwran School Class photo c.1900

At Easter, the custom of 'Clapping Week' was prevalent in the rural areas of Anglesey and North Wales, and was yet another reason for having to close the school. The tradition involved children visiting neighbouring homes and farms, chanting a traditional rhyme and "Clapping for Eggs" – often with a wooden egg-clapper. The collected eggs - sometimes many dozens or more - were taken home and for a time, displayed on each family's dresser.

The rhymes varied slightly from district to district, but went along the lines of :

"clap clap gofyn wy
I hogia' bach ar y plwy"

(clap clap ask for an egg,
for little children on the parish.)

[Interestingly, the custom, (which had died out by the 1960s), has recently been revived on Anglesey in the Beaumaris area.]

And in addition to the bad weather closures, in December -

"Many of the poorer children are absent this week as it is the custom here for the parents to go round the farms asking alms for Christmas".

Parents frequently got into trouble with 'the magistrates' for not sending their children to school regularly, but it was not apparent that this had any significant long term effect.

Owen as Pupil Teacher

Children would normally have left school at the ages of around thirteen or fourteen but it is considered likely that Owen was encouraged to stay on by the Head Master, who recognised a talented individual amongst his pupils.

The first mention of Owen as a pupil teacher (which the Head Master abbeviated to P.T.) was the Government report on June 22nd 1889 when he was fifteen years old :-

Extract from School Log Book - June 22nd 1889

176

1889.

Government Report.

Dated —— June 22 nd. 1889.

"The failures in the Writing of the third and sixth standards, and Arithmetic of the third, fourth, fifth, and sixth standards are very numerous, though the aggregate results in the elementary subjects are fair. I regret that no grant can be recommended for English. The school, I am sorry to say, is but very feebly conducted, and the manner in which caps &c. are now huddled together is very obstructive to discipline. Better means, such as I suggested to the Board's Clerk, should be at once provided for the accomodation of caps &c. Several of the school-room doors cannot be closed, as some of them are without locks or handles or both. This defect should also be at once remedied. Infants in most respects backward."

Head-Master Richard Llewellyn Thomas

Assistant Mistress Elizabeth Owen

Pupil Teacher William Owen

Clerk to the School Board. R. W. Pierce

And again in the Government Report dated June 12th 1890

"W. Owen has passed fairly."

Throughout the next three years whilst Owen was a pupil-teacher at the school, he occasionally features in the Head Master's reports.

October 22nd 1890

"The mother of Annie Jones (Tai Lawr) called in school on Wednesday afternoon after the children had been dismissed, to complain that her girl had been sent out of her class, and punished by the P.T."

April 13th – 17th 1891

" The P.T. examination is to be held on Saturday, the 18th inst."

June 8th – 12th 1891

"W. Owen, the P.T. [was absent] on Thursday and Friday, being laid up with the Influenza."

June 15th – 19th 1891

"W.Owen, the P.T. was absent through this week owing to illness."

June 18th 1891 (Government Report)

".... W.Owen, the Pupil Teacher, has passed a very creditable examination."

January 14th 1892

An important letter from the RSPCA was received - *see* panel 1.4 *on page 23.*

June 3rd 1892

"Wm. Owen, the P.T., was absent on Friday owing to illness."

June 10th 1892 (Government Report)

"W. Owen has passed fairly but should attend to Geography."

August 1st – 5th 1892

"A letter received by the Master on Thursday from Mr Ino Jones, Chemist, complaining that his son, Rd. Jones had been kicked by Ino Owen Rowlands. Mr Jones also complained of the treatment his children receive at the hands of Wm. Owen, the P.T. I Warned Wm. Owen not to touch the children on any account whatsoever."

August 22nd – 26th 1892

"A Complaint was made on Monday by Robt. Pritchard (Sadler) that his children were punished in school by the master, and by the P.T."

September 19th – 23rd 1892

"Information was received on Monday that Wm. Owen, the P.T. had been awarded the First Prize in an examination for Pupil Teachers open to all England, in connection with the "Teacher's Aid".

January 30th – February 3rd 1893

"Wm Owen, our P.T. has this year again won the prize (of £1-10-0) for the best essay offered by the Society for the Prevention of Cruelty to Animals."

June 13th 1893 (Government Report)

"William Owen - Pupil Teacher"

On June 6th 1893 is the penultimate entry for William Owen.

"Wm. Owen our P.T., left us on Tuesday afternoon, having been appointed Assistant Master at the Garth Board (Boys') School, Bangor."

1893.	195
May 29th - June 2nd	All classes commenced the new year's work this week.
June 5th. – 9th.	Wm. Owen, our P.T., left us on Tuesday afternoon, having been appointed Assistant Master at the Garth Board (Boys') School, Bangor.

Penultimate entry for William Owen - June 6th 1893

Oct. 9th – 13th.	A meeting of the Board was held at the school-room on Monday evening, wher it was announced that Wm. Owen, formerly P.T. at this school had passed th Queen's Scholarship Examination in the Second Division being No. 787 on the general list.

Final entry for William Owen - October 1893

October 9th – 13th 1893

"A meeting of the Board was held at the school-room on Monday evening , when it was announced the Wm. Owen, formerly P.T at this school, had passed the Queen's Scholarship Examination in the Second division, being No. 787 on the General list."

Footnote, February 5th – 9th 1894

"All the Children of Mr Ino Jones (Chemist) were withdrawn from school on Friday, so as to be taught at home by their father."

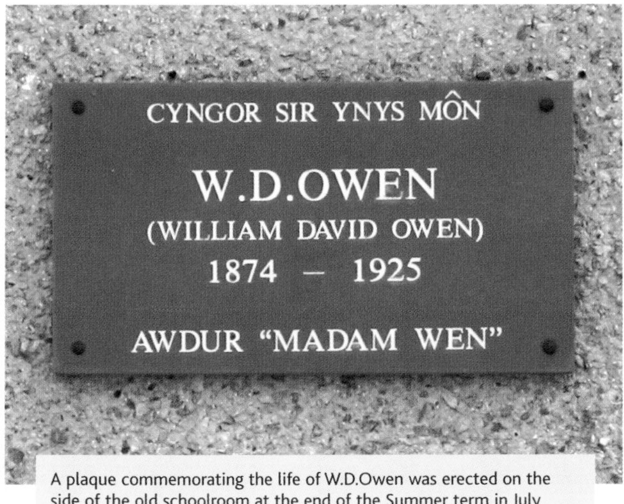

CYNGOR SIR YNYS MÔN
W.D.OWEN
(WILLIAM DAVID OWEN)
1874 – 1925
AWDUR "MADAM WEN"

A plaque commemorating the life of W.D.Owen was erected on the side of the old schoolroom at the end of the Summer term in July 1988. It was unveiled in an opening ceremony by Mrs Haulwen Morgan, Owen's great-niece, who still lives on Anglesey. The ceremony was organised by the Anglesey County Council's Central Services Dept. as part of a programme to honour Islanders who have made a valuable contribution to the way of life on Anglesey.

{The Chronicle, August 6th 1998}

RSPCA

The problem of cruelty to animals crops up in the log book on occasions. For example, the Head Master notes on 27th November 1882 -

"Had to punish four boys for ill-treating a donkey & took advantage of the occasion to warn the children against cruelty to animals."

The RSPCA was founded in 1824, although it did not receive its Royal warrant until 1840. From 1883 to the early 1970's all branches, including the regional branches, held essay competitions in schools across the land, in order to try to raise awareness of the need for humane treatment of animals. A Local branch had been set up in Caernarfonshire and Anglesey in the late 1880s and continues to this day.

In 1891, Owen entered the competition, 'the objective of which was to inspire both children and adults to be more aware of their fellow creatures and to treat them humanely. On this occasion, the title was 'The duty of man to the animal creation' and the winner was William Owen who, on January 14th 1891 won a special prize of £2. The Head master proudly recorded this in the school log book :

"A letter was received from Miss Mary Rathbone, Glan y Menai, on Thursday morning intimating that the Special Prize of £2 offered by the Royal society for the Prevention of Cruelty to Animals, to P.T.'s [Pupil Teachers] & Monitors for the best essay on "The Duty of Man to the Animals Creation" had been won by Wm. Owen, our P.T. here out of over 160 candidates."

Unfortunately, no national or local records exist which might shed further light on Owen's prize-winning essay, but it is clear that the event was a considerable achievement.

The RSPCA must have found the essay competitions immenseley important as they ran annually until the early 1970s, with tens of thousands of schools competing up and down the country.

Owen in fact won the prize in the following year too, although the winning amount was less – only £1 / 10 shillings on that occasion. (£1.50p).

{107}

1.2 *Garth Primary School, Bangor*

According to the school logbook, [*a] William Owen began teaching at the Garth Primary School in Bangor on Thursday June 8th 1893,

"Mr William Owen, from Bryngwran, commenced duties here instead of Mr Rd. Thomas, [who] left. He took the iii & iv s.s. from now to the end of July, when all the teachers will change their classes."

The Garth School was situated on Garth Road and was built in 1848 as the British School. [*b] It established a high standard of education and was used from 1854 for teaching practice by the Normal College. It became a Board school in 1871 and was closed in 1946. It was listed grade II as a building of special character in 1988, as "a rare survivor of a mid-nineteenth century British School." [*c]

In 1893 the school had a total of 144 pupils on the books, (although attendances were often well down on those figures), and taught both boys and girls.

As was the custom in the logbooks, the head master, Lewis D. Jones, [*d] made several reports on Owen's progress throughout the eight months that he was there.

Monday 26th July 1893
"I examined the iii s. The reading was very weak, I advised the teacher to confine himself to a given number of pages & master them. The spelling also was extremely backward; arithmetic sightly better than spelling. Of geography very little was done, & not much grammar: in fact the class did very badly. I gave instructions to the teacher on each of the subjects."

Friday 1st September 1893 – Owen has been moved to take a lower class:

The teachers changed their classes this week. Wm. Grace taking the iii & iv, J.R.Clayton the v-vii, and Wm. Owen the i & ii.

Wednesday 13th September 1893
"I spent the whole day with W.Owen in ss i & ii. The discipline is rather slack & defective & the boys are getting slow & inattentive."

Wednesday 4th October 1893
" I went thro' s i this morning, testing the work. The teachers have had one month with their new classes. The reading in this class was not at all good, the boys repeat the words in an unnatural tone & halt and spell the words. The attention to the work is not satisfactory. The notation is also bad & they count their fingers and make strokes on their slates in working the sums. Tables and Mental Arithmetic are not satisfactory. The writing is good.

In the afternoon I took the ii s. The class subjects were very well done, but the reading was faltering and careless. The writing was only fair, pencils were not pointed and the slates wanted re-ruling.

The arithmetic was badly done. The boys newly removed from s. I have not received the attention they ought to have and are falling behind. This class did not show the progress I expected to find. I gave some hints to the teacher who works hard but the slackness of his discipline is against his success."

Friday 6th October 1893
"A half holiday was given in the afternoon because W.Jones and W. Owen had passed the Queen Scholarship examination."

Friday 13th October 1893
"I spent the week with W. Owen in i & ii and W. Jones in iii & iv."

Friday 9th February 1894

"William Owen, assistant teacher left us to day to go to College, having won a Queen's Scholarship last July."

Garth Primary School, Bangor, 2009. The Old School has been converted into Housing Association flats.

BANGOR
BRITISH SCHOOL
FOR FIVE HUNDRED
CHILDREN
ERECTED 1848

Slate plaque detail from gable end of old school building.

*a Garth School Logbook, Gwynedd, Archives (Caernarfon). **{108}**

*b 'British' schools were normally supported by non-conformists and 'National' schools by Anglicans. The 1870 Education Act permitted School Boards to be created which were elected locally to create and administer schools by levying a rate. Boards were abolished by the 1902 Education Act and elementary education became the responsibility of Borough Councils. **{109}**

*c CADW Listing particulars, record No. 3988.

*d Lewis D. Jones, was better known by his bardic name 'Llew Tegid'. ('The Lion of Tegid'; Llew = Lion; Tegid is the name of the lake just outside the town of Bala in Snowdonia, where he was born in 1851). He became Head master of Garth school in 1875, where he remained for over a quarter of a century. Lewis was a staunch supporter of the National Eisteddfod of Wales, where he also conducted. He was an expert on Welsh folk songs and wrote the Welsh words to numerous traditional English folk songs. He died in 1928. **{110}**

1.3 *Bangor Normal College*

Bangor Normal College, was described as a "Residential College for the Training of Teachers" and was situated in Upper Bangor, overlooking the Menai Straits. It was founded in 1858 and developed in response to a shortage of teachers in Wales in the 1840s. Students lived at the college, which was principally funded by government grants, although the students had fees to pay, and there were also subscriptions and donations from many private sources.

1893 – admitted.
Owen was one of 153 candidates who sat for admission at the Scholarship examination in July 1893. 11 passed in the first class, 76 in the second class (including William Owen) and 22 in the third class. Those in the the third class were not admitted, and of the 87 available candidates, Owen was one of 30 admitted in January 1894. [*a]

1894 – first year student.

In the first year, William Owen, passed his examinations in the first division. The results were stated as follows: *b

Drawing – 2
Mechanics – E.P. [Elementary Pass]
Electricity – E.P.

1895 – graduated.

In the second and final year, William Owen, was one of 19 students who graduated in the First Division in 'midsummer'. The results were stated as follows: *c

Geometry – Pass
Mechanics – Pass
Electricity – Pass
Drawing – Full certificate of Competency.

The list of graduates in order of merit, shows that W.Owen was placed 10th out of 30 in the class. The index of all students of the College for that year states – 'Owen, William, from Bryngwran Bd. School appointed to "Joys' Green Bd. Lydbrook Glos".'

Jones, Ernest	Rhosllanerchrugog Bd.	Rhosllanerchrugog Bd
Jones, George	Manchester, Grange st. Bd.	Manchester, Smedley Rd. Bd., Cheetham
Owen, William	Bryngwran Bd.	Joys' Green Bd, Lydbrook, Gloster
Owen, William R.	Llanberis Bd.	Neath B
Parry, Griffith J.	Penmorfa Bd	Ferndale, Higher Grade

*a Report dated March 1894
*b Report dated March 1895
*c Report dated March 1896

BANGOR NORMAL COLLEGE

FOR THE

Training of Teachers

FOR

ELEMENTARY SCHOOLS IN WALES.

REPORT

FOR THE YEAR ENDED MARCH 31ST, 1894.

BANGOR:

PRINTED BY NIXON AND JARVIS, BOOKSELLERS AND STATIONERS.

1894.

1.4 *Joy's Green School, Gloucestershire*

Joy's Green was (and still is) a rural hamlet in the Forest of Dean in West Gloucestershire, close to the Welsh border. Its larger neighbour, Lydbrook, barely a mile distant, on the other hand, was quite a large industrial village, (pop. 2640 in 1905) and was famous for the production of tin plate and for iron & coal mining. The Lydbrook railway viaduct, and the close access to the river Wye, also contributed to its importance as a loading place for Forest coal.

It is not surprising then, that the Board school at Joy's Green was a substantial building, serving a far wider catchment than its location in the tiny hamlet would suggest.

Sadly, the school closed in August 2008, when the pupil numbers had dropped to below 20. However, the Log Books survive in Gloucestershire Archives and reveal some interesting facts about the school in the time that Owen took up his first appointment there, at the age of twenty-one, after graduating in Midsummer 1895.

Joy's Green Board School opened in 1883 and had junior, mixed and infants departments with places for 227 children, rising in 1894 to an average attendance of 287. [*a] In the school logbooks, [*b] the first mention of Owen is in the staff list for October 1896, where he is listed as 'Assistant Teacher' under the Head Teacher John Davies (who was reputed to be a strict disciplinarian). Owen is also included in the Kelly's directory listing of 1897 which is illustrated below.

SCHOOLS.

Board, Joys Green, under the Forest of Dean United District school board (mixed), built, with master's residence, in 1882, for 277 children; average attendance, 200 mixed & 80 infants; John Davies, master; William Owen, assistant master; Miss Caroline Gardiner, infants' mistress

National (mixed & infants), enlarged in 1872, for 262 children; average attendance, 132 mixed & 86 infants; Charles Thomas Bishop, master

In 1897, apart from the one week's holiday in June, for Queen Victoria's diamond Jubilee, the log book also noted that 'some families were nearly destitute because the tin plate works closed for 6 months'. [*c]

The entry for 30th August 1897 notes that *'Mr Owen will receive his certificate in due course'* but he is barely mentioned again save for two minor entries in November – *'Mr Owen resumed his school duties on Wednesday morning'* and the following week *'Mr Owen is now in the New Classroom, with the first standard in the charge of Ada Roberts* [a second year teacher] *and one of the new monitors, while he takes the 6th and 7th standards.'*

Owen's place of residence has proved a difficult challenge to track down. It is likely that he was boarding either in the village of Joy's Green, or nearby, but there was no census during his short time there, and the electoral rolls have proved unhelpful.

Owen remained at the school for two and a half years, until in February 21st 1898, the Log Book records that *"Mr Owen, Certificated assistant, leaves us today for Clay Lane National School, Derbyshire"*.

*a A history of the county of Gloucester, Vol 5

*b Gloucestershire archives, S208/1 logbook 1896-1923 **{111}**

*c Joy's Green County Primary School, Reunion booklet, 1993

Photographs of Joy's Green from the period are few and far between. These pictures of Joy's Green School and the Class Photo are from c1903. This is slightly later than when Owen was there but provide an accurate reflection of what the school was like at that time.

1.5 *Clay Cross School, Derbyshire*

Owen was appointed to 'Clay Lane National School' in February 1898 at the age of 24. *[a]

The Clay Lane township was (and still is) is principally a rural area of North Derbyshire, approximately five miles South of Chesterfield. The village, along with several surrounding villages, was gradually incorporated into the one administrative entity of Clay Cross, and grew due to the enormous coal mining developments in the area by the Clay Cross Company which had begun in the mid-nineteenth century. "A town of modern growth, the centre of a large coal and iron district. Pop. 8358." *[b] Today, Clay Lane village is effectively only a small part of Clay Cross town.

There were several Board schools in the district, administered by the Clay Lane United District School Board. This board, of seven members, had been formed in 1873 and covered the local villages of Clay Lane, Pilsley, Stretton, Tupton, North Wingfield, Egstow and Woodthorpe. *[c]

According to local directories of the period *[d] , a portion of the Clay Cross Board school "has been fitted up as a science school with a well arranged and very complete laboratory" and "will hold 130". This was in addition to the senior boys department, which had an average attendance of 185, and the senior girls, which had an average attendance of 188.

The first written record of Owen in Clay Cross, is an advert in the Derbyshire Courier [weekly newspaper] of August 1900 for the new "School of Science, Clay Cross" in which Owen is listed as "W. OWEN, 1st Class Trained Certificated Teacher".

The Log Book for the 'Clay Lane Board School' (senior boys department 1892-1907) sheds no light on Owen as a teacher at all, and if there ever was a separate log book for the science school, (part of which is now the Adult Education building), it has not come to light.

The next record of Owen in Clay Cross is the 1901 census, which lists him as a 'teacher' boarding at 38 High Street in the home of Elizabeth Hibbert and her adult son, Harry.

Owen was one of four boarders – Owen, Edward Huddleston, William Smith and Joseph Richards. (There is no sign of his future wife, Gwendolen, at this point, - she is listed in the 1901 census as living with her aunt in Hornsey, Middlesex).

However, he did not stay there long, as later on that year he had moved to the nearby village of Pilsley, where the electoral rolls for 1901 through to 1905 show his address as Elm Walk, Pilsley.

In 1903, a School Management Committee of 9 members was formed for the united district of Clay Lane (and the six other villages). John Henry Unwin was appointed clerk to the managers, and there were two attendance officers. The formation of this small group was to have a significant impact on Owen in the years to come.

Sometime during his time at Clay Lane, Owen met and fell in love with Edith Gwendolen Empsall, also believed to be a teacher in the Clay Cross area. Despite considerable research, it is disappointing to report that she has not been found listed by name in any of the official records still available. {112}

CLAY LANE U.D. SCHOOL BOARD.

COUNTY COUNCIL DISTRICT SECONDARY SCHOOL.

SCHOOL OF SCIENCE, CLAY CROSS.

STAFF :—

HEAD MASTER :—F. COWLING, F.C.S., Science Honours, Chemistry, Physiography, Hygiene.

ASSISTANTS : S. CROOKES, Inter. BSc. 1st Class London University. A.I.E.E.

C. HAWTHORN, B.A. (Honours) London University.

W. OWEN, 1st Class Trained Certificated Teacher.

VISITING TEACHERS : E. STOLLARD, Diploma, Sheffield School of Cookery.

H. SMITH, 1st Class Dressmaking Certif. City and Guilds.

The next Term commences SEPTEMBER 3rd.

Application for admission must be made at once.

JOHN H. UNWIN, Clerk.

School Board Offices, Clay Cross, Aug. 20th, 1900.

Advert from the Derbyshire Courier of August 1900.

Elm Walk, Pilsley, 2009. These houses are a very short walk away from the primary school.

The Clay cross Board schools complex was very extensive. Since it closed in 2009, only some of these buildings are now being used - most are behind security fencing awaiting redevelopment.

The building on the left (see p10 for a modern view of this building) became the Senior Boys' School and the building on the right, was the Mechanics Institute, which later became the Higher Grade School. Behind these two were the Infants' School and the Senior Girls' school.

Nevertheless, In the summer of 1904, on the 9th of August, William and Gwen got married in Holyhead. They returned to Derbyshire where WD continued to teach at Clay Cross Science School. Gwen, however, as a married woman, was now prohibited by law from teaching in a government school and this may have been her opportunity to make a career move into journalism.

In 1906, the Owens moved out of Pilsley to the adjacent hamlet of Woodthorpe, where WD appears on the electoral rolls as an 'Occupation Voter' at 'Coldwell, Parish of Woodthorpe'. It is likely that they were boarding there, in one of the properties belonging to an Arthur Stone.

In the absence of a log book for the Science School, we must assume that Owen's time there as a teacher, passed without incident. At some stage, Owen joined the management committee and the first (and only) written mentions of Owen are not as a teacher, but as 'one of the school managers',*[e] when in September 1907 he is noted as having 'checked the registers' in the Clay Lane Board School (later to become Clay Cross Council School). He continued to perform this duty in various schools between 1907 and 1909, {113} and in September of that year is again noted :

"Dr Duncan and Mr Owen (two of the managers) called in to look at the desks referred to in the Head [master's] report".

These are the first signs that he was moving away from teaching into management and administration – a path that would lead him to change his career.

After some moving around in rented properties, by 1910 William and Gwen were once again living on the outskirts of Clay Cross at 'Coldwell House, Woodthorpe, Old Tupton', a location which seems to be synonymous with 'Coldwell Farm'.

The decade that Owen spent in Derbyshire was most important to him. Between the ages of 25 and 35 he continued to teach and then moved across into school administration; he met, courted and married his wife, Gwendolen; and he decided to change his career to the law. But even bigger changes were afoot as William and Gwendolen had decided to leave the rural life behind and move to London.

Coldwell Farm, Woodthorpe

*a According to the school logbook of his previous school, Joy's Green.

*b Bartholomew's Gazetteer of The British Isles, 1904.

*c Kellys Directory of Derbyshire,1899

*d ditto

*e Log Books, Clay Lane Board School (later Clay Cross Council School) Senior Boys dept. 1892 and 1907. (Derbyshire Archives, D6194/1/3 and D6194/1/4).

1.6 *Muswell Hill and the Law*

Gwen had been living with her aunt in Hornsey, North London, before she came up to Derbyshire to work as a teacher in Clay Cross. It is no surprise therefore when her husband wanted to study law and chose the University of London, that they should eventually return to the area.

At the time Owen was there, the University of London was the largest in the country, and had over 4000 registered students. These included resident 'internal' students and non-resident 'external' students. Due to the absence of more detailed records, it is believed that Owen would have been an external student, studying by distance learning techniques, in which the University was one of the pioneers.

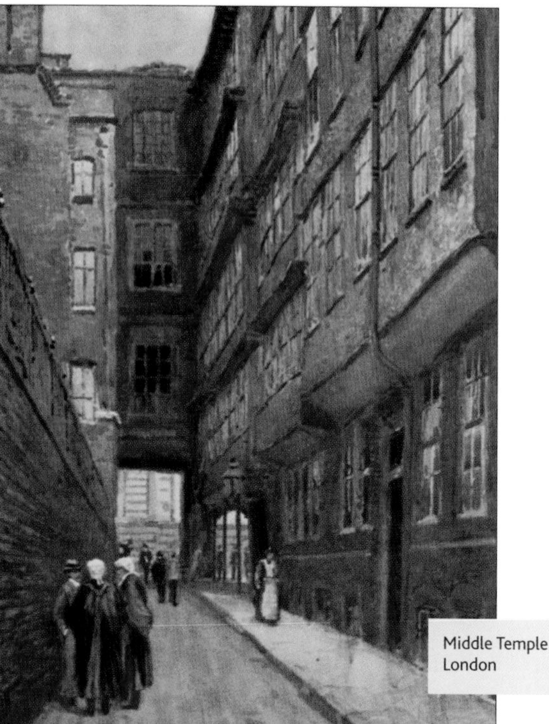

Middle Temple Lane, London

The records of the University of London are still available in an index for 1836-1926 but they are inconclusive concerning the subject of our research. The records show that 'William Owen' sat an intermediate law exam in 1906, but there is no record that shows whether he passed the exam or not. {114} However, one must presume that he did, in order to be able to continue with his studies.

Middle Temple is one of the four famous 'Inns of Court' providing support for barristers and student barristers. Its principal campus is just off Fleet Street in central London. The admissions register of Middle Temple states that Owen was admitted to the Inn on 11th November 1905 at the age of 30 and was subsequently called to the bar on 17th November 1909. Beyond that, and some personal information we already know about his home and education, the entry tells us little new information.

However, the photograph of Owen in his wig & gown (the only known photograph of Owen in existence) does give us further confidence in these dates. It was taken in the studios of J.W.Gorsuch of 48 Junction Rd. Holloway, London – only a few minutes away from Muswell Hill. Gorsuch ceased in business in 1911 (he is said to have gambled away his earnings on the horses) {115} so this photograph must have been taken between 1909 and 1911. This ties in neatly with Owen's dates at Middle Temple.

There are several "William Owen" entries in the University of London index.

Owen, Stanley J.: B.A. 22, King's. Owen, Thomas E.: B.A. 14.
Owen, William *(formerly* Owens) : B.A. 64.
Owen, William D.: M.B., B.S. 13. Owen, William H.: LL.B.* 98. Owen, William John : B.Sc. Eng.* 16. Owen, William John : B.A.* 24; Ped. 24.
Owen, William R.: B.A. 95.
Owen, William S.: B.A. 52.
Owen, William T.: B.Sc. Eng. 24, Univ. C.
Owens, Llewelyn A.: B.Sc.* 00.
Owens, Patricia M.: B.A.* 25 & Pod. 26, King's.
Owens, William : *(see* Owen).
Owens, William: B.A.* 26.
Owens, William J.: B.Sc.* 25, King's. Ower, Ernest B.Sc. Eng.* 15, Impl. C.-C. & G.C.
Owsley, George C.: M.B. 00.

The entry for "Owen, William D." appears, but as an M.B., B.S (A Batchelor of Medicine & Surgery awarded in 1913) whereas in the very next entry, even commencing on the same line, "Owen, William H." received the LL.B. (Batchelor of Law) with honours in 1898. There are no other Batchelors of Law amongst the William Owen entries, and no other 'William Owen' entries with more relevant graduation dates than 1913. Is it possible his name has been omitted? or is it possible that the entries for these two William Owens have been editorially confused? After this amount of time it is practically impossible to know.

The Law Lists {116} shows the following entries which would be consistent with a 1909 University of London graduation :

1910 & 1911 – Owen, Wm, [Middle Temple] 17 Nov 1909

1912 – Owen, Wm, M 17 Nov 1909; New Ct, Temple EC, N Wales and Chester circuit

1913-1920 - Owen, Wm, M 17 Nov 1909; N Wales and Chester circuit

The records of examination results from the period are now stored at the Institute of Advanced Legal Studies in London {117.iii}. These show that Owen sat his final Bar exams in 1909 and gained the following results (the maximum marks are shown in brackets) :

Real Property:	86	(170)
Law and Equity 1:	88	(170)
Law and Equity 2:	72	(170)
General Paper A:	24	(60)
General Paper B:	39	(60)
General Paper D:	44	(60)
Grand Total:	353	(690)

It should also be noted at this time, that he is still listed as plain William Owen, without his subsequently adopted middle name 'David'.

Sometime between 1910 and 1911 William and Gwen moved to a house in Muswell Hill, a Middlesex village barely 2 miles away from Hornsey, where she had lived with her aunt ten years previously. The 1911 census records him and Gwen as being the only two residents of 89 Sutton Road, Muswell Hill on that day [*a]. Sadly, the ownership details of the time are no longer in existence, as the house is now owned by a property company, and the deeds of that period have long disappeared. It is therefore not possible to establish whether the house was owned by Owen, or merely rented.

Sutton Road, Muswell Hill c1915

Muswell Hill is now simply thought of as a suburb of North London. Back in the eighteenth, and for most of the nineteenth centuries, it was a village of detached villas and mansions standing in large grounds. Careful development, following on from decades of its use by Londoners as a 'country retreat' continued, and even in the early twentieth century – when the Owens lived there – it remained a largely unspoilt area, characterised by houses being built of 'good materials, to high standards, during an interesting architectural time, resulting in distinctive and attractive Edwardian period houses.' *b Its population in 1904 was a little over 5000, and its nearest attraction is Alexandra Park (which also includes the seven and a half acre Alexandra Palace). See photo on page.78.

There seemed to have been quite a strong Welsh community in the Hornsey district and there were several Calvinistic Methodist chapels in the area where the Owens might have worshipped. These included Wood Green Chapel; Holloway Chapel; the more prestigious Charing Cross chapel, or the 'tin' chapel' (a temporary chapel) in Pembroke Rd, only a few streets away from Sutton Rd. *c

Attempts have been made to try to establish which of the chapels the Owens attended, in order to shed more light on their dates in Muswell Hill, but unfortunately, nothing definitive has been found.

I have suggested throughout that the principal reason for moving to London, was William's desire to study law, but the facts suggest that he probably studied off-campus. Is it possible that the real reason that William and Gwen returned to London, was that Gwen's journalistic career needed to bring her closer to Fleet Street? This subject is explored in section 1.7 following.

Owen of course later went on to study as a solicitor and what little we know about this is shown in panel 1.5 alongside.

*a 1911census.co.uk. (N.B. The house is visible on Google 'street view' and reveals it as a two-storey terraced villa)

*b 'A History of Muswell Hill' by Ken Gay. Hornsey Historical Society 1999

*c information courtesy Hornsey Historical Society.

Detailed information about Owen's activities as an independent barrister, has not survived. Although listed as being on the North Wales and Chester Circuit, the records of his case load, or of what Chambers he was attached to, have not been located. Institutions such as The National Archives, The Ministry of Justice and The Bar Council have also been unable to shed further light on his career. He does not appear in the Case Law 'bibles' of Butterworth's or Tolley's and it is therefore likely that the work he carried out would have been fairly mundane. Indeed, the fact that he decided to become a solicitor gives an indication that his workload as a barrister was not heavy.

The records of the Law Society show that Owen passed the Solicitors' final examination in March 1923 and was admitted a Solicitor of the Supreme Court of England & Wales in May 1923. His address at the time was given as 'Ashton' Rhosneigr and his results are as follows: (The maximum mark is shown in brackets).

Conveyancing:	100 (225)
Equity:	102 (225)
Common Law and Bankruptcy:	134 (225)
Probate, Divorce and Admiralty:	116 (225)
Combined Total:	452 (900)

We know from the record book of the clerk to Anglesey Council, that Owen had an new office built in Rhosneigr in June 1923, but the precise location is unclear.

From his diary (section 1.8) one can see that Owen acted as a general solicitor, with licensing and conveyancing issues being specifically noted. At a time when Rhosneigr was growing significantly, after the war, the buying and selling of property would have provided a solid workload. Whether William David Owen would have continued as a solicitor after the success of 'Madam Wen' is an interesting subject for debate.
{117}

[Panel 1.5]

1.7 *Gwen's Publishing Career*

Edith Gwendolen Empsall was the daughter of artist John Empsall and his wife, Margaret, (née Ladyman). She was born in Italy in about 1876, *a but in 1881, by the time she was six years old, she was attending private school in England and boarding with two schoolmistresses in Salford, Lancashire. By 1891 she was a sixteen-year-old pupil teacher in Ashton under Lyne and, in 1901, she was a 'Government Teacher and Journalist' living with an unmarried aunt in Hornsey, Middlesex, both her parents having died when she was in her teens.

According to William Owen's contemporary obituary in 'Y Cloriannydd' *(The Evaluator)* (see section 1.9) Gwen was a teacher in Clay Cross when they met, but despite considerable research with the various schools in the area, {112} no records have been found which categorically confirm this. However, at many of the schools, Assistant Teachers seemed to come and go with alacrity, so the likelihood of the story being true has a high probability.

After her marriage in the summer of 1904, Gwen would have been prevented by law from being able to teach, and it appears that she followed a journalisic career. This was already evident in the 'Profession or Occupation' column on the census entry for 1901, as noted above.

According to her brief obituary in the November 21st 1962 issue of 'Y Cloriannydd', (see page 41) she worked in Fleet Street as a sub-editor of the magazine Woman's Weekly, which was established in 1911. The same writer claimed that she was also a sub-editor of a magazine called Home Companion and that, for a short period before World War One, she edited a publication called the Holiday Mail.

Although there is no digital archive for any of these publications, some attempts have been made to verify these claims – see following panels 1.6 & 1.7.

Gwen, of course, has been included with W.D. throughout these pages where appropriate, but little is known about her life after her husband's death in 1925. In W.D.'s diary he notes that a bungalow is being built for them by Henry Jones and it is believed that this is 'Laneton' on Sandy Lane *b.

The bungalow 'Laneton', is clearly visible in the centre of this old Francis Frith postcard from the mid 1930s, which looks over Sandy Lane, Rhosneigr, towards Broad Beach.

The deeds of this property {104} show that on June 10th 1926 – some 7 months after Owen's death – the property was sold to Edith Gwendolen Owen of 'Ashton' Rhosneigr, and Henry Jones of 'Morlais', Beach Road, Builder.'

It is not known for how long Gwen actually lived in the bungalow but in the 1929 electoral roll, she is shown as living in Llanfaelog at Pentre Traeth, the house of Hugh and Margaret Hughes, where she was probably lodging, {118} and in October 1931, 'Laneton' was sold to Miss J. L. Williams of Malltraeth.

Gwen's obituary also states that she lived for a time in Valley and Caergeiliog but further details of her life and activities are outside the scope of this work

One Rhosneigr resident who knew her, remembers her as a "dotty old lady" who could still turn her hand to writing.

She recalls that Gwen used to write lots of letters and pin them up in the windows of the bungalow. "They were very odd letters", she said, "probably political in nature" as she recalls one particular occasion in the early 1930s.

She remembers when Megan Lloyd George came to Rhosneigr on 7th April 1931 to open the Water Works. She was called on by her father at the official reception at the Bay Hotel, to lead Miss LLoyd George away through the kitchen and out of the back, to avoid the attentions of Gwen, who was disrupting proceedings at the front.

One member of the family described how Gwen "went a bit eccentric" after her husband had died. She remembers how "she thought she could talk to the birds and regularly walked round the lanes in Rhosneigr twittering to them".

Sometime in the mid - late1950s, Gwen went into Park Mount old people's home in Llangefni – now part of Anglesey County Council's Education services dept.

Edith Gwendolen Owen died in 1962 at the age of eighty-six and is buried with her late husband in Gwalchmai Uchaf chapel.

Water Tower in Course of Construction.

Park Mount, Llangefni.

Home Companion

This title was published by Fleetway Publications Ltd of Farringdon, London, and ran between 1897 and 1941. The Journal is a fairly general women's-interest magazine, with typical content including several serials, household hints, agony aunt letters and replies, knitting and crochet patterns and reader's household tips. Adverts range from 'Atora' suet to 'Magneto' corsets.

The names of editorial staff for the period examined were absent and there was no evidence in the copies examined of any reference to Gwen, although editorials quite clearly state 'from your Editress'. However, unsigned articles abound in this journal and as part of the same publishing group for which she is known to have worked, it is quite probable that the workload was shared between the available staff.

Woman's Weekly

Also published by Fleetway Publications Ltd of Farringdon, London, this weekly journal contained a wide mixture of romantic stories, household hints, poetry and children's tales and claimed to be "a paper devoted to fashions and household interest and fine, real-life fiction".

The journal started publishing in 1911 and extensive random checks have been carried out in the first few years (until 1916).

[Panel 1.6]

There are very many unsigned stories in the magazine througout this period, but in the edition of October 26th 1912 the first of several stories appeared under the title of 'Adventures in Nursery Rhyme Land' by Edith G. Owen (see illustration overleaf). These stories continued to appear in the first half of 1913.

Woman's weekly is still published today, [*c] but unfortunately their records do not go back that far so it is impossible to determine what her other contributions to the editorial material was, or to get any idea of when she stopped working at the journal.

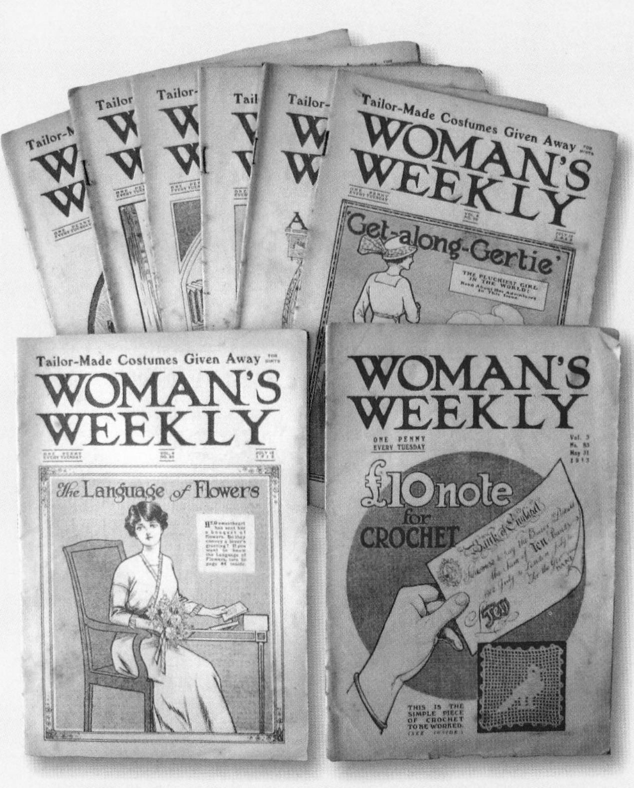

LET THE CHILDREN READ THIS PAGE.

ADVENTURES IN NURSERY RHYME LAND

THIS STORY CAN BE BEGUN ANY WEEK.

By EDITH G. OWEN.

"Oh, my!" cried Mother Hubbard. "What a very nice little box! What ever are those funny little things in it?"

"Oh, yes! What ever are they?" exclaimed the Old Woman. "Let me look!" And she got hold of Jack's arm so suddenly that he nearly upset the box.

"Oh, my patience! You very nearly broke the spell just then! They're my Magic Beans!" he said almost angrily.

"Well, I didn't know that, did I?" the Old Woman answered. "Besides, what good are Magic Beans, anyway?"

"Just you wait and see," said Jack quite good-temperedly as he took a bean out of the box, and, making a little hole in the ground, put the bean into it.

"You want to get to the top of the cliff, don't you? All right, then. But you must follow my instructions exactly, you know. Can you do so, do you think?"

"Why, of course we can!" cried both the old ladies together, as they tossed their heads.

"Very well, then," Jack replied. "Now shut your eyes tight and say your 'twice-one-are-two' three times without stopping. Then when you get to 'twice-twelve-are-twenty-four' third time, open your eyes and——"

"*What?*" they both asked.

"Oh, you'll see!" said Jack. "Now, are you ready? Now or never! Now or NEVER!" he added so loudly that the two old ladies were awf'ly startled. So they shut their eyes tight, and started saying their "twice-one-are-two" as fast as anything. Each meant to get to "twice-twelve-are-twenty-four" third time first, you know.

"Hi! Stop!" cried Jack to Mother Hubbard. "You said 'twice-eight-are-sixty.' Start again. Keep your eyes shut tight."

So Mother Hubbard had to start

again. And the Old Woman was so pleased that she opened one eye—the farthest one from Jack. But he saw it, bless you!

Mother Hubbard Jumps out of the Bean-stalk

"There now! You've spoilt it!" he said. "It was growing beautifully, and now it's stopped. I shall have to use another of my precious, precious beans."

He took another from his box, and put it in another little hole which he made in the ground.

"Now then, shut your eyes tight and start again! No nonsense this time, mind!"

So the old ladies screwed up their eyes as tight as tight, and began to say their "twice-one-are-two" very slowly and carefully.

And all went well until Mother Hubbard got to her "twice-eleven-are-twenty-two" third time. Then she suddenly opened her eyes and screamed:

"Oh, I can't keep 'em shut another jiffy!"

Of course, the Old Woman opened hers as well, though she was just in the middle of her "twice-twelve-are——"

"Oh, my! What a *splendid* bean-stalk!" she cried.

"Yes, but she's been and gone and done it," said Jack.

"Done what?"

"Made it stop short just three feet from the top!"

"Well, *there!*" Mother Hubbard exclaimed, holding up her hands. "Just as if *that* does any good when you don't finish your 'twice-one-are' properly."

"I can't possibly waste another bean on this job," went on Jack. "I've got ten bee-utiful princesses to rescue from castle turrets, not to mention seven steeplejacks who have got stuck fast on weathercocks. So another bean on this job is quite out of the question. Can you jump three feet?" he asked.

"It all depends whose feet," Mother Hubbard replied. "I couldn't jump three of some of the feet I've seen *shoes* for."

"If you mean *my* shoe," began the Old Woman.

"Now then, now then, now then!" shouted Jack. "If you start quarrelling the Beanstalk will vanish, and then where will you be?"

"Well, as we don't happen to be Polar bears," the Old Woman answered, "I don't see what good your silly old Beanstalk is to us, anyway!"

A little frown came out on Jack's forehead, but he sent it away at once, and a smile came round his lips instead.

"Madam, will you kindly step into the lift," he said ve-ry, ve-ry politely. And there, at the foot of the Beanstalk, a queer little door had opened suddenly.

"Oh! Oh! Oh! Oh! Oh!" the old ladies said as they skipped backwards like nice elderly frogs. "Oh, we don't want any more lifts!" said Mother Hubbard. "No, indeed! It was Bluebeard's lift that landed us down here," added the Old Woman.

"Well, please yourselves," Jack replied; "but the Giant's Valley isn't the safest place in the world for two nice, attractive ladies like yourselves."

Jack's Beanstalk grows fast

"Giants! Giants!" they screamed. "Why didn't you tell us that before?" And they hopped into the lift in double-quick time, and at once Jack started it going.

"Ow-ow-ow! What's happening? Oh, I think I'm sea-sick!" It was poor Mother Hubbard who spoke. "Oh, is my bonnet on straight?" she asked in a shaking voice as she peeped at herself in the mirror on the wall.

"Mind! It's going to stop!" Jack warned. And stop it suddenly did.

"Very nasty that—stopping, I mean," said the Old Woman. "Do I look like fainting?"

"Of course you don't!" snapped Mother Hubbard. "If anybody is going to faint, *I* am!"

"*Please,* ladies," pleaded Jack, "don't mention it! You see you are still three feet from the top of the cliff. Now, who is going to jump first?"

"You!" said Mother Hubbard to the Old Woman.

"No, you!"

"I sha'n't!"

"You'll have to, because it was you who stopped the Beanstalk from growing with your silly ways!" The Old Woman sounded very cross indeed.

(*Continued on page 853.*)

Holiday Mail

Only one edition of this sixteen-page 'journal' appeared, dated 15th July 1914. This of course was just a fortnight before the official start of the First World War, so it is unsurprising that no further issues were published in succeeding weeks.

'Holiday Mail' was subtitled 'The New Weekly Journal To Attract Visitors to Holiday Resorts' and in it there are at least two articles by Gwen. It was published by the National Holiday Bureau whose head office was at 155 Fleet Street, London. The bureau was the central organising office and registry of all hotels, hydros, furnished and boarding houses at the holiday resorts in Great Britain and also published directories of these establishments.

Unfortunately, there are no editorial or other staff listed in the publication itself but the principal article (effectively the 'editorial') is entitled "Where Shall we Stay ?", and is signed "E.G.O."

This article discusses the need for its clientele to promote themselves throughout the year, and these days that would be considered a fairly standard self-promotional message – simple fare for the first issue of any magazine.

On pages eight and nine, "The Golden Sands of Anglesey" was a 2-page article promoting the Island, including the villages of Menai Bridge, Beaumaris and Rhosneigr. Although unattributed, the writing is highly likely to have been by Gwen.

[Panel 1.7]

Y Cloriannydd (The Evaluator), November 21st 1962, page 4

Death of Mrs W.D. Owen

Mrs Edith Gwendolen Owen, widow of W. D. Owen, the author of the novel "Madam Wen", died on Friday, in Cefni Hospital, Llangefni, aged 87.

Mrs Owen was a sub-editor in Fleet Street, London, on the women's magazines "Home Companion" and "Woman's Weekly".

For some six months before the First World War she was the editor of "Holiday Mail".

She lived for periods in Valley, Rhosneigr and Caergeiliog.

The funeral was in the graveyard of Jerusalem (Calvinistic Methodist) Chapel, Gwalchmai, on Tuesday.

*a Although born in about 1876, her exact date and place of birth is not clear. The relevant column in the 1881 census is not filled in; the 1891 census gives 'London'; the 1901 census states 'Italy' and the 1911 census states 'Lancashire, Rochdale'. Her birth certificate has not been tracked down.

*b Laneton was the eponymous village in "Laneton Parsonage" an 1846 novel by Elizabeth M Sewell -, described as "a tale for children, on the practical use of a portion of the church catechism".

*c IPC Media, archives – ipc media.com

The Bay Hotel was built for Henry Cole (the son of the artist J.H.Cole) and opened for business in 1904. It had no drinks licence until the mid 1920s when Mr Cole purchased the licence from the Sheep Inn in Pencarnisiog which was closed, and its licence transferred to the Bay Hotel. We can see from Owen's diary entry of February 9th 1925, that he was interested enough in the deal to record it.

1.8 *Diary Extracts*

Selected and mostly verbatim extracts from W.D.Owen's diary for 1925 – the year that 'Madam Wen' was published, and the year that he died.

Many of the extracts relate to Owen's business as a solicitor, but in this, his 21st year of marriage, it is clear that William and Gwen were not living together. It is also noticeable that there are lots of entries in the diary, over many months, for "Supper at 7 Beach Rd" or similar. *a

February 1925

Mon February 9th
"licensing sessions at Valley. Bay Hotel got removal of Sheep Inn License."

Mon 16 February
"Sarah (Elmbank) to stay. Up all night with mam."

Thurs 19th February
"Gwen sent for me. went up in the evening & gave her £7. Called at Warrenside on the way back."

Sat 28th February [monthly comments section]
"very little fresh work came in."

"Gwen finished her cash."

"mother ill."

March 1925

Sun 1st March
"went to see O.G.O.'s wireless." [probably Owen G.Owen of Morfa Hill]

Sun 14th March
"Gwen called." (evening) "Gwen came in – gave her £2 and promised £10 for next week."

Thurs 19th March
"Gwen down re mortgage. 7 Beach rd after supper."

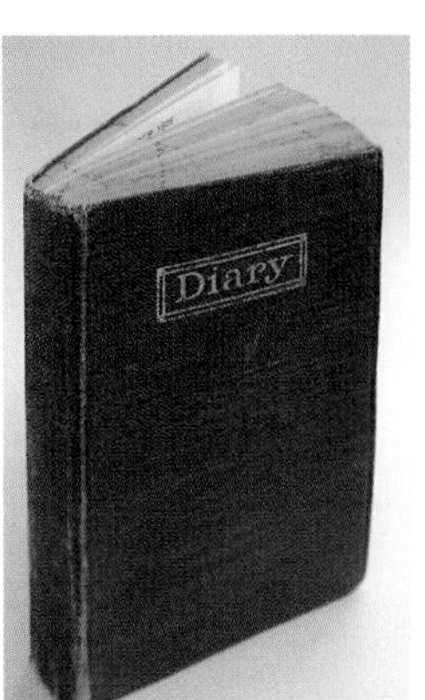

Fri 20th March
"Gwen – gave her £10."

March – notes
"Drains cut up High Street."

April 1925

Fri 10th April (Good Friday)
"called at the Bay."

"Played golf with W Rts FW & Tom Owen – then tea at the Bay. WR & WDO 3 and 2."

"Aching jaws all day."

Sat 11th April
"another bright day"

"filled up the motorcycle and went to Bryngwran."

Mon 13th April (Easter monday)
"(played golf in pm)"

May 1925

Fri 1st May
"A cold day."

*" Mr Wm Hughes West View.
Miss Owen Rts."*

"Proof of 78 pages of Madam Wen received & returned."

"Gwen sent message a second time".

Mon 4th May
"Gwen came down and signed mortgage deed. Gave her 10/-"

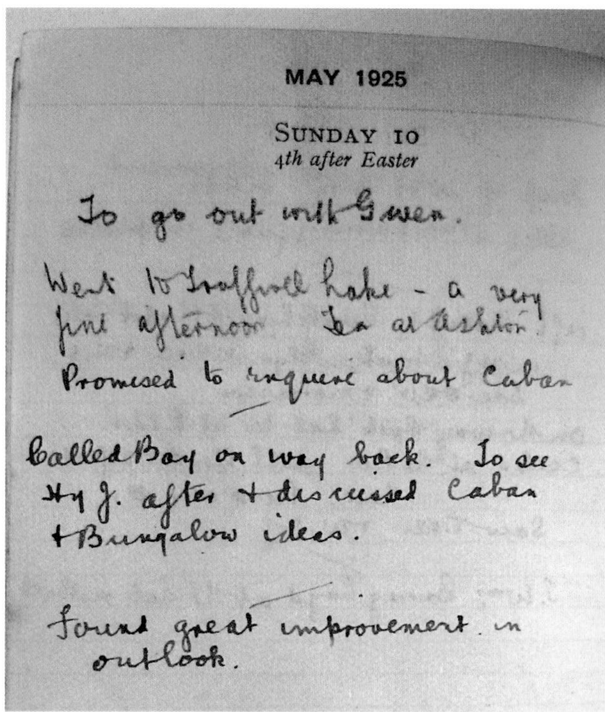

MAY 1925

SUNDAY 10
4th after Easter

To go out with Gwen.

Went to Traffwll Lake - a very fine afternoon. Tea at Ashton.

Promised to enquire about Caban

Called Bay on way back. To see Hy J. after & discussed Caban & Bungalow ideas.

Found great improvement in outlook.

Sun 10th May

"To go out with Gwen. Went to Traffwll lake – a very fine afternoon. Tea at Ashton. Promised to enquire about Caban."

"Called Bay on way back. To see Hy.J. after & discussed Caban & Bungalow ideas."

"Found great improvement in outlook"

Sat 13th May

"Called Ashton – Gwen 30/-. Promised to go tomorrow aft. for a walk."

Mon 25th May

"Drove to Mynachdy with Gwen. (Walter W 16/- leaving 2/- for a station run)."

Sun 31st May

"Worked out a new plan of a bungalow."

June 1925

Sun 7th June

"Aft. went with Gwen to see plot 11. She was dissatisfied."

Tue 16th June

"Went to see asbestos work at pavilion."

"Afterwards (even.) at 7 Beach Rd. W. Lewis there. R.Hughes (Bay). Gwen came in after supper."

"second instal. of proofs of Madam Wen received."

Wed 17th June

"aft. proofs of 'Madam Wen'"

"even. proofs. Gwen came in."

Fri 19th June

"posted proofs 'Madam Wen'"

Sat 27th June

"Called at Ashton. 30/-"

Sun 28th June

"aft. with Gwen on plot 11. Tea at Ashton. New plan of bungalow drawn. Hy. J to supper at Bronant then to Braich yr Orsedd, Avondale & 7 Beach Rd."

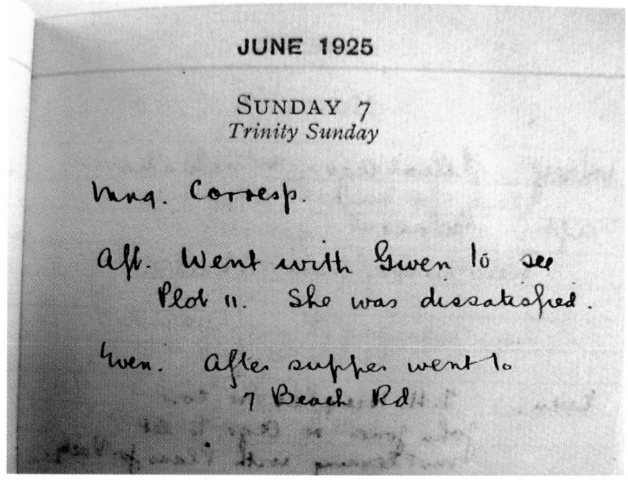

JUNE 1925

SUNDAY 7
Trinity Sunday

Mng. Corresp.

Aft. Went with Gwen to see Plot 11. She was dissatisfied.

Even. After supper went to 7 Beach Rd.

June (memo)

"arrangements made this month for erecting a bungalow. Plot 11 bought & stuff ordered. plans passed."

July 1925

Tues 7th July

"foundations cut for bungalow."

Wed 8th July

"proofs of last chaps Madam Wen received."

Fri 10th July

"Proofs Madam Wen sent."

"Hy J here re alteration of plan. Expecting G who didn't come."

Sat 11th July

"not well – slept badly."

Sun 12th July

"With G on the common. 30/- for last week."

"Not well – bowel trouble. Slept badly."

Fri 17th July

"Attended sale at Bay Hotel – Wave Crest. [*b] *Met Mackensie Roberts-Jones (solr.)."*

Sun 26th July

"After tea, Gwen came. went to Bungalow site & back for tea, then Ashton. Called at the Bay."

Tue 28th July

"Played 15 holes with RAR. Very tired after it & went to bed at 10pm."

Wed 29th July

"went to bed early – not well."

memo for July

"not much new good work."

"progress with publication of Madam Wen to be out in September."

August 1925

Sat 1st August

"still not well."

"Gwen came – gave her £1. went to the bungalow with her then started a walk but turned back."

"Zara House completion."

Sun 2nd August

"better today."

"even. – Gwen. gave her remaining 10/- for last week."

Wed 5th August

"Gwen came & stayed. Talk about Religious & ethical matters."

Mon 10th August

"Not well. Corresp."

Tues 11th August

"Y Genedl – Barmadaethau" [decisions]

"Bungalow a second time.

Thurs 13th August

"G called. we had porridge together. Went to 9 Beach Rd & then to 7 Beach Rd."

Sun 16th August

"Gwen came – stopped A Thompson in the street & we quarrelled."

Mon 24th August

"Gwen called & promised to come again at 9pm."

August memo

"Much progress made with the bungalow. Roofed, made into rooms (partition)."

"Fair amount new work came in."

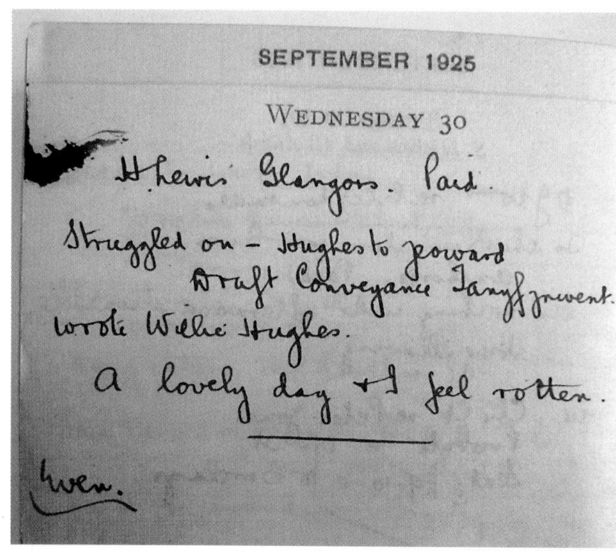

SEPTEMBER 1925

WEDNESDAY 30

H. Lewis Glangors. Paid.

Struggled on – Hughes to Yeoward Draft Conveyance Tanyfynwent.

wrote Willie Hughes.

a lovely day + I feel rotten.

Gwen.

September 1925

Fri 4th September
"aft – no work. Went to bungalow."

"even. – Slacking. Not well."

Fri 5th September
"mother not well"

Tue 8th September
"whole day spent on the bungalow. Gwen down about the colouring – arranging about the outside finish."

Sat 12th September
"Gwen in at supper time. Went with her to Ashton. (£2) being 30/- this week's & 10/- arrears."

Tue 24th September
"Not well. Put off Llangefni."

"Had a bad night with temp of 103. Gwen came."

Sat 26th September
"Wm Rlds declined to advance on 5 Bch. Terr."

"Still unwell."

Tues 29th September
"Did nothing in the afternoon – unwell."

Wed 30th September
"struggled on. Hughes to Yeoward draft conveyance Tan y Fynwent."

"A lovely day & I feel rotten."

September memo
"Health fair till end of month then collapse."

October 1925

Fri 2nd October
T. Hughes Tynllan executed deeds. Posted them to Tynmawr Mynydd."

[in a busy diary, It is noticeable that there are no entries between 3rd and 21st October]

Thurs 22nd October
"First copies of 'Madam Wen' received." [Written in a very weak hand].

Tues 27th October – the last entry in the diary.
"Hughes to Yeoward. Rcd. £360 balance of P M draft on Barclay. Sending £360 to bank. Sent £8 to E. O. Jones."

[William David Owen died on 4th November 1925.]

*a 7 Beach Road, ('Morlais' - 'The Voice of The Sea') was the home of Henry Jones the builder.

*b 'Wave Crest' was the name of the hotel at No.4 & No.5 Beach Terrace.

*c Zara House, at the bottom of Beach Rd. has been renamed Morwennol *(Sea Swallow)*.

1.9 Obituary

Y Cloriannydd (The Evaluator)

November 11th 1925

Losing a Lawyer

Mr W. D. Owen, Rhosneigr

After a long period of ill-health, Mr Owen died on Tuesday and the news brought grief to a wide circle. His career had proved that he was a man of ability, possessed of a fine mind and great commitment.

He was the son of William and Jane Owen, formerly of Tynfranen (sic), Bryngwran; his elderly mother is still alive and lives with her two daughters in Bronant, Rhosneigr.The son became a pupil-teacher in Bryngwran School, then he attended Bangor Normal College, gaining a first class certificate after two years. Then he became a teacher in a secondary school in Clay Cross, where he met an able girl, who was a teacher there at the same time, and who became his wife.

After that, he studied for the Bar and passed to become a barrister but his health was weak and it was in the hope of becoming stronger that he came to Rhosneigr; seeing that he would do better as a solicitor, he studied for that position and passed easily.

For while he looked after the Soldiers' Pensions Office in Llangefni and, when that closed, he set up as a solicitor, opening a branch-office in Llangefni on Thursdays. He was rapidly gaining a good position in his profession but had failed to come to town for about five weeks.

He was a man of high literary taste, having read many English classics. He wrote many Welsh sonnets and he enjoyed studying the characteristics of the [Welsh] language. A fortnight before he died Wrexham Press published his book "Madam Wen", a romance based on the tradition of that "lady" in the Llyn Traffwll district. The book was in our hands when we were told of the death of its author; three days previously we had written to thank him for it.

He was characterised by justness and purity of purpose; he hated every form of insincerety; he was one of the most obliging of men. He had strong natural sense and a good judgement. He acknowledged very recently that it was to the Sunday School that he was most indebted for his desire for knowledge. He lost his father when he was a small child and took good care of his mother; after he left home a week never went by without her receiving a letter from William.

The Funeral

The funeral of Mr W. D. Owen, solicitor, Rhosneigr and Llangefni, took place on Saturday, the interment being at Gwalchmai Chapel, when the Revs. O. R. Owen, B.A., W. H. Jones, Hebron,.and R. Thomas, B.A., Bont Newydd, took part in the service.

The mourners included:—The Widow; Misses E, and S. Owen (sisters); Mrs Jones, Ty Croes, Bodorgan (aunt); Mrs Jones, Malltraeth; Mr and Mrs Owen, Elm Bank, Rhosneigr; Mr and Mrs Jones, Arosfa, do.; Mr and Mrs Jones, Morlais, do.; Messrs Griffith Owen, John Owen, David Jones, Llandudno Junction; William Jones, Bangor; Tom Jones, Ty Croes, Bodorgan; Owen Jones, Llanfair P.G.; Capt. Ellis Roberts, Caernarfon.; Messrs David Charles Roberts, Colwyn Bay; D. Owen, Bryn Meini; John E Roberts, Conway; Wm. Griffith, do., and Richard Roberts, Pentretraeth (cousins).

There were also present.: Messrs W. Rowlands, Griffith Rowlands, R. J. Evans, and Henry Hughes (deacons of Paran Chapel); Dr. O. J. Parry Edwards, Bodedern; Messrs W. Hughes, auctioneer, Bodorgan; O. T. Owen, Rhosbadrig; H. S. Cole, Bay Hotel; O. J. Hughes, clerk of the Holyhead Union; R. Ll. Hughes, Meyrick Arms, Bodorgan; J. Hughes, stationmaster, Llangefni; Isaac Parry, Caernarfon; O. G. Owen, Morfa Hill; Walter O. Jones, Hugh Pritchard, E. O. Jones, Frank Williams, D. Llewelyn Jones, Walter Roberts, Bank; and R.E. Owen, Llangefni.

Wreaths were sent by: Mrs W. D. Owen, Mrs and Misses Owen, Bronant; Mrs Jones and family, Ty Croes, Bodorgan; Mr and Mrs Owen and Willie, Elm Bank; Mr and Mrs Jones and Megan, Arosfa; Mr and Mrs Jones and family, Morlais; Mrs Roddick and family, Bryn Awel; Mrs Jones and family, Plas; Mr and Mrs Jos. E. Jones, Edge-lane, Liverpool; Mr and Mrs Hughes, Avondale; Miss Hughes, Ynysfor; Rhosneigr Ratepayers' Association, Mr O. G. Owen, Morfa Hill; The Anglesey Golf Club; Mrs Harrison, Bryn Tawel; Miss Owen, Elm Bank; Mr and Mrs H. S. Cole, Bay Hotel; the Brethren of the Cefni Masonic Lodge (4086), Llangefni.

1.10 *The Florence Nightingale Connection*

WDO's first story "Elin Cadwaladr", published in 1913, contains several important threads relating to poor health and sickness and whilst such storylines may well have been prompted by the general problems of the era, I believe that there is another link which influenced him, one much closer to home.

The reader will come to see how WDO's stories have been influenced by his surroundings, but perhaps one of the more subtle influences on him was Elinor (or Ellen), the elder of his two sisters. For several years, whilst WD was in his formative teenage years, Ellen worked in Anglesey, and later in London, for the Verney family and subsequently for the renowned nurse and medical reformer of the age, Miss Florence Nightingale.

It is not easy to piece together the correct chain of events relating to Ellen's employment by Florence, partly due to the absence of full information, and partly due to the absence of dates for some of the information we do have. However, some of Florence's letters to Ellen Owen, (whom Florence calls 'Nelly'), have survived, {119} as has an interview conducted with Ellen herself in the early 1950s (shown in panel 1.9 below). {120}

Florence's own life and work has, of course, been comprehensively documented and analysed in several significant biographies. These draw upon the enormous amount of correspondence and notes she left behind on her death, and are stored in various public and private archives, including those at Claydon House, Bucks. {121}

Several of these items are reproduced here, by kind permission of their owners, (see references section).

Through the examination of these documents, and the published biographies, it is possible to learn a sizeable amount relevant to the life and working conditions of Nelly Owen. We can see for instance, that Florence took an interest in Nelly's wellbeing and family and even, on one occasion, specifically asked after her brother William whilst he was still at school. However, we should first set her employment in context.

THE LATE
MISS. FLORENCE NIGHTINGALE.
L.S.Co. No123.

Florence Nightingale was born on the 13th May 1820, and named after that beautiful Italian city which was her birthplace. She was the younger of Mr William Shore Nightingale's two daughters – her elder sister being

Parthenope (or 'Parthe' for short). Her father was a wealthy landowner of 'Embley Park' in Hampshire and - what became their Summer House - 'Lea Hurst', in Holloway, a small village near the town of Matlock in Derbyshire *a. Florence spent most of her childhood and adolescence between these two properties.

Even from a young age, Florence was a prolific letter-writer, writing to many members of her extensive family (and later, her staff) about every subject under the sun.

Aside from her nursing career, one of the major events of Florence's life occurred when Sir Harry Verney, of Claydon House in Buckinghamshire, fell in love with Florence after the death of his first wife, and in the summer of 1859 asked her to marry him. However, she refused him. Barely a year later, he had courted and married Florence's elder sister Parthenope.

As may be expected, considering the enormous influence her work had in the areas of Health and Sanitation, Florence's standards were very high. Her ideas of cleanliness and hygiene were said to be strange to her contemporaries and her standards exacting - this also extended to her staff. *"Florence has strange ideas about maids"*. writes her mother, Fanny, in 1864. {122}

After their mother, died in 1880, a reconciliation between Florence and her sister Parthe took place (they had not been particularly close for years) and for the first time almost since childhood, they became good friends again. Florence began to visit Claydon but Parthe suffered with arthritis and as her illness worsened and she became a cripple, Sir Harry relied on Florence more, and she gradually took an active part in the management of the estate's affairs. This is why many of Florence's letters from this time are written from Claydon, rather than from her home at South Street, London.

This 'Midland Railway official' postcard of Lea Hurst dates from pre-1923 and is captioned :-
"Lea Hurst
The Home of Florence Nightingale,
Whatstandwell Station,
Midland Route,
London Manchester and Liverpool."

Claydon House, Buckinghamshire

Ellen (Nelly) Owen was born in 1867 [*b] and would have left school by her middle teens. Her recently widowed mother was starting to make a living as a dressmaker and her brother William and younger sister Sarah, were still at school. Nelly would have had little choice but to try to find work.

The Verney family were major landowners with a number of properties on Anglesey at that time and had a sizeable complement of staff. Margaret Verney (née Hay Williams) was one of Sir Harry's daughters in law and lived at Plas Rhianfa, on the banks of the Menai Straits (between Beaumaris and Menai Bridge) [*c] and the family also had a holiday house at Rhoscolyn, known as 'Plas Rhoscolyn'.

And so it was that sometime around 1885, Nelly began to work for the Verneys as a housemaid at Rhoscolyn, and later at Rhianfa.

'Plas Rhoscolyn' has little changed externally in the 100 years between these two photos, and is still owned by the Verney family.

Margaret Verney must have thought quite highly of Nelly, for it is clear that she had recommended her to Florence Nightingale, who on April 12th 1886 writes :

"do you know, I shall be so pleased to try that girl you mentioned - the little housemaid at Rhoscolyn". {V1}

Florence wanted her to be a *"half housemaid and half kitchen maid"* at her South Street home in London and was *"very glad...of the prospect of having Nelly Owen"* {V2}

> Very glad am I of the prospect of having Nelly Owen. I have written to your good Mrs. Thomas to send her up, if possible, on Tuesday or Easter Wednesday - for later on the trains are so crowded, let alone

The trip to London from Anglesey on the train just after Easter 1886 would have been quite a journey for Nelly, and Florence expresses concern to Margaret over her welfare. She also enquires as to *"the momentous question of beer"* – had Nelly *"either beer, or beer money ?"* {V2} A question that remained unanswered.

Nelly passed her interview, although her health at the time had not been good, and commenced work with Florence Nightingale in London shortly afterwards.

Florence obviously cared deeply that her young staff were well looked after and arranged for them to go to church, and to *"take a little run in the park every day"* and (in Nelly's case) to take cooking lessons. {LA1} Florence also checked that Nelly had asked her mother for a Welsh prayer book and Bible. However, Nelly didn't have a Bible, and was presented with one by Florence herself – The inscription on the flyleaf reportedly reads *"To Ellen Owen with Florence Nightingale's fervent prayer that we may both be kept for the Master's use. August 1886"* [*d]

At the time Nelly started working for her, Florence was sixty-six, had already lost many friends and relatives to old age and her deluge of correspondence, and correspondents, was starting to dry up. However, she still retained an active involvement with medical matters of the Government of the day – particularly in the work of sanitation and hospital nursing. It is hardly surprising that her lifelong interest in such things would have influenced her staff too.

Florence Nightingale had a succession of maids, housemaids and household staff and always took a keen interest in the detail of what went on. In many ways, this must have meant that working for her was quite demanding, and indeed as was commonplace at the time, the tone and phraseology of Florence's notes and correspondence to and about her staff, could on occasions be interpreted as a little patronising - *"I send you your quarter.* [*e] *Was it you who told me that you put "the Sovering" into the Savings Bank?"* {H6}

During 1886 and 1887, Florence continued to write to Margaret Verney about Nelly's progress, and on several occasions, Nelly shows concern over Margaret's children, Lettice and Ellin, with whom she had obviously struck up a good relationship whilst in Anglesey. *"Might Nelly Owen come to see Miss Ellin and Miss Lettice for a few minutes sometime ?... It would make her so happy"* {V5} she asks, although when she did eventually go, she was late - *"You know she is a little stolid. I could not get her off, tho' she had a cab."* {V6}

There are other references to Nelly's *"slowness"*, *"denseness and indifference"* {V7} in particular when Nelly is being encouraged to go home to Anglesey for her summer holidays. She does not seem to be very keen to do so, and Florence expresses her concerns in a number of letters to Margaret Verney:

"the difficulty of getting her to take a walk in the park – or to dress for tea – or to care about Church or Class – or to make progress in cooking – she cooks & then falls back. She had rather grub all day & all evening in the Scullery – or(sic) to read or make her own pretty frock". {V7}

And she blames herself for Nelly's demeanor – *"of course a great deal of this must be our fault."*

When Nelly does go, there is obvious relief in her letter to Margaret Verney. *"Nelly Owen is gone home."* she writes, continuing *"she is certainly very wilful – but so steady – she never wants to go anywhere."* {V8}

Nelly worked increasingly in the kitchen, and occasionally Florence ventured into the kitchen herself. On 23rd September 1887 she wrote to Margaret Verney *"I found Nelly (the kitchen maid) on a cool day popping everything into the refrigerator as if it were a larder".* What she said to Nelly, is not recorded. {123}

There are also occasions when Nelly helps at the Verney household when they come to London, and it is also of note that Nelly spoke Welsh with Margaret Verney – *"I am sure that it must be a great pleasure to you to have a talk from Mrs Verney in Welsh"*, writes Florence in January 1888 {LA2}

Florence had always taken immense pains over her household which was clearly highly organised, with no detail being too small to be of interest. According to one of her biographers, Mrs Cecil Woodham Smith, -

"The duties to be performed in the house and in the Kitchen at every hour through the day were marked on a chart. The food was ordered by Florence herself and she was very particular as to quality. In March 1889, [when Nelly had been with her for about three years], she wrote to a new Butcher for *"a fore quarter of your best small mutton. I prefer four year old mutton".* The following week she wrote *"the neck 'ate' better than the shoulder tho' off the same piece"* and she placed a further order for *"13 to 14 pounds of good sirloin of beef to try".* {124}

In late summer of 1889, Nelly spent two weeks home on Anglesey and Florence sent her a long letter in which, among other things, she enquired about her brother William, who was fourteen and still at school at the time:

"And now will you not write me a nice little letter & tell me how your brother is getting on with the new school master?
I hope however you had him at home for a part of your holiday"
{H3}

And now will you not
write me a nice little letter
& tell me how your brother
is getting on with the new
school master? I hope however
you had him at home for a
part of your holiday

If Nelly had told her brother that the famous Florence Nightingale had been asking after him, it could not have failed to have had an impact on him. However, the absence of any written response to Florence Nightingale, (which would have been saved in the archives), indicates that Nelly probably didn't reply.

Nelly shows increasing levels of responsibility in Florence's household, - she is entrusted with choosing *"a good couple of fowls, trussed as I said, that is the breastbone not broken"* {LA4} and by October 1889 was acting as Florence's Housekeeper.

"And I shall not tell you what to get for me. You shall order what things you think I shall like best. We shall bring with us eggs but no chicken. We may perhaps bring cream." {LA6}

Florence's taste in food was said to be fastidious. Each day's menu was submitted to her and she made suggestions and criticised the previous day's dishes. *"remember I am a small but delicate eater"* she wrote. {125} An example of her attention to the smallest detail is shown in the instructions for Minced Beef and for Roasts (see panel 1.8).

Florence continued to spend more time at Claydon, and this meant that some of her staff in London became under-utilised. Correspondence with Margaret Verney in April 1890 revealed that Nelly was leaving – but it is not clear whose decision this was. Margaret writes :

"If you have not found any suitable place for Nelly Owen by the time we return to London about the 15th, I am sure I could find her a situation by talking it over with Mrs Hunt, she has a registry office in Duke St, where so many of our friends inquire (sic) for servants. How good you have been to Nelly Owen, she will never be so much considered again."

She continues : *"If I can hear of another Nelly Owen, I will let you know, alas cooks are most difficult, I do not know of one, Maude recommends Miss Paget, who interests herself in getting servants places, I believe she is Sir James' daughter, if I can see her for you, pray let me know."* {V10}

In May 1890, after a long illness, Parthe died and her passing brought Florence even closer to the Verney family and to Sir Harry. She spent most of the summer at Claydon and as one might imagine, eventually became more and more involved in the management of the Claydon estate including its surrounding villages, and its sanitation and water supply.

Minced beef for my dinner

"The beef must be from the under-cut of the sirloin; mince the beef over a plate which must catch the juices which fall. The meat must be uncooked. Sauces and gravies are not to be thickened with flour. The bones of the meat are simmered down with vegetables to make the stock, which is then reduced to make the sauces. Use plenty of herbs for flavouring. Minced veal must be dished up with potato or rice, [but] the potato or rice must not come higher than the veal; there must not be a hole with the veal in it. It must be garnished with small thin pieces of fried rolled bacon round. The little bits of veal are not mashed but separate tender bits with sauce poured over—really a very delicate dish."

"Roast pheasant must be hung not too near a good fire and basted every minute or two with good butter for an hour. Roast chicken must be larded all over. Roast neck of mutton must be very small, never above 6 1/2 lbs. - not too thin. Streaky fat in the lean makes good mutton. Half the battle is in trimming the fat. The fat near the bone should be left to soak down into the meat. A nice brisk fire and 1 1/2 hrs doing. Not too near at first. Keep on basting every minute or two in the tasty way, a little salt, flour, butter." {126}

[Panel 1.8]

It is probable that Nelly went to work for Margaret Verney for a short time, - possibly for the summer months back on Anglesey, but in September of 1890, Nelly was back in London acting at least in some part as Florence's cook. *"I send you wages for 7 weeks at £16 a year with my very best wishes"... "Now you are our little cook I suppose"* she writes. {H4}

A gap in correspondence regarding Nelly ensues, and, in April 1891, the ten-yearly census shows 'Ellen Owen' in the employ of James D. Hill of Onslow Gardens, Kensington – an Australian Merchant and Shipowner. This was a bigger household than Florence Nightingale's with twice as many servants and whilst it is possible that Nelly has seized an opportunity – it is perhaps more likely that the Hills were well acquainted with the Verneys, and the opportunity was by word of mouth and only a temporary arrangement.

Some time afterwards, Nelly must have returned to the Verney family, as a year later, in January 1892, Florence writes to Nelly asking her to return to South Street as her cook.

"I believe Mrs Verney has kindly given you messages from me asking you if you would like to come to me as cook for a time at 10 South Street. I should like you to come to me on the [letter has blank space here for date to be entered later] *or as soon as Mrs Verney can spare you. And I shall be glad to see my little Nelly again."* {LA7}

Margaret Verney responds (from Rhianva), on behalf of her sister Maude, *f by confirming that Nelly can return to London on the 13th January:

"It is among the minor mercies of life that Nelly Owen is really so charming – so anxious to serve us all, she is quite content & happy to come to you on the 13th the day we all leave; & I am inviting her mother to come & stay here on monday that Nelly may see her. Maude has been giving her £20 wages I believe." {V14}

Nelly did not stay for long though. By August of 1892, Nelly had decided to leave Florence Nightingale's employment for good and, for a time at least, return to Anglesey. One of the last letters Florence wrote to her was not a happy one {LA8} :-

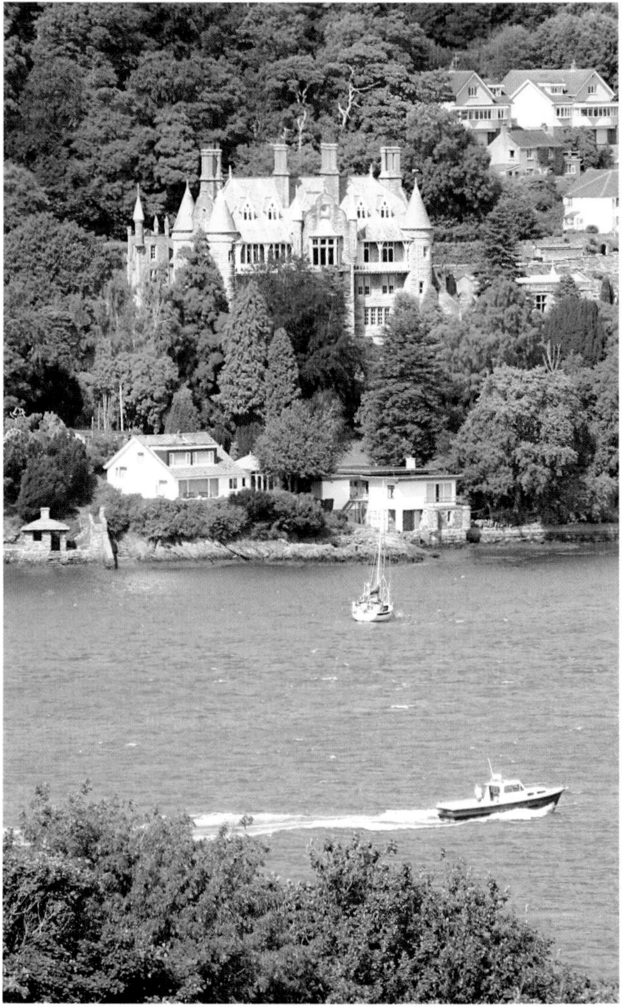

Plas Rhianfa, on the banks of the Menai Straits, was built by Sir John Hay Williams, the second Baronet of Bodelwyddan, between 1848-1851 as a summer retreat for the family. It is now listed grade II* and is officially described as "A seaside villa with turrets, fish-scale roof tiles and balconies, influenced by the chateaux of the Loire Valley."

Sir John's elder daughter, Margaret, married Edmund Hope Verney which is how, through inheritance, the Verneys came to own the Rhianfa estate – just over 5000 acres worth in 1872 - which they occupied until the late 1950s.

At the time of writing, (early 2009) Plas Rhianfa, is for sale with a guide price of over £3.25 million

address.
God bless you both –
F.Nightingale

I will write again

Not one word, Nelly – not even a line with your books; which I have only just received.

Not one word, even to give me your address in Anglesea –

1. *I enclose a cheque for the whole £ 9. 13. 10d you will see that leaves you £1.2.3d in hand which you will hand over to Mrs Broome who comes tomorrow (Tuesday)*
2. *You will of course show her all your places in kitchen, scullery, larder and housekeepers room. And I know you will show them her <u>clean</u> and <u>tidy</u>.*
3. *You will leave all the books when paid, with the tradesman. But <u>your</u> book you will return <u>me</u>, please, by Tuesday's (tomorrow's) post.*
4. *Ask Frances for a packet of envelopes to replace those you lent me and*
5. *Ask her for your and Kate's cab money to the station. – I suppose you go together –and for what it will cost you from the Anglesea Station to reach your home. Kate [*8], please tell her may take hers, out of the overplus of board wages, 3 weeks, I gave her. And she must keep an account for me.*

Kind regards to Kate and tell her to write to me from home and give me her address.

God bless you both – F Nightingale

I will write again.

However, Florence did not bear her any ill will and even after she had left, Nelly was offered help with a place and references. In October 1892 she writes : *"My dear Nelly Owen, Mrs Frederick Verney and I suppose that you are still in want of a place."* ... *"Mrs Verney knows an agency which she says might be helpful. She has been there & thinks they would take trouble for a 'servant well recommended'. They now have kitchenmaids wanted but, she says, not high wages."* {H5}. However there is no record to show if Nelly took up this particular offer.

Sir Harry Verney died in 1894 and after his death, Florence visited Claydon less and by 1896 she had retrenched to South Street. Her spirit remained strong though at least until the turn of the century, at which point her eyesight failed completely and her declining state of health eventually gave out. On 13th August 1910 , at the age of 90, Florence Nightingale died in her sleep.

In keeping with her wishes, she was buried in the family grave at East Wellow, in Hampshire, and though her memorial is only two lines on the family tombstone, "F.N. Born 1820. Died 1910", her legacy to the world has been immense.

Nelly's employment after her time with Florence Nightingale is not recorded in detail, but it is known from her 1951 interview, that she went on to work for Maude and Sir Frederick Verney, and later in Liverpool for Mr. Thomas E. Greenshields, a Scottish Shipowner. She returned to Rhosneigr in 1904 to look after her sister Sarah, who was ill with pneumonia.

The sisters lived with their mother in 'Bronant 'on the High Street from about 1904 onwards, and after their brother died in 1925, and their mother in 1927, they spent many years in semi-retirement, undertaking dressmaking alterations and taking in visitors for the summer. {127}

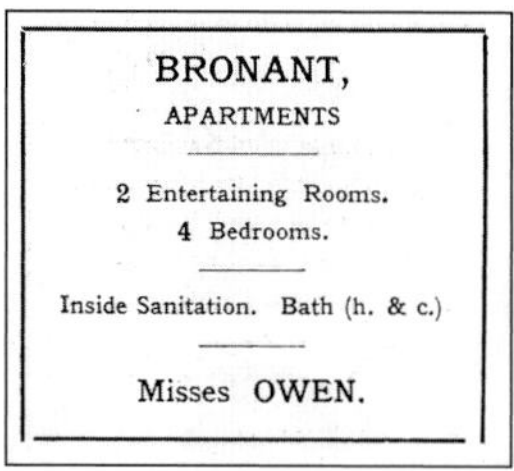
BRONANT,
APARTMENTS

2 Entertaining Rooms.
4 Bedrooms.

Inside Sanitation. Bath (h. & c.)

Misses OWEN.

Nelly died in 1954 and is buried with William and Gwen in Gwalchmai. According to the Paran Chapel records, Sarah died in 1960 and Bronant was sold later the same year by Margaret Jones of 'Arosfa' – Sarah's cousin and next of kin, but her place of burial has not been traced. {128}

The two sisters are remembered by several living Rhosneigr residents, and some later photographs of them have also come to light.

"Sarah Owen was very lame, with a 'club foot'. She wore a special elevated shoe and used to send me to the beach to bring her a bucket of seawater so she could bathe her feet in it."

"They always wore black Bombazine dresses – they had no electricity or lamps for years."

"They used to be black with soot from the fire – even though they were dressmakers"

"There was a shed at the back of the house [Bronant] which was open to the elements. I think it had been used as a TB shelter originally."

Sarah (L) and Ellen (R) in the garden of Bronant, circa 1950

*a Coincidentally, Matlock is only a few miles from Clay Cross, where WD spent many years as a teacher.

*b Ellen's date of birth varies. The Bryngwran school logbook states her date of birth as 28/6/1867. She is 14 on the 1881 census and 24 on the 1891 census which corroborates 1867. However her memory had faded by the time she was in her eighties, as in her interview she states that she was born in1863, which is incorrect.

*c Plas Rhianfa is entitled 'Rhianva, Bangor' on the Verney notepaper.

*d The whereabouts of this bible has not been found. The inscription is quoted by Ellen in her 1951 interview.

*e It was customary at the time to hire domestic servants by the year, in which case wages were paid quarterly.

*f Maude Verney (nee Hay Williams) was Margaret's sister. By an unusual coincidence, Margaret married Edmund Verney and her sister Maude married Edmund's brother, Frederick. Both were sons of Sir Harry Verney, Florence Nightingale's brother in law.

Frederick Verney graduated from Christ Church College Oxford in 1870 and became a Deacon at St Mary's Church, Sheffield, marrying Maude in the same year. In 1873 they moved to Middlesborough, where he took the curacy of St John's church. However, he relinquished his Holy Orders in 1875 and joined the Army, where he gained the rank of Lieutenant in the Buckinghamshire Yeomanry Cavalry. He later became a barrister and then a JP, first in Buckinghamshire, later in Derbyshire.

Maude and Frederick employed Nelly Owen as a kitchenmaid for a time but precisely when is unclear, as the letter of appointment (which was written from 'The Lodge', Old Lakenham, Norwich) **{H1}** is dated October 13, but has no year. It is thought likely that the letter was sent sometime after May 1890, when Parthe Verney (nee Nightingale) died, as the letter is written on black-edged mourning paper.

Maude & Frederick Verney lived for many years in Pleasley, on the Derbyshire/Nottinghamshire border, just a few miles East of where 'Lea Hurst' was located. Frederick was first noted as 'Lord of The Manor' in 1899, succeeding William E Nightingale (Florence & Parthe's father) who occupied the title from around the 1850s. **{129}**

*g The reference to 'Kate' is believed to be Kate Jones, also an employee of Florence Nightingale at that time.

(L-R) Ellen (Nelly), Sarah & their mother Jane on the steps of 'Bronant'. circa 1910.

Worked for Florence Nightingale

Rhosneigr resident's link with famous woman.

Eighty eight year old Miss. Ellen Owen who lives at Bronant, Rhosneigr is one of the very few surviving people who knew Miss. Florence Nightingale.

Born in 1863, Miss. Ellen Owen entered the service of Miss. Nightingale at the age of 16 as a kitchen maid, when the founder of the present day nursing service was living in semi-retirement at No. 10, South Street, Park Lane, London.

In a long and interesting interview with our correspondent, Miss. Owen, a small sprightly lady whose mental powers and memory have remained undimmed, related her experience as a servant in the home of a woman whose service to mankind have been deeply etched into the history of this country.

It was obvious that Miss. Owen still retained some awe, mixed with a deep affection and respect for Miss. Nightingale, and her story was continually punctuated with examples of the great lady's kindness and devout attitude to life.

Sitting on a well-cushioned chair in the kitchen of her home in Rhosneigr, Miss. Owen said: "I will never forget her. There are so many little things about her that remind me of my girlhood days, 65 years ago when I worked for Miss. Nightingale in London. Whatever else I tell you, I must say this - She was a kind and gentle lady who loved everyone. No one was too humble to Miss. Nightingale. She had a kind word for everyone - the wicked as well as the good.'

When Miss. Owen entered the service of Miss. Nightingale, the Lady of Crimea was suffering from ill-health after her experiences at Scutari and other places where the sick were allowed to rot and die until Miss. Nightingale happened on the scene.

"She always had her meals on a tray in her room," Miss. Owen went on. "She was often ill with fever and sometimes was unable to sit up, but with all her suffering she had a smile for us. I remember her saying one day that the reason for the lack of medical stores in the Crimea was because no one kept any accounts.

"Nellie," she would say, "Always be economical and try to save. Keep accounts always."

"I have kept accounts to this day." Miss. Owen said.

Religious instruction for staff.

Miss. Nightingale was obviously keen on her staff receiving religious instruction, and every other Sunday Miss. Owen accompanied by another servant, would attend divine service at St. Thomas' Church, Park Lane, London.

"After every service she made me go to her room and recite the text and tell her about the sermon. I suppose she picked me because I was the youngest member of her staff and the lowliest of all. She would frown at me if I forgot what the preacher had said or if I did not give the text properly. When I left her service, I was 23 years old, she presented me with a Bible which she signed for me."

Miss. Owen produced the Bible and the inscription on the fly-leaf read: "To Ellen Owen with Florence Nightingale's fervent prayer that we may both be kept for the Master's use. August 1886."

There was an old crossing sweeper who used to sweep the roads from South Street to the Park He was an Irishman who had served in the Crimean War, and Miss. Nightingale remembered meeting him out there. When she saw him she brought him into the house and they had a long talk. After that she gave him sixpence every week. All the staff got to know him but we never learned his name, so we used to call him 'Sixpence'. Miss. Owen related.

"But that was like Miss. Nightingale. She was kind and never forgot a person."

Miss. Nightingale, Miss. Owen said, used to occasionally take a walk from South Street to the Serpentine or to Lady Verney's house, which was also on South Street.

"She was very poorly, but she never let it get her down. She liked to go to the Verney's house who were related to her."

The staff at 10 South Street in Miss. Owen's day consisted of Cook, Mrs. Nield; parlour maid, Frances Groundsal; personal maid, Lizzie Coleman; handy man, William Healey; between maid, Lizzie Whittingham; kitchen maid, Miss. Ellen Owen. Miss. Ellen Owen's wage was £22 per year.

Miss. Owen left Miss. Nightingale's service to work for Sir Frederick Verney and later worked at 45 Canning Street, Liverpool for Mr. Greenshields, a wealthy Scotch shipowner. Forty seven years ago she returned home to Rhosneigr to look after her sister, Miss. Sarah Owen, who was ill with pneumonia.

"I have not been to London since 1886, and I have only been to Liverpool once since leaving there 47 years ago. I am happy here in Rhosneigr." she said.

Miss. Owen was born in Bryngwran at Cerrig Cynrig and her brother, the late Mr. W.D.Owen, was a well known barrister.

Today, Miss. Owen, who lives with her sister that she came home to nurse, does all the cooking and shopping, and in the summer takes in a few visitors. Apart from the use of glasses for reading, she is in good health, and puts down her longevity to hard work and good food For 47 years she has been a popular figure in Rhosneigr, and the local residents are proud of their link with a famous woman.

(1951)

[Panel 1.9]

Editor's Notes:

(i) This article has been transcribed from a photocopy of a handwritten original, Unfortunately, the title of the journal or newspaper in which it may have been published has not been traced and the author's name is not known.

(ii) In the original, the word 'Miss' is followed by a full stop, signifying the abbreviation of 'Mistress'. This convention is rarely used these days.

(iii) There are several date inconsistencies in the article, for example :

(a) According to several earlier censuses, and the school log book, Ellen was born in 1867 (not 1863).

(b) It is also documented that Ellen started work for Florence Nightingale in 1886, when she was about 19, not 16.

Notwithstanding these minor errors, this is a fascinating piece of Rhosneigr history.

Elin Cadwaladr

Elin Cadwaladr tells the story of David Charles, a young preacher, and his sweetheart, the eponymous heroine. They drift apart when he goes up to Oxford and becomes involved with Politics. He serves for a short while as the minister of a prestigious chapel in a London suburb but loses his religious conviction and begins to practise law. He is chosen as a parliamentary candidate but, shortly before the General Election, Elin Cadwaladr becomes seriously ill. David's return to Anglesey leads to a momentous decision which will change his life forever.

8360

No.............................

RHOSNEIGR WESLEYAN CHAPEL.

On Wednesday, March 1st, 1905,

A GRAND DRAW

Will take place, when a Splendid

New Piano, Value £20,

WILL BE DRAWN FOR.

Proceeds towards clearing the debt on the above Chapel.

TICKET—SIXPENCE. **Books of 22 Tickets, 10/-**

Winning number will be published in the *Gwyliedydd* of March 8th, and the *Liverpool Echo* of March 4th.

Secretary – J. O. WILLIAMS, 6 Beach Terrace.

Treasurer—THOS. WILLIAMS, Gadys House.

Samuel Hughes, Printer & Stationer, 45, High Street, Bangor.

2.1 *Introduction to Elin Cadwaladr*

When first published in the (predominantly) Welsh language newspaper 'Y Genedl Gymreig' (The Welsh Nation), the story was originally entitled 'Dychweliad y Crwydryn' and subtitled 'Taro Tant a Newid Cywair' ("The Return of the Wanderer" or "Strike a Chord and Change Key"). This is clearly a rather a long and cumbersome title. The story took up two full length columns of the weekly broadsheet newspaper for 30 weeks during the latter half of 1913, an important achievement for a new author. Owen would have been in his late 30s at this time.

The story is set primarily in the imaginary village and parish of Bryn Siriol ('Pleasant Hill'), in Anglesey, near which a holiday village has been built for visitors from the towns of England. It is likely that Llechylched Parish, the villages of Bryngwran and Rhosneigr, and the surrounding areas were all combined to form the setting for the novel. (An index to the place names used is shown in **panel 2.1** on page 65)

Serialised novels were a common feature of the Welsh press from the 1840s onwards, when Welsh translations of American temperance novels began to appear in many of the Welsh denominational publications (see also **panel 2.2**). Many of these were anonymous or appeared under pseudonyms. {201} Indeed, had the annotated and corrected compilation not come to light (see below), it is probable that it would never have been attributed to Owen at all. There is also the tantalising possibility that there are other works of Owen's in existence, yet to be found – a subject touched on in the biography.

Although it has been identified that several serialised stories later appeared as published books {202} "The Return of the Wanderer or Strike a Chord and Change Key" was never published in book form, (in Welsh or English). However, Bangor University Archives have what appears to be a full compilation, cut from the newspaper, glued onto pages and loosely bound into a scrapbook. It is likely, although not known for absolute certainty, that this had been assembled by its author.

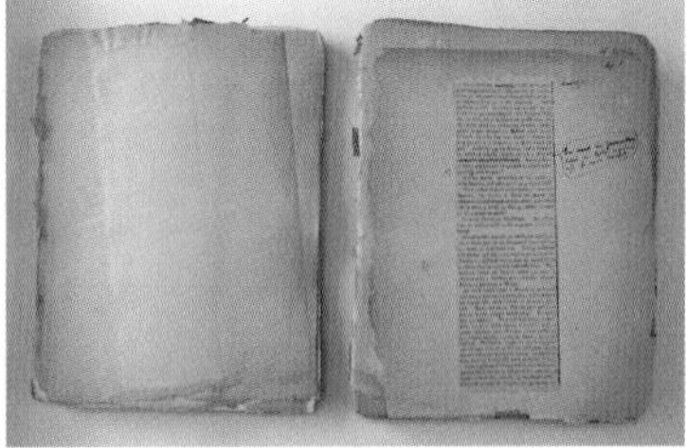

At the top of page one, typed in capital letters is the story's new, much crisper title, 'Elin Cadwaladr'. This is what WD clearly planned to call the story on its publication in book form. Many of the pages have been corrected or annotated, as if the author was preparing to have the novel published. Most of the changes (some of which are visible in the photographs), are simply minor corrections to the original text (for example, see {203}).

The handwritten name and address of the author appears top left 'William David Owen, Seaforth, Rhosneigr, Anglesey' and top right, in a different hand is the name & address of 'John E. Roberts, 15 [Mellor ?] Rd, Cheadle Hulme, Cheshire'.

Roberts, who could obviously read Welsh, was originally from Anglesey and is thought to have been one of Owen's cousins {204}.

The story is slightly longer than 'Madam Wen', and had it been published, would in all probability been received with acclaim. (A more detailed analysis of the comparison between the two stories has been included in section 4, panel 4.11)

Presented here for the first time in English, therefore, is an abridged version of William David Owen's first romantic novel "Elin Cadwaladr".

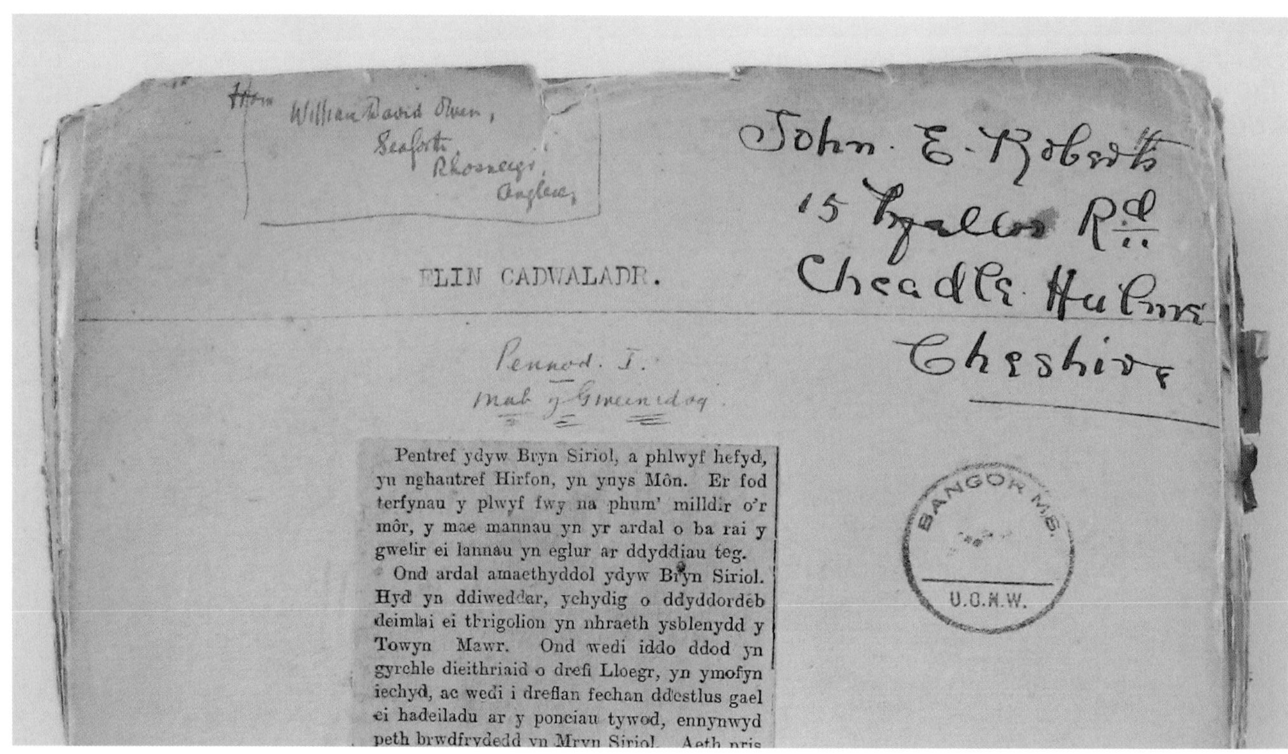

William David Owen,
Seaforth,
Rhosneigr,
Anglesey

John E. Roberts
15 [illegible] Rd
Cheadle Hulme
Cheshire

ELIN CADWALADR.

Pennod. I.
Mab y Gweinidog

Pentref ydyw Bryn Siriol, a phlwyf hefyd, yn nghantref Hirfon, yn ynys Môn. Er fod terfynau y plwyf fwy na phum' milldir o'r môr, y mae mannau yn yr ardal o ba rai y gwelir ei lannau yn eglur ar ddyddiau teg.

Ond ardal amaethyddol ydyw Bryn Siriol. Hyd yn ddiweddar, ychydig o ddyddordeb deimlai ei thrigolion yn nhraeth ysblenydd y Towyn Mawr. Ond wedi iddo ddod yn gyrchle dieithriaid o drefi Lloegr, yn ymofyn iechyd, ac wedi i dreflan fechan ddestlus gael ei hadeiladu ar y ponciau tywod, ennynwyd peth brwdfrydedd yn Mryn Siriol. Aeth pris

BANGOR MS.
U.C.N.W.

Index of names & places

Translations of Welsh Names & noted events in Elin Cadwaladr.

Bodawel : Breeze Abode
Bryn Siriol : Pleasant Hill
Bryn Tawel : Quiet Hill
Cymanfa Ganu : Singing festival
Dolydd Ivan : Ivan's Meadows
Ffos Wen : White Ditch
Gwynfryn : Whitehill
Nant y Fron : Brook of the Breast of the Hill
Neuadd Lwyd : Grey Hall
Noson Lawen : Soirée / evening of entertainment
Seiat : Fellowship Meeting
Tan y Fron : Under the Breast of the Hill
Traeth Mawr : Big Beach
Ty Du : Black House
Ty Hen : Old House
Y Blaid Werinol : The People's Party
Y Llecyn : The Place or The Spot
Y Pant : The Hollow
Y Rhiw : The Hill

[Panel 2.1]

Prejudice against fiction

There was a great deal of religious prejudice in the 19th century against fiction. It was thought that it would pollute the minds and undermine the morals of young people. The authors of the Welsh serialised novels from the latter half of the nineteenth century, strove to reverse this prejudice against literature, by creating novels of the highest moral standards.

In Elin Cadwaladr, W. D. Owen is following this tradition, and the two main characters in the story clearly conform to the pattern of characterisation in such moralistic tales. As E. G. Millward writes in his article 'More 19th Century Novels':

... The young Welshman could be a lover (love stories were extremely popular) but he had to be a pure lover. So also, the object of his love; she is faultless, preparing herself to be an angel in the house. These novels end with a happy marriage, a double marriage sometimes, as in 'Enoc Huws'. 'True love' finds victory in the end. After tribulation comes bliss (in this world, note), as long as we remain honest, hard-working, kind and true to the highest principles and the best religious standards. Bliss, tribulation, heroes and heroines, undoubted scoundrels. Characterisation in the popular novel is black and white ..

{205}

[Panel 2.2]

The rural aspect of central Rhosneigr from c1904. The Glan Neigr on the extreme left of this old postcard provides a fix to the location of these fields, which are now almost completely covered by houses.

Chapter 1 *Starting to Preach*

The story is set in the rural village and parish of Bryn Siriol in Anglesey. A holiday village has recently been built within the parish near the 'Big Beach', which receives frequent summer visitors from the cities of England.

Bryn Siriol is a village, and also a parish, in the hundred of Hirfon, on the island of Anglesey. Although the parish boundaries are more than five miles from the sea, there are places in the district from which its shores can be clearly seen on fine days.

But Bryn Siriol is an agricultural district. Until recently its inhabitants took little interest in the splendid sands of the Big Beach. But after it became a Mecca for strangers from the towns of England, in search of health, and after a trim little townlet was built on the sandbanks, some enthusiasm was kindled in Bryn Siriol. The price of butter went up. The price of eggs rose too...

The people of the parish are people who work hard, and live hard. They laugh when they see the Englishmen of the Big Beach walking miles in all weathers through the heather and ferns after a small white ball. They laugh just as heartily when they hear the English talking about health rules and the relationship between sick cattle and consumption.

But let no-one jump to the conclusion that the people of Bryn Siriol lack sense. They are astute and thoughtful people; men of mental abilities stronger than the usual amidst country folk and wise, skilful women.

The village has two rows of cottages, one each side of the main road. The majority of the houses in the village are small one-roomed shacks, open to the roof. There are some better houses, designed and built more like the houses of the Big Beach. Indeed, the parsonage and the schoolmaster's new house would adorn any small town in England ...

David Charles, the handsome son of the minister of Engedi Chapel [*1a] in the village, delivers his first sermon in his native chapel. It is well received and his father and the deacons are pleased with him. So, too, is the beautiful and devout Elin Cadwaladr, who plays the chapel harmonium and who is obviously fond of 'Davy'.

The author also tells how many of the Bryn Siriol's young people have had to leave their native village in order to make a living and how they make frequent return visits, having done well in life.

The centrality of the chapel in village life in Wales a century ago is clearly portrayed, as is the status conveyed by being made a deacon and the importance of chapel values. Humility is obviously regarded as an important virtue as, at the end of the service (and the end of the chapter), taking their cue from Morris Jones, an old deacon, none of the other deacons presumes to congratulate Robert Charles on how well his son has conducted himself on his début in the pulpit. Morris Jones beats about the bush with phrases such as, "*God has been good to us tonight,*" until he finally brings himself to say, "*I was glad to hear the boy do so well tonight. He was fine.*"

The characters introduced are David Charles, son of Robert Charles, 'Bryntawel' *['Quiet Hill']* minister of the chapel Engedi, a handsome and charismatic young man whose heroes are not film stars and sports personalities but the well-known preachers of the day, Elin Cadwaladr, a beautiful and emotional young woman who plays the chapel harmonium; Rev. Robert Charles himself; his wife, Mary Charles, a native of Bryn Siriol, godly, capable and highly respected; and Morris Jones, an old deacon and Robert Charles's friend.

*1a - Engedi has no Welsh meaning, but in Hebrew means 'the spring of the young goat'

Chapter 2 *Parry's Shop*

The following day a number of the men of the village meet in Parry's shop, the discussion centre of the village *2a, to discuss the previous night's sermon. Although a deacon, Parry is not narrow-minded, is interested in sport and is a skilled billiards player. Price the Schoolmaster and Robert Edward, the Carpenter, join Parry in a discussion on the previous night's sermon. The schoolmaster, largely to goad the carpenter, maintains that David's sermon contained a great deal of 'new thinking' whereas Robert Edward is adamant that it was totally true to the Scriptures. Price goes on to suggest that, after he has spent time at Oxford, David will turn his back on preaching and may even turn to politics! The argument becomes heated and John, 'Dolydd Ivan', *[Ivan's Meadows]* *2b tries to act as mediator. Eventually it is Parry the shopkeeper's suggestion that David is very clever and is sure to succeed in whatever field he chooses, which calms things down.

The talk then turns to the possibility of having a billiard table in the chapel schoolroom, as Mr Prichard, minister of Libanus Chapel, is proposing to do. Opinion is divided as to whether billiards is the work of the devil or whether it will be an innocent pleasure which will keep the young people in the chapel and away from the pub. Parry's only daughter, Grace, enters the shop with her cousin, Elin Cadwaldr of 'Ty Hen' *[Old House]*. Grace is described as comely but not a deep thinker whereas Elin is beautiful, well-bred, intellectual and thoughtful. She expresses the opinion that, while she is not against the game of billiards in itself, she would not wish to do anything to upset the minister or the older members of the 'big seat' *2c like Morris Jones.

Paran Chapel, Rhosneigr, showing pews and the 'Big Seat' at the front.

*2a - Parry's shop is interestingly described as the "Areopagus" of Bryn Siriol. The Areopagus was originally the highest judicial court in ancient Athens, but is used here in the context of an assembly of persons gathered together for a common purpose.

*2b - The tradition of using a forename, followed by a place of residence instead of a surname, still persists in many places (including Rhosneigr) today. This method of naming is used throughout the novel.

*2c - in Nonconformist chapels, the 'big seat' is at the front of the chapel, immediately below the pulpit, and is where the deacons sit.

Chapter 3 *Leaving Home*

David's trial year as a preacher comes to an end; his preaching has been acclaimed throughout the county. He spends the morning of his last day in Bryn Siriol before going up to Oxford, with his father, who gives him spiritual advice. David has made frequent visits to Elin's home, 'Ty Hen', during the year, and, in the afternoon, his mother makes it clear that she has set her heart on his marrying Elin.

That evening, he calls at 'Ty Hen' – *a low-ceilinged, humble, tenant farmhouse, situated in a hollow on the edge of the mill stream, bordering the fen and reached by a narrow stony path* - to say his goodbyes to Elin and discovers that she is visiting an elderly neighbour.

David walks to meet Elin at nearby 'Bodawel' *[Breeze Abode]*. When they meet, he pulls her into his arms and confesses that he has loved her since childhood and that his achievements, past and future, mean nothing without her love. He also confesses that the fights he used to have with Tom Evans, 'Gwynfryn' *[White Hill]*, when they were schoolboys, were about Elin!

In this chapter, Elin's father, John Cadwaladr, a widower, is described as a cold man, interested in worldly advancement. Elin however has received a good education in a school in Liverpool and her ability to speak English is of great use to her father in selling and buying animals. Elin is an astute businesswoman - the idea of selling their beef cattle and keeping dairy cattle in order to supply the needs of the new resort was hers.

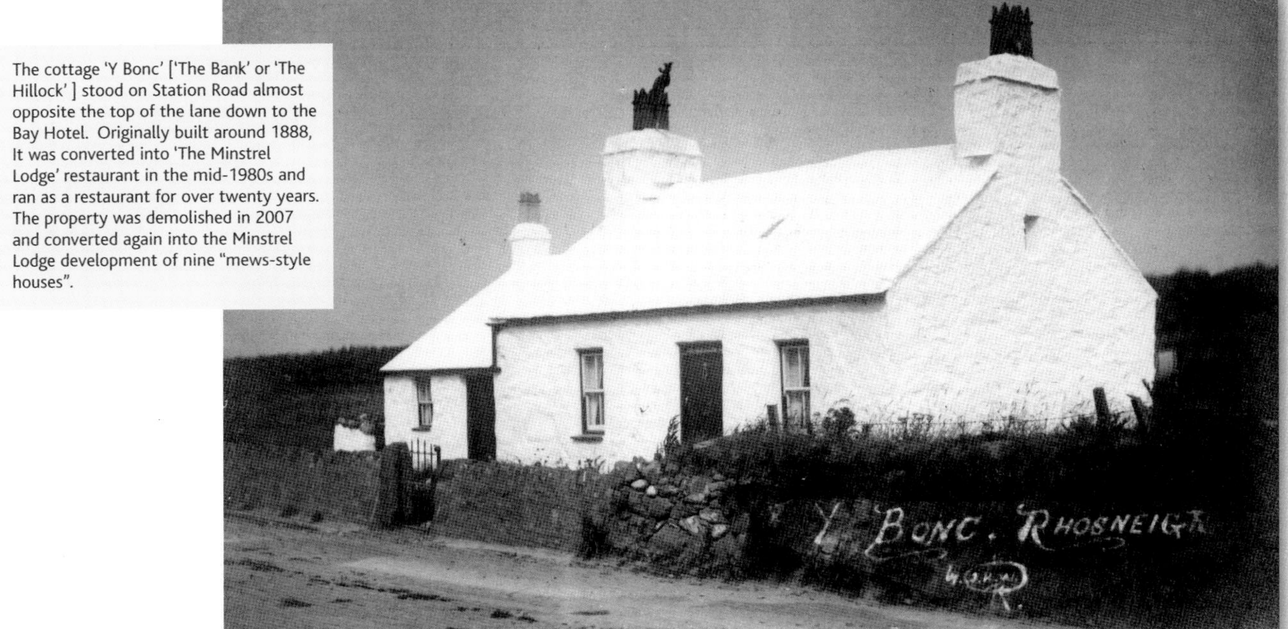

The cottage 'Y Bonc' ['The Bank' or 'The Hillock'] stood on Station Road almost opposite the top of the lane down to the Bay Hotel. Originally built around 1888, It was converted into 'The Minstrel Lodge' restaurant in the mid-1980s and ran as a restaurant for over twenty years. The property was demolished in 2007 and converted again into the Minstrel Lodge development of nine "mews-style houses".

Chapter 4 *Disappointment*

It is noted that because of pastimes such as golf, rowing and fishing and because the girls are engaged in seasonal work in the new resort, chapel congregations are much smaller in the summer, to the distress of men such as Morris Jones and Evans, 'Gwynfryn'. Even Elin's father, John Cadwaladr, comes under criticism from some, for selling milk to the visitors on Sundays. However, interest in chapel events increases again in the autumn, with 'big names' coming to preach at the harvest services, a musical festival at Libanus and preparations under way for the grand Christmas concert.

Meanwhile, David is thoroughly enjoying his first term at Oxford but writes regularly to his parents and to Elin. Mrs Charles and Elin spend at least one evening a week in each other's company and both are longing for the time when Davy comes home for the Christmas holidays. Three weeks before Christmas, Mary Charles receives a letter from her son saying that he has accepted an invitation to spend Christmas with the family of his friend, Harries, in Pembrokeshire. She is extremely upset and remembers admiring references in David's letters to Harries's sister, Dorothy. When Elin is shown the letter she tries to hide her own feelings, to defend Davy and to comfort Mrs Charles, breaking down only after Mrs Charles has left. However, Elin's attempts to defend Davy have made Mary Charles think she doesn't care about him any more.

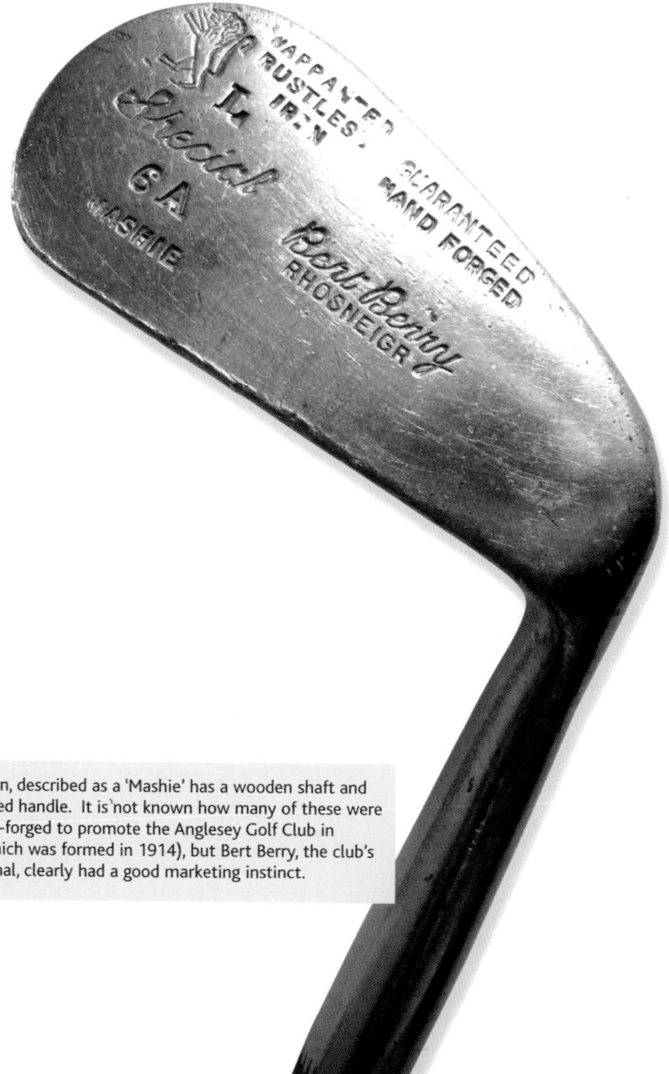

This No.6A iron, described as a 'Mashie' has a wooden shaft and leather wrapped handle. It is not known how many of these were specially hand-forged to promote the Anglesey Golf Club in Rhosneigr, (which was formed in 1914), but Bert Berry, the club's first Professional, clearly had a good marketing instinct.

Chapter 5 *Land of Song*

During the all-male committee meeting to make plans for the grand concert, a tenor, Eithinog Huws, is suggested by the Chairman, Parry, as the 'guest star' and is accepted, although little is known about his credentials. Tom Evans, 'Gwynfryn', who has recently qualified as a Doctor, is chosen as the concert's Master of Ceremonies.

There is a piano and an American organ in 'Gwynfryn' and a copy of the 'Piano Tutor' is frequently seen in the drawing room. *Who then, could say, in the face of facts like that, that Miss Jennie Evans, Gwynfryn, is not an authority on all things musical?* It follows therefore that Dr Thomas's sister, Jennie, is suggested as an accompanist along with Miss Beaconsfield Thomas.

Miss Thomas is the daughter of Welshman, Mr Beaconsfield Thomas, (wealthy occupant of 'Hazel Dell', built on a hill above Bryn Siriol) who was formerly known as Thomas Thomas, and who went to England with neither craft nor education, but made his fortune and changed his name to reflect his changed circumstances.

Both girls are rejected, however, in favour of Elin Cadwaladr. They subsequently become 'comrades in adversity' and see Elin as a common enemy.

Miss Beaconsfield Thomas visits Jennie Evans at 'Gwynfryn' just before Christmas and Tom overhears her telling his sister that David Charles is not coming home for Christmas and has given Elin up. Tom quietly leaves the house to visit 'Ty Hen' and speak to Elin's father.

Bryn Siriol is described as a musical parish. There is much light-hearted satire in this chapter. Parry, for example, is considered 'musical' because he once knew a famous tenor and follows the careers of well-known singers. Elin is described (without satire) as having musical talent combined with skill and knowledge.

Other musical people in the village include the non-Welsh speaking newcomer, Miss Beaconsfield Thomas, who has five letters after her name, all musical; Hugh Griffith, the sexton; Thomas Thomas, who leads the singing in Engedi; Richard Jones, 'Y Pant' *[The Hollow]*, three times secretary of the Cymanfa Ganu *[singing festival]* and Price the Schoolmaster who was almost forgotten because he is modest about his talent as a singer.

Chapter 6 *Dr Evans' visit*

Elin spends a miserable three weeks after discovering that David is not coming home for Christmas. Apart from going to chapel on Sundays, she leaves the house only once, to go to the shop, where she encounters Miss Evans and Miss Beaconsfield Thomas. The two girls lose no time in paying Elin back for the perceived insult of the night of the committee meeting, initially pretending they haven't seen her, then treating her as though she doesn't exist and finally pointedly listing all those young people who are coming home for Christmas. Elin feels that the whole village must be pointing the finger of scorn at her but, when asked by her father why David hasn't called at the house, she manages to act as though nothing is amiss.

Tom Evans visits 'Ty Hen' in order to ask John Cadwaladr's permission to pay his attentions to Elin but is embarrassed when he finds both father and daughter at home. Elin tactfully withdraws to the kitchen while Tom, sweating profusely and half in Welsh, which he has largely forgotten, and half in English, of which John Cadwaladr understands barely a word, tries to get his message across. When John Cadwaladr finally understands what Tom wants, after telling him that Elin is spoken for, he mischievously suggests that Tom should tell Elin himself and calls her, leaving the room and leaving Tom yet more discomfited. Tom confesses to Elin that he, too, has loved her since schooldays and tells her something of his prospects as a doctor. In telling him that she is not free, Elin is careful to spare his feelings. Later, on the night of the grand concert, in which the guest tenor proves a disappointment, Tom and Elin support one another, much to the chagrin of the two malicious young ladies.

It is three weeks into the New Year before Elin receives a letter from David, telling her of the human suffering he has seen in the industrial areas of South Wales. Rev. Charles receives a more detailed missive on the same topic, revealing Harries's increasing influence on Davy and the former's conviction that socialism is the answer to all the world's ills.

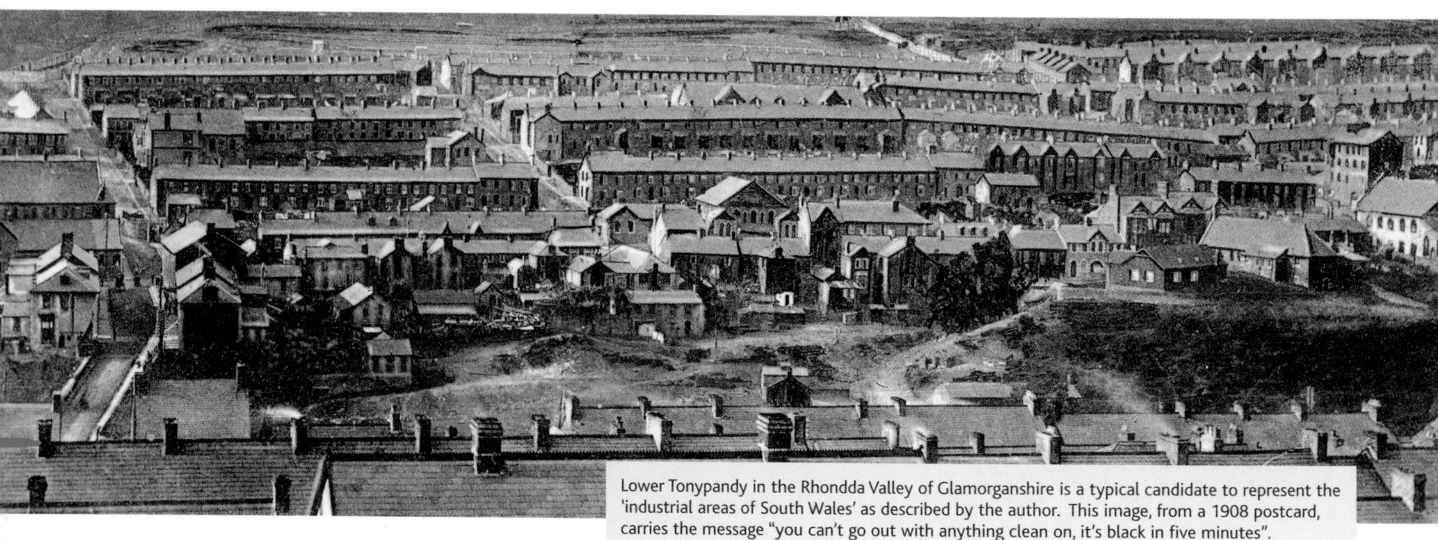

Lower Tonypandy in the Rhondda Valley of Glamorganshire is a typical candidate to represent the 'industrial areas of South Wales' as described by the author. This image, from a 1908 postcard, carries the message "you can't go out with anything clean on, it's black in five minutes".

Chapter 7 *Wandering Far*

When she continues to receive affectionate letters from her son, Mary Charles quickly recovers from the disappointment of not seeing him at Christmas. Elin's hurt is deeper, however. She is aware that Dorothy Harries possesses some quality that earns David's admiration, while she herself apparently does not, and her confusion is compounded by the change in David's mother's attitude towards her. When David comes home at Easter he and Elin spend time together but her feeling that something has altered between them remains.

David is coming into contact, and exchanging ideas, with people from all corners of the British Empire and from the Far East. His mind is being expanded, which is a good thing, but in criticising the narrow-mindedness of many Christians he comes to reject Christianity itself. At the same time, he becomes more and more involved in political thinking, seeing capitalism as the cause of the suffering of the poor, religion as the great deceiver which misleads the suffering thousands, and socialism as the solution to all the world's ills. David himself is aware of how much his attitude to spiritual matters and the old standards has changed but, in order to avoid hurting Elin and because he is sure she will disapprove, does not tell her of his feelings or of his intention to study law. At the same time he feels he is deceiving her and this makes him uncomfortable in her presence. [*7a]

Having obtained the sum of money he requires to study law from his mother, David returns to Oxford and Harries, but is aware of the concern in the eyes of his father and Elin. When Harries greets David on his return to Oxford they exchange greetings in Welsh. However, they eventually resort to English to converse because the enormous differences between their two dialects make it easier to converse in English than in their native Welsh.

*7a - The similarities between Owen's personal life, and the events in his novel are, in this writer's opinion, too close to be coincidental.

Chapter 8 *Between the Two Harvests*

The period in summer between 'the two harvests' is, in rural areas, often a time for outings and social gatherings. David finishes college, having been invited to be the minister of an English chapel in a London suburb and, that summer, a garden party is held in the grounds of 'Neuadd Lwyd' *[Grey Hall]* in Bryn Siriol. It is hosted by the owner, Samuel Thomas Gruffydd, who has made his fortune outside Wales but has returned to his native village, still a thorough Welshman. The new seaside resort is the product of his ideas and his funding and the garden party is an opportunity for the village people and the visitors to get to know one another. His home 'Neuadd Lwyd' was formerly owned by non-Welsh aristocracy but is now said to be the home of *'a Welshman who is worthy of it'*.

David is in the company of Elin, Grace Parry and her father and Price the Schoolmaster. Dorothy Harries, however, has engineered an invitation to the event through the host's daughter, Olwen. Dorothy proceeds to monopolise David and to give the impression to everyone present that she and David are engaged. Elin sees through her but David naively feels that he has to be polite to the sister of the friend who has done so much for him and, when David accepts an invitation to spend the evening at 'Neuadd Lwyd', Elin is powerless to intervene. Meanwhile, one of the village girls, Lizzie Ellen, 'Y Rhiw' *[The Hill]*, is taken ill and coughs up blood, causing several of the other girls to faint. The sick girl asks for Elin who capably takes charge of the situation.

Towards the end of the chapter, Price the Schoolmaster and John Gruffydd 'Dolydd Ivan' (both champions of Elin) are discussing Dorothy Harries's behaviour. John Gruffydd asks Price who the girl is and is told, *"The sister of that boy who is busy making a Socialist of Davy."* Price also describes Dorothy as *"some flibberty gibbit from South Wales."* Both men can see through her and think that Davy is making a fool of himself and will make a mess of things if he carries on like this.

Chapter 9 *The Family Quilt*

Lizzie Ellen is the daughter of William and Betsan Williams, a kind and well-liked couple who have already lost their two older children to tuberculosis. Their home is 'Y Rhiw', which is an old farmhouse with dampness, windows which don't open, and one room, used as a bedroom, which has no window at all. Lizzie is lying under a patchwork quilt which has never been washed and which is kept for special occasions, having been last used on the deathbeds of her brother and sister. She is very frightened when Rev. Robert Charles calls and reads her the same Bible passage that he read to her sister Kate shortly before she died and Betsan is convinced that she is about to lose a third child.

Fortunately Dr Tom Evans is at home, and it is rumoured that he wishes to return to Anglesey to work. He calls regularly to see Lizzie, tells her she must eat well and start to go out in the fresh air and insists that Betsan gets a carpenter in to ensure that all the windows in the old house can be opened. The newly qualified Dr Evans understands that without these changes, the house is a breeding ground for TB. [*9a] He also manages to persuade Betsan to remove the germ-laden quilt, saying that it is too hot for summer. As Tom leaves after one of his visits, he meets David Charles and asks him if it is true that he is engaged to Dorothy. Little does David realise when he promptly replies, "Nothing of the sort!" that his answer is a source of great disappointment to Tom!

*9a In the character of Dr Evans, Owen explores the changing attitudes in the medical world to the treatment of TB.

Chapter 10 *The Fellowship Meeting in Engedi*

Nevertheless, rumours that David is seeing Dorothy every day during her stay at 'Neuadd Lwyd' are rife. David is criticised all the more because he is a minister of the Gospel and is tried and found guilty by the villagers before he ever realises that he is on trial! The same gossip-mongers make sure that Elin is aware of what is, supposedly, going on, and Elin eventually tells Ann Thomas, wife of Thomas Thomas the Precentor [*10a], that she wishes to hear no more about Davy Charles.

Ann, who sells yarn for knitting stockings, loses no time in making it known throughout the village that it is all over between Davy, 'Bryn Tawel' and Elin, 'Ty Hen'. Elin turns her attention to her books and to the various societies to which she belongs; her opinion is always respected.

A 'seiat' *[fellowship meeting]*, is held in the chapel to make a final decision on the question of the billiard room and feelings run high on both sides. In those days, it was unusual for a woman to speak in the seiat but, towards the end of the proceedings, Elin delivers a well-researched and well reasoned speech in favour of the billiard room, changing the opinions of many who were in opposition. The very last speaker is the old deacon, Morris Jones, who, with tears in his eyes speaks at length about the house of God as a place which is to be honoured and respected. He ends by saying that he knows Elin will do nothing to dishonour the house of God and, therefore, asks the congregation to support the proposition. The proposition is carried but, long before he finishes speaking, Elin bursts into tears and so do several others. All go home subdued and the plan is quietly shelved!

*10a The Precentor is the person who leads the singing of the congregation.

Billiards & Fellowship

The 'seiat' gives the author an opportunity to develop the characters of some of the deacons.

Mr Beaconsfield Thomas is a sort of 'honorary member' of the 'Big Seat' 'who is not expected to humble himself by kneeling publicly!' He gives generously to the cause *(People's donations are made public in an annual report so that other members will see what he gives!)* but he is 'not present that night'.

Richard Jones, 'Y Pant' is looked on principally as the chapel's clerk rather than one of its spiritual leaders.

Rev Robert Charles is very uncomfortable and plays no part in the discussion [giving an indication that he is not a very strong leader].

Parry the Shop is much less confident in front of his fellow deacons than he had been in the shop but speaks out bravely in favour of the billiard room.

Robert Edward the Carpenter condemns the idea vehemently citing the 'curse of the tavern' as his main reason against it. However, the author tells us that people generally take little notice of his opinion because he drifts in and out of the chapel at will. When he is outside 'the fold' he curses chapel-goers and religion but, each time he 'repents' and returns there is no-one more fervent.

Price the Schoolmaster speaks in favour of the room, emphasising that the whole point of the idea is to keep the young people away from the tavern and declares that the billiard-room in Libanus is a complete success.

John Griffiths speaks in favour (but there are no details); William Williams, 'Ffos Wen' *[White Ditch]* feels it is a step in a dubious direction and Richard Ellis, the old man from 'Bodawel' feels the same.

Evans 'Gwynfryn' is against the billiards room. He is described as bombastic, opinionated, fond of laying down the law, incapable of accepting the opinions of others and very unlike his son, Tom. He also has a horrible habit of laughing mockingly at his opponents. He condemns the young people and says they would be better off reading their Bibles and attending chapel more regularly than playing billiards. It is his attitude that brings Elin to her feet.

Morris Jones is the very old, well-respected deacon. He begins by saying he is only a poor, humble stone-cutter. He tries desperately to move with the times and to say that, if Elin is in favour, the billiard-room must be all right – but his humility, his bewilderment, his sincerity, his love of his Saviour and his respect for his place of worship carry the day against the proposal in a way which Evans Gwynfryn's bullying and bombastic tactics could never have done.

BILLIARD EXPRESSIONS.
A KISS OFF THE CUSHION.

A Bamforth's postcard from the 'Billiards' series dated 1914. The double-entendre caption perfectly represents the dichotomy of the chapel elders.

Chapter 11 *The Minister of Crouch Park*

David spends a year as the minister of the Presbyterian chapel in Crouch Park, a respectable London suburb *[11a]. Little is required in terms of pastoral or missionary work and he soon makes a name for himself through his excellent sermons which attract large congregations. When a friend calls to see David and tells him of the intention to invite him to preach in 'big meetings' in Engedi Chapel back home, David realises that his preaching in Crouch Park is merely a form of acting and that he cannot stand in Engedi's pulpit as a hypocrite. He visits Pembroke Harries, who is practising law in Lincoln's Inn *[11b], and his friend invites him to join him some time, in addressing a meeting of miners in Bakewell Heath.

David is in mental and emotional turmoil as he finds himself unable to reconcile his Socialist leanings with his post as a Presbyterian minister. He feels that philosophy, science, history and socialism all lead him away from religion and there is no-one at hand to point out that there is much in what he believes which is not incompatible with the teachings of the New Testament. David thinks of Elin every day and tries to write to her to explain the turmoil in which he finds himself but, remembering that she seemed distant the last time he was home, and convinced that she will not understand, he fails to write the letter and the barrier between them remains. David resolves to give up his job, feeling Harries's suggestion that he should remain in the ministry and continue to draw his salary until he has some other means of obtaining an income, to be unethical. Having made the decision, he feels more at peace with himself and his principles.

*11a The author lived for several years in Muswell Hill, less than a mile away from Crouch End, which he retitles 'Crouch Park'.

*11b Lincoln's Inn is barely a stone's throw from where the author himself trained as a barrister.

CROUCH END PLAYING FIELDS AND ALEXANDRA PALACE.
No. 102.

Chapter 12 *The Church's Greed*

Dr Tom Evans has returned to Bryn Siriol to practise and has had a house built on the edge of the village. An eligible young doctor with his own home inevitably attracts the interest of the young ladies and Miss Beaconsfield Thomas's friendship with Tom's sister becomes even closer! In some circles Tom's name is also linked with that of Olwen Gruffydd of 'Neuadd Lwyd'. Tom tends his first patient, Lizzie Ellen, diligently, but she is too ill to be moved to a sanatorium before the cold weather sets in and it becomes obvious that she is dying. She asks for Elin, who is fetched and is able to comfort the dying girl. Lizzie Ellen rallies briefly but the next time Elin is fetched she is too late.

The sight of the dead girl's face arouses passionate feelings in Elin. She realises that tuberculosis flourishes in conditions of poverty and squalor, that landlords are making money from sub-standard housing at the expense of their tenants' health and that the landlord of Lizzie Ellen's home, 'Y Rhiw', is actually a deacon in the chapel. When Tom takes her home and tells her that he suspects Lizzie Ellen's younger sister, Maggie, has the same illness, Elin says that she feels the chapel should be putting into practice some of the Scriptural teachings which it preaches. She asks Tom where they can start to try to make a difference and he asks her to try to get rid of Betsan Williams's quilt!

Chapter 13 *Our Dear Sister*

David Charles meets Pembroke Harries to make their way to the miners' meeting in Bakewell Heath but, having renounced his faith and told the chapel officials of his intention to resign, he feels nothing but emptiness and has no appetite for Socialism. On the same day, crowds gather in Bryn Siriol for Lizzie Ellen's funeral. The weather is atrocious with driving rain and a bitingly cold wind in the cemetery. Mary Charles is concerned for the health of her husband, the minister, who has been suffering with a cough and who looks extremely unwell.

From the window of 'Tan y Fron' *[Under the Breast of the Hill]*, a picturesque but poor cottage, a young girl named Mary Roberts, who also has T.B., watches the funeral procession, fearing that hers will be the next. Her parents decide to ask for the help of S. T. Gruffydd, 'Neuadd Lwyd', to take up Dr Tom Evans's suggestion to send her to a sanatorium.

On the road between 'Y Rhiw' and the village there is a small cottage on the side of the lane. It is called 'Tan y Fron'. Motorists from the Big Beach and from Holyhead stop to look at it in admiration.

"Isn't it sweet?" say the girls without exception.

"Very pretty," confess the men, with less enthusiasm.

The Welsh, too, like to sing the praises of the yellow cottages of their fathers. Such a one is Tan y Fron. It nestles attractively in a garden of trees and bushes like a beautiful tea-rose among the leaves, like a pretty bower in a summer garden.

But Tan y Fron is the cottage of a labourer. And its beauty is only external. Henry and Margaid Roberts chose it as their home not for its antiquity or its yellowness or its beauty but because there was no other shelter available that they could afford on the wages of a labourer.

Although considerably altered inside from the two cottages it once was, externally, this group of buildings has little changed. Known as 'Maen Hir' *[Monolith]* after the standing stone in the field opposite, it lies on the main road between Llanfaelog and the small hamlet of Engedi. This style of Welsh cottage is typical of Anglesey which made this hard to identify, particularly as some of the trees have now disappeared. However, the bend in the road and the cottage in the distance, are other features which are still present.

Chapter 14 *The Red Banner*

David and Harries reach Bakewell Heath, a depressing industrial town, and have a cup of tea in the house of Wilkins, the Ruskin scholar who has arranged the meeting (and who likes the sound of his own voice) before proceeding to the meeting itself. It is held in an upstairs room of the George and Dragon, from which emanates the smell of two hundred clay pipes and a similar number of mugs of beer. David is called to speak first, to the disappointment of the men, who were expecting Harries. David has no idea, initially, what he is going to say, but his natural skills as an orator and an actor come to his rescue and he soon captivates his audience. He uses the words – society – labour – capital – wealth – need – taxes – burdens – privileges and so on, and no-one, not even Harries, guesses that he is speaking about the turmoil in his own heart and his own search for the truth. Harries and Wilkins also speak but David has completely outshone them. The papers the following day carry the story, adding the fact that the promising young speaker is from Anglesey and is currently the minister of Crouch Park!

David has barely had time to consider the negative effect this might have on his family before a telegram arrives asking him to return home as his father is dangerously ill with pneumonia.

The postman, 'Thomas Hughes the Post', is introduced. He is extremely critical of David and is busy showing the titbit of news to everyone he meets in the village. Indeed: *Nothing of this level of interest had happened in Bryn Siriol since the son of 'Y Llecyn' [The Place] shot himself after his father married the maid.* Having been shown a copy of the newspaper, Parry the Shop manages to retrieve the copy which has been delivered to the minister's home before it can be opened and read, aware of the distress it would cause David's family.

Chapter 15 *The Wooden Shacks*

John Griffith, who farms 'Dolydd Ivan', has reached an age where he feels he should take a wife. His mother is anxious for him to marry Miss Ann Pritchard, 'Ty Du' *[Black House]*, but it is obvious that John is not keen on the idea. One day, John is ploughing near the road when a gipsy woman passes by and insists on telling his fortune. [*15a] She tells him that he is soon to wed, that the girl has a fair complexion and that he will have to pass wooden shacks on his way to her house. These clues point to the same Miss Pritchard, and John is so distressed that, for some days, he is unable to eat or sleep. One evening he confesses his problem to Price the Schoolmaster.

On the evening of Christmas Day there is to be a get-together at the Parry household. After tea, John Griffith and Price go for a walk together to 'Nant y Fron' *[Brook on the Breast of the Hill]*, which is the other side of the village from Engedi. Price leads John along a path which is unfamiliar to him and they end up by some wooden shacks. To John's surprise they are the warehouses behind Parry's shop. They go in and, during the course of the evening, John and Grace Parry find themselves alone in the kitchen under a sprig of mistletoe. More than one kiss ensues and the wedding quickly follows.

Elin visits Grace frequently in 'Dolydd Ivan' and, one evening, Grace asks her whether she still hears from David and, when Elin says that she does not, tells her all the rumours which are being spread about David, mainly by Thomas Hughes the Post and Robert Edwards the Carpenter, and asks her why she does not give up on him and marry Dr Tom. Elin defends David valiantly and Grace uses the tactic of telling her that Hannah Beaconsfield Thomas has her eye on the doctor, to try to get her to change her mind.

*15a There is a suggestion at the end of this chapter that Price the Schoolmaster set up the gipsy.

Chapter 16 *Recollections*

David arrives home to find his father fighting for breath. Robert Charles recognises his son but, by morning, has lost his battle for life. David stays with his mother for a week after the funeral. They reach an understanding and, when he leaves Bryn Siriol to move in very different circles back in London, it is with her blessing. During the time that he is at home, he does not make any attempt to look up his old friends. Elin would like to see David and comfort him but gets no suitable opportunity to do so.

Some time after the funeral, David is once again the subject of gossip and criticism in the village. In particular there is a heated discussion in Parry's shop, in which Robert Edward (the Carpenter) and Thomas Hughes (the Postman) do not have a good word to say about him. John Griffith 'Dolydd Ivan' says that David has disappointed him more than any man he has ever known; Price (the Schoolmaster) sticks up for him but only because he enjoys playing Devil's advocate and only Parry genuinely tries to stand up for him. Little is said against him in Elin's hearing, however, since such is the regard in which she is now held that people are anxious to spare her feelings. Elin is now described as a mature young woman whose opinions are respected and who is now far above the petty spitefulness of Jennie Evans and Hannah Beaconsfield Thomas. She is however aware of the gossip but her love for David remains as strong as ever and she frequently thinks of the evening when he told her he loved her. True to her resolution to do something practical in the fight against tuberculosis, she approaches her landlord, Sir Hugh Blakeley, to request that new cowsheds be built. The access road to the house is also improved and soon people come from near and far to see the 'model dairy'. Business expands and other farmers are forced to improve their standards in order to compete.

Dr Tom Evans risks angering many by saying that the health provisions in the new resort are sub-standard and that thousands of pounds need to be spent on improvements. The land-owners and residents of the Big Beach complain that he will ruin the place, while the villagers fear a rise in taxes. In heated meetings, two of the English residents of the Big Beach, Mr Goodenough and Captain Weeks, treat the almost monoglot Welsh farmers as though they are savages! S. T. Gruffydd manages to persuade the residents of the new resort of the wisdom of the plan but even he has to confess that persuading the villagers to pay increased taxes to develop the holiday village is going to be no easy task!

This view towards Llanfaelog shows a small group of cattle grazing at the side of the Maelog lake. This land, owned by the Maelog Lake Hotel, forms part of Tywyn Llyn *[Duneland by the Lake]* common which was finally subject to a scheme of regulation in 1946 under the Commons Act of 1899. Considerable attention was given to this subject during the early part of the 20th century - there was much concern over the issue of 'enclosure' and there are vast quantities of correspondence in the archives on the subject. Even in the more recent past, 'private' signs erected at the lakeside by the J.W.Lees brewery in the 1990s caused some controversy.

Chapter 17 *Election*

S. T. Gruffydd has made enquiries regarding a place in a sanatorium for Mary Roberts but, such is the demand that no place is available. However, he has seen a special shelter in an exhibition in London and has ordered one for Mary. Within a fortnight it has arrived and been erected in a suitable position in the garden of 'Tan y Fron'. It is designed to ensure that Mary gets the fresh air she needs. Nourishing foodstuffs are sent twice a week to Mary's home from 'Neuadd Lwyd' and shortly, other villagers begin to follow suit. Within a month Dr Tom is very pleased with his patient's progress. S. T. Gruffydd's good name in helping the Roberts family, however, is overshadowed in the minds of the villagers by his support for improving the facilities at the Big Beach, thus causing their taxes to rise:
It was strange how the sixpence in the pound tax that was threatened, outweighed every other consideration, narrowing and shrivelling the minds of people whose characters were normally noted for their tenderness and kindness. But so it was.

Typical open-air TB shelter as described by the author, although unfortunately no photographs of local shelters have been traced. This shelter was in use at the Papworth Village settlement in Cambridge. {206}

This situation is soon eclipsed by another problem which arises in the parish. For the last six years, Mr Beaconsfield Thomas has represented Bryn Siriol as its County Councillor, having been returned unopposed. The villagers had supposed that such a fine figure of a man would make an excellent representative but had been disappointed. The men cast about among themselves for someone to stand against him. When one of the village children suggests John Cadwaladr they seize upon his name and persuade him to stand for election. Elin fears that her father will be out of his depth in the job but dutifully supports him, despite the way in which the supporters of both candidates slander the other :- John Cadwaladr is said to be *miserly, almost illiterate and to have treated his wife badly,* while Mr Beaconsfield Thomas is said to be *heavily in debt and to have a second cousin who sells cockles with a mule and cart!* However, so anxious are the farmers to get rid of their erstwhile idol that John Cadwaladr wins the election by a substantial majority but the bemused farmer has no idea how to cope with his new role!

Chapter 18 *Politics*

David is making a name for himself in the legal profession and the villagers of Bryn Siriol gradually allow themselves to feel proud of him again. David himself has not seen Elin for some considerable time and, though he thinks of her with tenderness, he believes that the path he has chosen has led him away from her and that it is pointless to dwell in the past. Dorothy Harries ensures that she sees David regularly in the hope that frequent proximity will enable her to win him.

One day, Sir Hugh Morgan, who is well known in the political world, calls to see David and asks him to join the club of the political party to which he belongs. David has become disillusioned with Socialism and is tempted to accept Sir Hugh's offer as he feels he will be more comfortable in his party. [*18.1]

Sir Hugh tells him that an M.P. is about to retire and there will be an opportunity for him to become a parliamentary candidate. David asks for time to think about it, visits Harries and tries to persuade him to join him in Sir Hugh's party but Harries's socialist convictions are too strong.

Back in Bryn Siriol, Mary Charles has received a letter from David telling her what has happened and she feels more cheerful than she has done since her husband's death. She hastens to reply, telling David the local news. Mr Beaconsfield Thomas has gone bankrupt, almost ruining Evans 'Gwynfryn', from whom he had borrowed money, in the process. Elin is going to pay for Maggie Williams, 'Y Rhiw', to go to a chest specialist; Mary Roberts, 'Tan y Fron', is doing well; rumour has it that Olwen Gruffydd is going to marry a rich man from Liverpool and John Cadwaladr has given notice to the County Council that he is going to raise the question of the county's dairies in the next meeting!

*18.1 Translators Note: This chapter is extremely confusing. The party, which Harries supports, is referred to as 'y blaid werinol' *[The People's Party]* though the words 'socialist' and 'socialism' are always used in connection with his beliefs. The party which David is asked to join is not named, and the members who are mentioned are believed to be fictitious, but it is said at one point that its members are more David's sort of people, which suggests, perhaps, that they are more middle-class. His mother approves of his change of heart and even Harries does not seem too horrified by it. It is likely, therefore, that the party in question is the Liberal Party.

Chapter 19 *Company in Dolydd Ivan*

Grace, 'Dolydd Ivan', is an excellent hostess and there is always a welcome in her home. Old Mrs Griffith loves having her there and is now hugely relieved that her son did not marry Ann Pritchard, 'Ty Du'. Even John Cadwaladr enjoys going there and he and Elin have supper there after his first meeting as a County Councillor. We discover that he has been very confused by the rules and that he had not given sufficient notice to raise the question of the county's dairies. However, we can see by his amusing and perceptive analysis of his fellow councillors that John Cadwaladr is no fool! (At one point he compares his fellow County Councillors to potatoes: champions, magnum bonums and little red ones! He also describes different kinds of speakers, the best being those who have something worth saying and who say it clearly and concisely).

A few days later, Grace invites Dr Evans to tea, tells him that it is all over between Elin and David and suggests that he approaches Elin again. Shortly afterwards, Tom visits Elin at 'Ty Hen' and asks her to marry him. He says that he has waited a long time and is not pressing for an immediate answer. Elin now feels that her hopes for herself and David are an impossible dream and that she might be wise to accept Tom's offer. She does not say, "No," and Tom tells her that he will call again.

Although originally built as a cinema in 1920, the 'Pavilion Picture House' became Rhosneigr's village hall - and the natural venue for all local meetings - from the late 1960s onwards. It was eventually demolished in 2007 to make way for the new Village Hall now in its place.

Chapter 20 *The Day of the Auction*

A year has passed since Mary, 'Tan y Fron', began to sleep in the open-air shelter, and she is growing so strong and healthy that the general opinion of the villagers is that *she could never have had T.B. in the first place*. Meanwhile, Maggie, 'Y Rhiw', is deteriorating rapidly. In the face of Betsan Williams's continuing opposition, Elin arranges for the specialist to call at 'Ty Hen' and see Maggie there. He tells Elin that most people's lungs show the symptoms of tuberculosis from time to time but that, when they have good food and housing and plenty of fresh air they are able to shake it off. Maggie, however, needs immediate medical attention in a sanatorium if she is to stand any chance. The next day, Elin travels to a private sanatorium less than forty miles away, taking the specialist's report with her, and the medical staff agree to take Maggie free of charge as the case, if successfully treated, will act as an advertisement for the sanatorium.

Following the bankruptcy, there is an auction of furniture at 'Hazel Dell'. John Griffith has been instructed by his wife to buy an iron bedstead and two saucepans but buys a basketful of gas brackets and lampshades even though he has no gas! The villagers turn out in force to inspect Mr Beaconsfield Thomas's furniture and, of course, find it wanting. The same day the news comes out that Price the Schoolmaster has inherited a fortune from an aunt in America.

Night air is the only air
at night,
Better open than closed
up tight.
Sleep in
Fresh Air
DRAWING BY WM. DONAHEY.
55268
COPYRIGHT 1920, BY THE CHICAGO TUBERCULOSIS INSTITUTE.

Chapter 21 *Talk of a Minister*

Engedi is without a minister for three years following the death of Robert Charles. In many ways there is no need for a minister since the deacons are perfectly capable of conducting the services. Eventually, however, visiting preachers start to be considered as potential ministers. A theological student named John ap Rhisiart, who delivers a challenging sermon, [dealt with in great detail in this chapter] is considered, but the majority of the deacons find him too intellectual. The other possibility is Rev. Deubwll Williams, who is an unremarkable preacher but a pleasant guest at mealtimes, when the chapel members take it in turns to play host to the visiting preacher.

John Cadwaladr's proposal to get the County Council to intervene in the matter of the County's dairies has been postponed so many times that he is heartily sick of it. Nothing further has been heard of Price's inheritance, although, two new characters, Dick Griffith the rabbit catcher and William Pirs the carrier, are introduced at the very end of the chapter as people who had started tugging their forelocks to Price in the street *'in case there was something in the story of his inheritance'*. However, neither character is ever mentioned again.

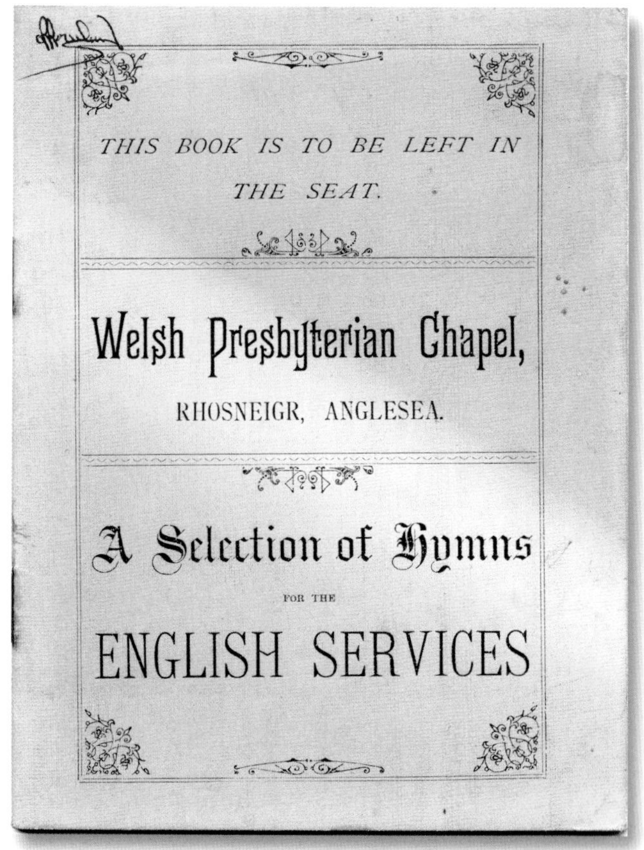

THIS BOOK IS TO BE LEFT IN THE SEAT.

Welsh Presbyterian Chapel,

RHOSNEIGR, ANGLESEA.

A Selection of Hymns

FOR THE

ENGLISH SERVICES

Chapter 22 *Old Friends*

After Dr. Tom Evans's departure, Elin sits for about half an hour as if in a trance, before rising and going out into the cold night air without waiting to don suitable clothing. Scarcely aware of what she is doing, she walks along the lane towards Bodawel, then, frightened even of the sound of her own footsteps, she leaves the lane and takes to the fields. She finds herself at the edge of the mill stream, in a spot where she and the other village children used to bathe. She sees the whirlpool where one of the village children drowned and feels afresh the horror of the tragedy. She remembers the competitions the boys used to have, her own desire that David should do well and the way that he always looked to her for approbation. Then her thoughts return to the present and the painful realisation that David has obviously not thought about her for years. One leap into the whirlpool and her pain would be at an end – but she dismisses this thought as cowardice. Her common sense tells her that there would be many advantages to accepting the doctor's proposal but her heart remains in thrall to the one who is seemingly so indifferent towards her. She decides to remain true to her own heart and to write a letter to Tom rejecting his proposal.

Elin is startled by a noise nearby and is relieved to find that it is Price the Schoolmaster, out hunting rabbits. On the way back to 'Ty Hen', Price confesses to her that his grand inheritance turned out to be only £100. She invites him in to see her father, and, on finding that John Cadwaladr has already gone to bed, presses him to stay for supper. The two have always got on well and respect each other's intellectual abilities but, when all the usual topics have been exhausted, Price tells her that he has loved her for years and asks her to marry him. Desperately anxious not to lose his friendship, she begs him to continue as before and forget that this conversation ever happened. It is not until very late that night when she sits down to write her letter to Tom Evans.

In a conversation with Price shortly afterwards, Dr Evans expounds the theories of Eugenics, that a man should choose as a wife a healthy, good-looking, intelligent girl who is likely to produce similarly healthy, intelligent children, and that love does not come into it!

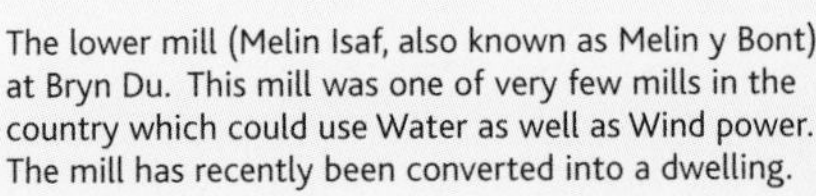

The lower mill (Melin Isaf, also known as Melin y Bont) at Bryn Du. This mill was one of very few mills in the country which could use Water as well as Wind power. The mill has recently been converted into a dwelling.

Evening in the Old Mill Yard (An Anglesey Scene)

Chapter 23 *The Staircase to Success*

Dr. Tom Evans takes a three-week holiday, his first since his return from London, touring North and mid Wales. He returns to Bryn Siriol much stronger in body and in spirit. The first person he sees on his return is Olwen Gruffydd, bright-eyed and rosy-cheeked as she holds the reins of a playful young pony pulling a trap. She does not need to ask him twice to accompany her to 'Neuadd Lwyd' for a cup of tea and, within a few weeks, everyone in the village knows that they are courting.

Meanwhile, David is busy climbing the ladder of success in London, dividing his time between his work and his political duties. He has been selected as his party's candidate for Newlea Marsh on the retirement of Wensley Parr [*23a]. The fact that a newcomer to the political scene has been selected to contest a safe seat is a measure of the esteem in which his party holds him. David is immersed in his work and is no longer beset by doubts and regrets, though he often thinks fondly of the narrow roads, earthen embankments, gorse bushes and rocky outcrops of Anglesey.

*23a. There is a detailed discussion in this chapter of the political styles of two other young politicians who had been fellow-students of David's, but this adds little to the plot

Chapter 24 *Changes*

Deubwll Williams's campaign to be the next minister of Engedi is gaining ground. He frequently visits the homes of influential chapel members and they, gradually, convert others. *There was pluck to be admired in Deubwll and, in many ways he'd have made a perfectly good minister in an area like Bryn Siriol. He was exceptionally faithful for months in his visits to the most influential families amongst his supporters, thus gaining much ground.* Shortly before the marriage of Tom Evans and Olwen Gruffydd, however, Deubwll happens to meet Olwen's father, S. T. Gruffydd, and overdoes the sycophancy, a characteristic which S. T. finds unbearable. He prevails upon Tom to have a word with his father; Evans 'Gwynfryn' quietly lets it be known that his opinion has changed; eventually Deubwll realises that his chances are over and turns his talents in another direction.

Maggie, 'Y Rhiw', comes home from the sanatorium alive and well. Having promised the Matron that she will share her new-found knowledge, she and her sister empty every drawer and cupboard in the house, much to her mother's horror, and give their contents a good airing in the sun and breeze. She also arranges for someone to come into the house, strip layers of wallpaper off the walls and whitewash them. Maggie's father, William Williams, who has aged before his time after losing three children, rejoices in Maggie's recovery, begins to believe that Death, the enemy, has taken from him its last sacrifice, and regains much of his zest for life.

Chapter 25 *The Threshold*

Price the Schoolmaster has decided to spend his legacy on a voyage to America. He calls to see Elin the night before the voyage and, although she has been feeling ill for about a fortnight, her imagination is fired by the idea of the trip and she speculates as to who his travelling companions might be. She tells him he might meet all sorts of rich or famous people travelling incognito, even, perhaps, an heiress searching for a husband!

Elin's illness worsens; she battles valiantly to do her normal share of the work but, within a few days, has to take to her bed. Dr Evans is away on honeymoon in Italy so John Cadwaladr goes to the village to fetch the locum, an inexperienced young Englishman. On the way he meets Mary Charles, who has noticed Elin's absence from her usual place at the organ in chapel and is worried when John Cadwaladr tells her that Elin has been in bed for some days. The young doctor calls at 'Ty Hen' but does not know Elin well and does not feel that there is anything seriously wrong.

The following day, Mrs Charles decides to visit Elin. She has not been to 'Ty Hen' for years and feels very uncomfortable but this awkwardness swiftly turns to concern when she sees how ill Elin looks. After speaking to Elin for some time she is shocked at Elin's passive acceptance of her illness and feels sure that some strange depression and indifference are part of her condition. Mrs Charles ensures that the maids take better care of Elin and promises to be back the following day.

Meanwhile, David's political campaign is about to begin and there is no doubt that it will be successful. His feet are on the threshold of the House of Commons and who can blame him for being enchanted by the prospect?

Maggie, 'Y Rhiw', calls to see her benefactress and, though somewhat reassured when Elin tells her that the doctors are sure she does not have any problem with her lungs, is shocked by Elin's appearance and walks to the town to try to get hold of the specialist. He, however, is in Scotland and will not be able to get to Bryn Siriol for some days.

Mary Charles decides that David must be told of Elin's illness and writes to ask him to come home immediately. He receives the letter on the morning of the opening meeting of his parliamentary campaign, in which he is scheduled to give an important speech. When he receives the letter he is immediately reminded of the last time he received such a summons, when he managed only to spend one night in his father's company before the end. The love which he once felt for Elin and which had been dormant for so many years, resurfaces. Although he believes that his treatment of her over the years will have killed the love Elin once felt for him, he feels that he must see her and so cancels his speaking engagement.

The long hours which he spends in the train give him the opportunity to take a long, hard, look at himself, and he realises that, in his selfish determination to succeed, he has overlooked the person who means most to him and he agonises lest he should arrive too late.

Chapter 26 *Breaking an Engagement*

David's first question when he enters the kitchen of 'Ty Hen' is, "How is Elin?" She is sleeping, and when, some time later, Mary Charles enters her bedroom, Elin says she has been dreaming that David has come home. This makes it easy for Mrs Charles to break the news to her. From then onwards, there is another faithful watcher by Elin's bedside. Past misunderstandings are cleared up, forgiveness is sought and freely given and David and Elin are reunited in love.

When the specialist finally arrives he pronounces that Elin has a rare and dangerous illness which has recently received considerable attention from doctors. There is nothing that can be done, however, except to continue to nurse her.

'Ty Hen' becomes a house of sadness. John Cadwaladr wanders aimlessly about the fields as if in anticipation of his loss. David withdraws from the election candidacy and tells Elin that he will not return to London until she can come and see him off at the station. He tells her that there will be other election opportunities and that the candidate's wife often earns more votes than the candidate himself! Although Elin smiles at this, David realises that she thinks it unlikely that she will ever be the candidate's wife. This gives David an idea which he loses no time in putting into practice. Within a few days a preacher comes to the house and, with Elin still in her sickbed and only John Cadwaladr and Mary Charles as 'guests', David and Elin are married. The bride sheds tears at the words 'to live together' and her heart bleeds with sorrow for the husband she is convinced she is shortly going to leave behind.

Chapter 27 *Company of Five*

The bride and groom sit in contented silence for some time after the marriage ceremony then Elin confesses that she is very tired and needs to sleep. David is hopeful that this is a healthy sign whereas his mother fears it is yet another indication that Elin is losing ground. She sends David on an errand to 'Bryn Tawel', feeling that a walk in the fresh air will do him good. It is a fine August day and David delights in the beauty of Nature and in the old, familiar pathways. He climbs to the top of the hill where he used to stand, as a boy, in a stone 'pulpit' and pretend to be a preacher.

The words of the marriage ceremony come back to him, their force redoubled, and he wants to declaim them to the bushes and rocks which he used to pretend were his 'congregation'. He seeks to explain to himself the confidence with which the prayer imbued him. Is it not in the nature of mankind to crave belief in a Supreme Being when in need of support or comfort? He wrestles with his unbelief; how sweet would be the knowledge that there really was a God who cared about him and about Elin!

On his return to 'Ty Hen', he discusses his doubts with Elin and she expresses her opinion, largely influenced by the sermon of the young student, John ap Rhisiart, on the relationship between man and God. David is amazed by the depth of her knowledge and the clarity of her vision and finds himself close to being able to share her faith.

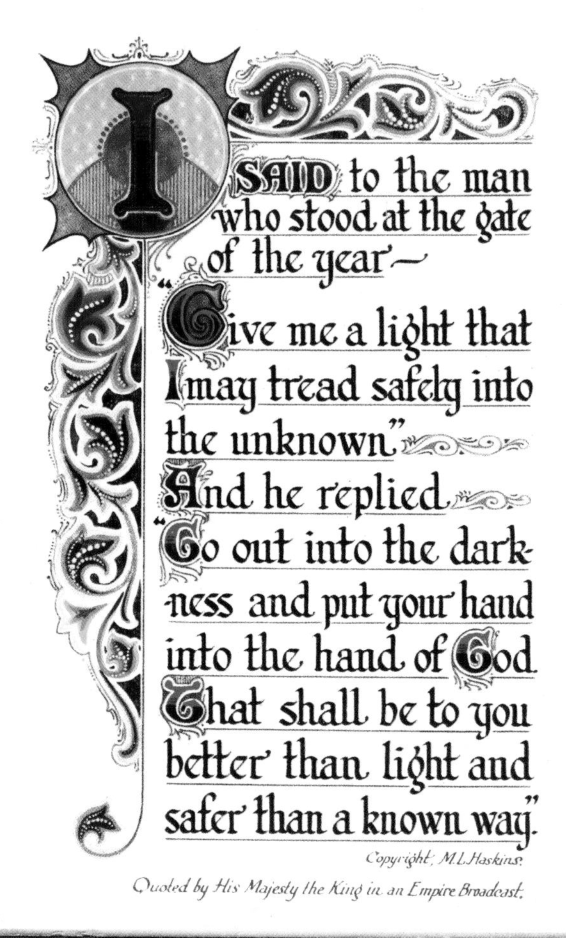
I SAID to the man who stood at the gate of the year—
"Give me a light that I may tread safely into the unknown."
And he replied,
"Go out into the darkness and put your hand into the hand of God.
That shall be to you better than light and safer than a known way."

Copyright: M.L.Haskins.

Quoted by His Majesty the King in an Empire Broadcast.

Chapter 28 *Searching for The Truth*

For some days afterwards, David spends time sitting on an old tree stump behind 'Bryn Tawel' considering his future. He has a successful career, which will make him a wealthy man, and he is sure that further opportunities will present themselves for political success. He is becoming increasingly confident that Elin will pull through and that he will have a wife with whom to share the fame and fortune which are within his grasp. However, Elin's words have removed the veil from his eyes and another voice is calling, a voice which is telling him to renounce all this and return to preaching. This is what he now wants more than anything but he dreads being selfish again. Will it be fair to condemn Elin to the poverty of a preacher's wife when he could offer her so much more?

Meanwhile, the villagers remain in complete ignorance of the wedding at 'Ty Hen'. One evening, Parry's shop is full and the talk is of Dr Evans and his young wife who are due to return from their honeymoon the following Saturday. Someone comes in with a newspaper and Johnnie, 'Y Pant', cuts across the general conversation from time to time to tell Parry how things are going in an important cricket match between Kent and Yorkshire. Johnnie is told to shut up about the cricket while the important subject of where Dr and Mrs Evans are going to live is discussed. Parry, who is trying to hold two conversations at once, becomes very confused and, when asked if he would like to be there, says, *"Where? The cricket ground or the piece of land near the parsonage?"* Moments later when Johnnie whistles loudly and says, *"Listen to this!"* no-one pays him any attention. Parry, however, insists on listening and there is silence. Johnnie reads:

Marriage -
August 15th, by Special Licence,
David Charles, Bryn Tawel, Bryn Siriol and Elin, only daughter of John Cadwaladr of Ty Hen, in the same parish ...

Johnnie is accused of making it up and told not to joke about such things until, one by one, the men of the village look over his shoulder and read it for themselves, in amazement.

Parry shuts the shop early that evening and takes the paper to show old Morris Jones. When the old man gets over his amazement he is delighted and tells Parry that his constant prayers for David have been answered. Less than ten minutes after Parry's departure there is another knock on the door and who should be standing there but David Charles!

"A good match" in Parry's shop

The village had been totally unaware of the visit of the strange preacher to 'Ty Hen' and the marriage of the two people whose names were so often on everyone's lips. The maidservants knew nothing about it and both John Cadwaladr and Mary Charles were well-known for keeping things 'close to their chest'. Therefore, the poor village was kept in the dark. In consequence it had satisfied itself with suppositions and it is probable that most of those suppositions were far from the truth.

That is why the news was so fresh when it came. There was no forewarning to mar its newness. No-one had the slightest idea. Even Thomas Hughes had to confess that it was 'news to him'.

And, when it did come, it was so unexpected.

There happened to be a shopful of people there that evening and somebody was saying that Dr Evans and his young wife would be coming home on the Saturday.

A newspaper had also come into the shop and Johnnie 'Pant' was interrupting the conversation every now and then to tell Parry how things were going between Kent and Yorkshire in an important cricket match.

"Where are they going to live, then?" asked Thomas Thomas. He didn't have the cricket teams in mind.

"I heard that S T wants to build them a mansion," said Robert Edward.

"Hundred and one in an hour and thirty-five minutes, Parry!" interrupted Johnnie enthusiastically.

"Pretty good, what!" answered Parry hurriedly, then, "Where will that be, I wonder?" with his eyes on Robert Edward and the imaginary mansion.

"There's talk that he's bought land near the Parsonage." It was Thomas Hughes who had heard this.

"That Rhodes is a boy, Parry!" said Johnnie in admiration that was almost beyond words.

"Fine fellow, what?" said Parry to appease Johnnie. Then, to Thomas Hughes, "Near the parsonage? What land, I wonder?"

"Would you like to be there, Parry?" asked Johnnie.

The poor shopkeeper was like a man trying to play two balls at the same time. "Like to be there?" The cricket pitch or the land near the Parsonage?

"Stop confusing things Johnnie, with your cricket and your nonsense," said Robert Edward. "We've got better things to do than listen to that sort of rubbish."

"Gossiping, you mean?" asked Johnnie, getting his own back on the carpenter.

Thomas Hughes had resumed the story of the doctor and everyone was listening intently, when Johnnie whistled aloud in astonishment.

When he got his breath back he said: "The - dear - Bishop – listen!"

"Shut your nonsense now, Johnnie!" Robert Edward was starting to lose his temper.

But Parry insisted on listening and demanded silence. Johnnie read hurriedly: "August 15th, by special licence, David Charles, 'Bryntawel', Bryn Siriol, and Elin, only daughter of John Cadwaladr, 'Ty Hen', in the same parish..."

"What?" asked Parry like a lost man.

"He's kidding us," said the carpenter, then, in a tone of impatient scorn, "that's what he's like."

"Yes, don't joke about things like that, my boy," said Thomas Hughes, sternly.

"Look here!" said Johnnie indignantly, waving the paper at the postman. Johnnie himself had practically been stunned out of his senses.

"Dear people!" said Thomas Hughes having taken a peep at the names.

"The Great Lord!" shouted Robert Edward, who was looking over Thomas Hughes's shoulder.

Parry leaped over the counter like a greyhound, his face as white as lime. "Father!"

Having astonished everybody with the discovery, Johnnie felt something of a hero. "That's what he's like, is he?" he said, maliciously to Robert Edward.

Dr Evans and his house were forgotten.

After the revelation had been discussed many times, someone was heard to ask, "Will she get better, I wonder?"

The answer was lost but Thomas Thomas was heard to say with heavy emphasis, "She's certainly been lucky!"

"Lucky? Yes. I should say so. He makes money like stones," said Robert Edward.

Everybody agreed and that's what made Johnnie's observation the more striking. He said heatedly,

"He's been lucky too. Doesn't that count?"

And, when they'd thought about it, no-one contradicted him ....

Chapter 29 *In the Newspaper*

Price the Schoolmaster, who has spent his £100 inheritance on the holiday in America, is told of the marriage by his housekeeper on the afternoon of his return. Another village news item is that Parry is to retire and the shop is to be taken over by Jennie Evans, 'Gwynfryn', who is to marry an old flame. Price loses no time in going to visit first Parry and then Dr Evans. He tells Tom that he has become engaged to Marjorie Ford, a wealthy heiress whom he met on the ship, having proposed and been accepted before he had any idea of her circumstances!

Price goes with Tom and Olwen to 'Ty Hen', where they are warmly welcomed by Mary Charles, John Cadwaladr is at his most sociable, Elin is much better, David has regained much of his old high spirits and they have a thoroughly enjoyable evening. After their departure, Elin is anxious to assure herself that David has no regrets about giving up his work in London and that he does not hanker after the comfortable lifestyle which Tom Evans and Price will now enjoy. David convinces her that he has not felt such contentment of mind for years as he has felt since the evening he went to see Morris Jones.

A few weeks later comes a day which will long be remembered in the history of Engedi. The chapel is full and, in her place at the organ sits Elin, 'the daughter of Ty Hen'. She still looks pale, it is true, but no-one can fail to be entranced by her presence. Morris Jones walks in, followed by David Charles and the rest of the deacons. David has become a fine handsome man. There is something of his father in his voice and in his bearing which draws a tear from his mother's eye, but he possesses a strength and a quality of leadership far greater than those of his father.

The preacher is on his feet and is reading out the first hymn. They are singing together of the name of Jesus; they will play together for ever the only harp which is worth playing.

This is a section from an early postcard of 'South Main Street, Rhosneigr' dating from approximately 1916. The Calvinistic Methodist chapel of Paran and the Chapel house are clearly visible on the Left Hand side.

Madam Wen

Madam Wen is based on the Anglesey legend of the same name and tells the story of the love of Morys Williams – an honest country squire – for Einir Wyn, a beautiful and intelligent woman of society who, unbeknown to him, leads a double life as the leader of a band of robbers and smugglers. After a number of daring adventures, there is dissention in the ranks, resulting in a clash of leadership and a murder with devastating consequences.

Section from Baugh's map of Anglesey c1795.

Perhaps the most interesting feature on this map is the clearly defined "road" running across the sands at Cymmyran from the Inland Sea, crossing the main bay of Rhosneigr, traversing along Broad Beach to Lion Rocks & Tyn Towyn before returning to land as it heads off to Aberffraw.

Note also that Llangwyfen church is not yet "in the sea".

3.1 *Introduction to Madam Wen*

The Madam Wen legend has been well-known on Anglesey probably since the 18th century and the first known written reference to it was in November 1897 by J.W. Huws which is shown in Appendix 5.1. However, it was not until the early 20th Century that it was brought together and popularised in a book. "Madam Wen" *[The White Lady]* is the title of a 188-page novel written by William David Owen a good decade before he began practising as a solicitor in Rhosneigr. The story was not his first, but was his most successful and best acclaimed work and was first published in serialised form in the newspaper Y Genedl Gymreig *[The Welsh Nation]* between January and July 1914. It took a further 11 years before the story first appeared in book form, in the winter of 1925, but sadly, W.D.Owen died shortly after it was published.

Madam Wen was written entirely in Welsh and, with the exception of a short interpretation, published in 2004 {301} has never before been translated into English. The following translation, which has been specially commissioned for this book, reveals the story to be a complex tale of smuggling, piracy and romance, set in and around the 'lakes' area adjacent to the village of Rhosneigr, where the author lived.

The book remained a quiet masterpiece for decades, being unknown by the English and partly forgotten by the Welsh. The exception being in some parts of Anglesey, where in the mid 20th century, most households would have been aware of its existence even if they did not possess a copy themselves. This changed in 1982, when the newly formed television channel for Wales, S4C {302}, chose Madam Wen as its first "big film".

Produced by Gwilym Owen (who is no known relation to the author) and directed by Pennant Roberts (who had just completed the 'Tenko' Japanese prisoner-of-war series for BBC), it was commissioned by the Welsh Film Board and was filmed on Anglesey during the spring of 1982. S4C first started broadcasting on November 1st 1982 and the first showing of the film was on December 26th the same year.

The film starred the Anglesey based actress Marged Esli as Madam Wen and John Pierce Jones as her romantic hero, Morys Williams. It became controversial for being significantly over-budget and for its attempts to depict a ship at sea in a storm, which were largely unsuccessful as the ship was so clearly a model, (see illustration on p.142). The film is still available for viewing at the National Library of Wales, in Aberystwyth {303}, but having viewed it, I can confirm that it could benefit from being brought up to date! (see section 4 for further information).

It has been difficult to decide what to include in this book about Madam Wen, however, I have tried to include the most significant parts of what I have found. The book and film reviews I have been able to track down, have been used almost in their entirety, and the novel itself has been compacted into an abridged form.

It is probably unfair to assess a full length novel based upon a shortened version, (a comparison of both stories by my translator appears in section 4) but it is certain that the story has considerable merit, although its strongly romanticised content, and tales of "derring-do", ring a little untrue to 21st Century eyes.

Here therefore, presented for your enjoyment and edification, is an abridged version of William David Owen's romantic novel – Madam Wen.

It proved quite a challenge to identify and track down some of the key elements in the story. In particular, Madam Wen's cave, as evocatively described in the author's foreword, and so intrinsic to the plot, proved in the end to be something of a disappointment. True, the cave is there close by the public footpath on the South Western side of lake Traffwll, but as the photo shows, it is quite small and easily overlooked amongst the gorse and brambles. On the other hand, it would make a perfect entrance to something bigger and better hidden....

3.2 Author's Foreword

Tradition had little to say about the career of Madam Wen and what it did say was misleading. Were it not for a discovery that was made some time ago it would not have been possible to write the chapters which follow.

To search for the home of Madam Wen one must go to the south-west of Anglesey, to an area which could be called the District of the Lakes. There are three lakes of substantial size, the biggest of the three being Traffwll Lake. The District of the Lakes is rather a remote place and little does the world know about its romantic quietness. If there is any truth in what is whispered in the area about the lady's magical visits to the scene of her erstwhile heroism, then it doubtless gives her independent spirit unmixed satisfaction to to see that the old lake and its surroundings continue to keep its secret undefiled.

To the south side of the lake and half encircling it, are the fields of Traffwll. Here, years ago, the gorse grew tall and thick, forming a dense forest, and, in the shadows of that dark forest lurked Madam Wen's cave at the edge of the water. The cave was an ugly enough place – as it appeared to us when we were children – to be a secret place or a hideout for anyone. All that could be seen was an enormous piece of rock, tall, strong and angular, standing squarely as if in the doorway, opposite the two smooth faces of the bigger rock, from which it had, at some time, been hurled. Between this and the steep faces of the rock, two narrow entrances meet at the far end. It was these entrances which were known for ages as 'Madam Wen's Cave'.

Late one summer's day, a man from the area was sitting on a tree trunk near the cave gazing at the silvery face of the lake. His meditations may have strayed back to childhood, when any mention of Madam Wen endowed the cave and its surroundings with a kind of magic. Whatever the reason, he was overcome by an urge to go and explore the cave. He remembered the empty echoes – frightening at the time – which arose when we, as children, stamped our feet on the floor of the cave, and he came up with the idea that there might be a space under the floor. The sound was the sound of emptiness.

It was somewhat stealthily, and fearing that someone would see him, that he took a mattock and a spade, went to the cave, and started to dig at the far end. It did not surprise him in the least when the tip of the mattock went straight through, revealing the true entrance to Madam Wen's underground hiding place. After two hours of hard work, he saw that there was a smooth plank of rock forming a sort of lintel over the door below.

After that he examined the cave thoroughly but, as a description of it appears elsewhere, it is not necessary to describe it here. Suffice it to say that the secrets of the cave were close to vanishing into oblivion because of the dampness of the place. Exceptional care was taken of what was found there, particularly the fragment of diary. That – on loose leaves - appeared to be the fruit of many hours of leisure, or perhaps hours of sadness, when Madam Wen sat in the solitude of her dark cell with time to consider how alone she was in the world. Doubtless it was then that she confided her secrets to the pages.

Having found out about the skirmish between her and Abel Owen, the pirate, he conducted further research in other areas, and it was found that the history of Abel Owen's stormy career had been recorded and was available. His unworthy career ended under the executioner's axe in London's Execution Dock in 1711. {304}

Much digging had been done in the fields from time to time searching for the hidden treasure of Wil Llanfihangel. It is probable that every generation of children from the area, ever since then, has dug in its turn after hearing the story. But no-one has ever been said to have found the earthenware vessel.

There are, in the story which follows, many facts which were obtained from time to time by families who had heard them from their ancestors. But it was not known to which period the different stories belonged until Madam Wen's diary formed a link - through the medium of the names – to unite the stories into a cohesive whole.

W.D.Owen

The travelling fairs were a regular and enormously popular form of entertainment during the late 19th and early 20th centuries. This photo shows "The Great Spanish Menagerie" believed to have been put on by "Barnum's [Beas]t Novelties" sometime between 1898 and 1905. {305}

Acts also visible on the photo include : "Gregralt's Spanish Menagerie" (or possibly Gregrast's – the photo is unclear);, "Absolutely Untameable Lions From Africa", "Captain Marco And His Famous Boxing Bear"; "Sealions"; and (on the right of the picture) – "The Largest Ballet Girl in the World".

Other acts known to have been present (from a second photograph not shown here) were "General Tiny Mite – the Smallest Person in the World" and the "Alarming accident of the Giant Lady in a Paris Motor Car".

Admission varied between 2d and 3d for adults (the direct modern equivalent being approximately 1p, but adjusted for earnings inflation, would now amount to approximately £5.14p){306}.

The location for this fair was the land at the bottom of Rhosneigr village, opposite where the Old Post Office stood and approximately where the house Ty Newydd now stands. In the distance, on the top right of the photo, can be seen Ynys Feirig (Starvation Island) on the far side of the bay.

Chapter 1 *The Boat Tavern*

The second week of October was the week of weeks for Siôn Ifan, landlord of the Boat Tavern, {307} *and the tenth day of that month was the high point of the year for him. Although the nights of the Tavern were important times, they faded into the shadows when it came to the feast day of St Michael, the parish saint. When Michaelmas arrived and people gathered in hosts on the church field, the beer flowed like rivers in the Boat Tavern, to the particular advantage of Siôn Ifan.*

The feast day brought all manner of traders to the village of Llanfihangel-yn-Nhowyn. They came with carts selling strange and exciting goods, along with sideshows offering boxing and wrestling matches and a fiddler who provided music for the people to dance.

Siôn Ifan was a man who was excellent at dealing with people. He had a quick mind and a skilful way of tempering his response to the degree of sobriety, or drunkenness, that he saw in the customer's behaviour. ...He had had plenty of practice and he sold his knowledge and his good sense, the same as his beer, for the pennies of those less talented than himself.

Siôn Ifan and Catrin Parri, his wife, [*1a] *had three sons, Dic, Ifan and Meic. When trade was brisk , ...the three helped the innkeeper with the casks of beer and the thirsty customers. But at other times, they mysteriously disappeared, and there was no sign of them anywhere near the tavern. No-one knew with any certainty what became of the three lads at times like that.*

During the evening, the merriment in the Boat Tavern became raucous, with several customers the worse for drink. Siôn Ifan asked two of the regulars, Wil Llanfihangel [*1b] *a long, thin strip of a man, supple and muscular, garrulous and sneering* and his friend Robin 'y Pandy', *[Robin the Miller] larger of size but slower of tongue* to leave. Wil protested loudly but was suddenly silenced when he saw a stranger standing near the door.

Not every stranger would have had the effect of silencing Wil so suddenly, as everyone of his acquaintance knew, but this was a man who immediately attracted attention. For one thing, he was approaching seven feet in height, making a dwarf even of Robin y Pandy and making the ceiling of the Boat Tavern look low. He was thickset too, amazingly so, creating the impression of a giant amongst men. His manner and dress alone would have been enough to draw attention to him in the kind of company that was in the tavern. It was not every day that a coat of expensive black brocade was seen there, its edges showing a handsome lining of gold, or a leather waistcoat with such intricate silk ornamentation. This, as well as the neat and costly wig of the strange man, made Wil and the others stare at him for a moment in silence.

But neither the initial amazement nor the silence lasted long. Too much beer had flowed - the class leveller had been at work breaking down the barriers between the common people and the gentry. To the obvious disgust of Siôn Ifan, Wil started jeering and mocking at the expense of the stranger, making fun of his uncommon stature, without sparing his bearing or his dress which marked him out as belonging to a higher level of society.

Siôn Ifan finally persuaded the two men to go, but outside, a fight was in progress, with two of the innkeeper's sons attacking one man, Twm 'Pen y Bont' *[Bridge End]*. Twm was less than five feet tall but almost as wide, and was holding his own until Wil joined in the fray, making it three to one.

Suddenly the enormous stranger appeared on the scene, separating the heap of men and setting Twm on his feet. He told Wil to go home quietly, and, when Wil refused and made to strike him, he picked him up bodily and hurled him over the hedge into a field. By this time, Siôn Ifan had discovered who the stranger was, but said not a word to his sons.

*1a. In 17th century Wales, only women in the very highest social classes adopted their husband's surnames on marriage.

*1b. The tradition of using a forename, followed by a place of residence instead of a surname, still persists in many places (including Rhosneigr) today. This method of naming is used throughout the novel.

Chapter 2 *The Squire and his Steed*

Morys Williams, squire of the Cymunod Estate, {308} for such was the stranger's name, was new to Anglesey, having only recently come into possession of his land there. Unbeknown to him, on the night of the feast day, he had angered one or two of the followers of the mysterious 'Madam Wen', leader of a band of robbers and smugglers.

He visited the Boat Tavern to try to find out the identities of the man he had thrown over the hedge the previous night and of Madam Wen, but got nothing out of the innkeeper Siôn Ifan. One of the maidservants he had hired locally, Nanni, from 'Allwyn Ddu' *[Black Allwyn Farm]*, one of the local farms, could have told him a good deal about both had she chosen to do so!

One morning, some time after his arrival at Cymunod, Morys Williams set off on Lewys, his enormous black horse, to collect rents which were due to him in the parish of Trefdraeth *[Beach Town]*.

The curtains of night had long since descended before the squire was ready to make his way home, his leather wallet heavy with the rent money of Trefdraeth's farmers. The night was not dark. But there, in a sudden bend in the road, Morys came face to face with three men on horseback, standing side by side, as if guarding the narrow way.

"Good evening," he said, waiting for an opportunity to pass them and as yet unaware of their intention. In response they pointed three handguns at his head. The squire put his hand on his own, a valuable weapon, shiny in its newness. On observing the three men more closely he saw that each one of them was wearing a mask.

It was the man in the middle who spoke first and, on hearing his voice, the squire felt that he had met him before. "If you give us that leather wallet without any fuss, you will be allowed to go on your way unharmed."

"Oho!" said the squire, who was used to making light of danger.

"Without any fuss, eh? What makes you think I've got a leather wallet at all?"

"We know full well you've got one," answered the robber. We know what's in it. There's no point in wasting any more time."

Morys laughed, his great voice resounding in the quietness of the evening. "What say you, Lewys?" he said playfully, but without taking his eyes off the thieves. The horse neighed excitedly, and began to move his feet eagerly. Morys noticed that one of the men was large and corpulent and rode a pony which was larger than those of his companions.

The highwaymen drew closer together. Morys tightened his grip on the rein. The black horse tossed and turned impatiently.

"We are waiting," said the man in the centre. "You might as well hand it over now as later. Someone else is waiting for you further on. Then there'll be no wasting words; you can take my word for it."

"Is that so?" retorted Morys, his blood warming. It gets better, Lewys."

"Don't mess with me," said the largest of the robbers viciously and, on hearing his voice, Morys remembered seeing him by the big chimney in the Boat Tavern on the evening of the feast day.

"Indeed," he responded. "That would be a thankless task." At that, Lewys felt the spur and leaped forward as if the robbers' ponies were merely summer insects in his path. In the confusion one of the ponies went down, the three robbers were thrown into disarray and, in agitation and disappointment, Wil Llanfihangel shouted, "Shoot him, Robin!"

Morys heard the sound of a shot as if at his heel and Lewys Ddu [Lewis the Black] galloped down the road like a deer in front of dogs, his huge hooves striking fire from the cobbles like sparks from a blacksmith's anvil. The sound of pursuit could be heard in the distance.

Before long the horse's keen eyes saw another band of men on horseback, large enough to fill the road to such an extent that it was impossible to pass. Morys did not see the danger. Lewys slowed his stride and whinnied nervously, as if he was telling his master that all was not well. And, as he approached, he looked to the left and to the right for a means of escape and his master understood that there was an obstacle ahead. There was no time to lose; they were caught like birds in a net and the robbers were upon them on all sides. Morys loosened the reins. "Take whichever way you choose, Lewys," he said.

On the right there was a stone wall and a row of blackthorn trees but, on the left, there was an earthen bank surmounted by a hedge, a leap of five feet. Lewys chose the bank, with the robbers at their heels. Perhaps the commotion confused him, or perhaps it was the narrowness of the road, but a hoof struck the top of the bank and he tumbled headlong into the ditch below with Morys spread-eagled on the field.

It was not long before the squire rose. He leaped up and stood beside his horse, his gun in his hand and his blood boiling. He could smell battle, but he felt no fear, only anxiety when he saw that Lewys did not get up at once.

When the robbers saw the extent of the problem, they were emboldened. Wil was in no hurry after gaining the upper hand. He took delight in taunting the squire about his intention to escape across the fields. The black horse continued to lie where he had fallen and Morys began to feel immense concern.

After some deliberation, Morys took a knife, cut the wallet free from the saddle and threw it to the robbers, who, having achieved their objective, galloped away, leaving him free to attend to Lewys.

Thanks to Morys's patience, his great strength, and the understanding which existed between the two, Lewys, whose leg was doubled under him, was eventually freed and was able to limp slowly home, his master vowing to avenge his injury in full.

Chapter 3 *Einir Wyn's Vow*

Soon afterwards, Morys crossed the Menai Straits and rode to Penrhyn, the home of his ancestors, for the most prestigious ball of the year. The host, Sir Robert Williams, welcomed his young kinsman warmly and, after Morys had related the story of his ambush, the conversation turned to Madam Wen. The baronet informed Morys that she was considered to be an enemy of the King's Men but not of pirates, robbers and smugglers. He was informed that she was both beautiful and educated, that it was some personal quarrel that had made her rebel against law and order and that it was her habit to rob the rich in order to help the poor. Morys began to understand why no-one among the general populace of the island was willing to divulge any information about her.

The two then entered the great hall where Morys was introduced to a number of new people and met several old acquaintances. Almost everyone was speaking English, and the young squire turned quickly when he heard a female voice speaking Welsh. *He saw two playful eyes behind an ivory fan and stared at their owner in mute admiration.* Sir Robert introduced the most beautiful girl he had ever seen as 'your kinswoman, Einir Wyn.' Morys remembered that she was a distant relation to his host and to himself, the orphaned daughter of the noble Wyn family of Gwynedd **{309}**. She had travelled all over the world and he had a faint memory that her father had once owned land, which he had lost.

Einir suggested that they should leave the dance hall at midnight and escape on horseback to the mountains. On the way, she called in a poor cottage to see an old couple whom she had been helping, then, as they rode, Morys told her about the ambush, the theft of his wallet and the injury sustained by his horse. Einir showed herself to be a skilled and fearless horsewoman, negotiating, in the moonlight, narrow, treacherous mountain paths which caused Morys's mount to baulk. On their way back across the sand, Morys spoke of the admiration he had felt as a boy, for Einir's father's prowess in the saddle, and she broke down as she told him how her father's property had been unlawfully taken from him. Morys was unable to refrain from telling her how much he had loved her from the first moment he had seen her but she told him that she was not free to return his love, being bound by a vow to win back her father's lands.

Chapter 4 *The Authority of the Cave*

Morys's maidservant, Nanni 'Allwyn Ddu', called at Wil Llanfihangel's tumbledown cottage on the edge of the fen to tell him that Madam Wen wanted to see him.

Wil made his way to Madam Wen's cave and gave the signal, the cry of a moorhen in the sedge. *He saw a light in the cleft in the rock and Madam Wen appeared with a lamp in her hand. She wore a grey mantle, the colour of the rocks, which fell loosely to her heels, making her look taller than she was.*

"Are you better, Wil?" she asked, placing the lamp on the stone bench on the left hand side of the cell.

Wil was about to ask 'better from what?' when he saw her eyes penetrating his very thoughts. He feared no man in the world but he quietened remarkably in her presence; it could almost be said that he was afraid of her. He'd had plenty of experience of her iron will and had seen her unrivalled courage on many occasions; he'd been a witness to her unswerving determination so many times that he had the greatest respect for her as a leader and as one to whom he owed obedience. Perhaps, too, Wil remembered at all times that his own fate lay in the palm of the hand of one who was so learned and knowledgeable and had such great influence.

"You don't look as if you've broken any bones," she went on, "but I was not at all pleased to hear about you and Siôn Ifan's lads quarrelling and fighting on the evening of the feast day and making an exhibition of yourselves. What'll happen one day,"- she said carefully and with emphasis – "as I've told you ten times before, is that the sheriff's officer will catch you. And then everything you've done will come out and nobody will be able to keep your head on your shoulders when hanging day comes round in Beaumaris."

Wil had nightmares about hanging in Beaumaris. He took the rebuke quietly like a naughty child caught out in a misdemeanour. He said not a word but he wondered why it was so difficult to do the slightest thing without its reaching the ears of the mistress of the cave.

The next half-hour was spent discussing the smuggling trade. Then, without warning, Madam Wen asked, *"Were you out on horseback one night?"*

Wil tried to deflect the conversation but she persisted, coldly and with deliberation, *"Was there a big band of you out one night?"*

"Well, yes," Wil answered, wondering which one of the expeditions it would be safest to disclose.

"Was the booty substantial?"

Wil was now in a difficult situation. There were three incidents to which she could be referring. *He answered lamely, "Not too much."*

"You got forty guineas or more?"

His heart leaped. It was obvious that she was referring to the encounter with Morys, the squire of Cymunod. That was the sum. So she knew nothing of the other two robberies. *"It was just over forty guineas," he answered readily.*

But his relief did not last long. The lady of the cave was in a vile temper.

"How far would you say it is from here to Cymunod?" she asked him.

"Barely two miles," he responded, like a little boy reciting a lesson.

"Would you consider the owner of Cymunod to be a neighbour?"

Wil felt that she was playing with him as a man plays with his dog, but how on earth could he avoid answering her? "Well, yes, as far as I know."

"As far as I know too. But tell me, was it in the name of Madam Wen that you went out so bravely to attack a neighbour and then to rob him?" What insult she could encapsulate in one sentence! Wil was amazed that such a thing could be done so effectively without a single swear word or oath. "You shameless rogues! A dozen or two of you attacking one man, a quiet neighbour! What has become of the rules I gave you when I became your patron? You greedy knaves! I'd like to know how many good works you've done during the last two months, how many favours to the poor, how many good turns to those in need."

The robber uttered not a word.

"I'm starting to tire of these foolish tricks," she said. "You fools, with your petty thieving and your drunken brawls! Listen! The next time I hear of such idiocy, it'll be the end of the band and the smuggling trade and I'll have nothing more to do with you. You know full well that you'd have hanged long since were it not for me."

Wil was well aware that the smuggling trade and the success of the band depended on her wisdom and knowledge and he was frightened lest the disaster to which she referred should befall him. He knew too that his own safety was the surer with her support ... Her authority was final and there was nothing to do now but accept the rebuke and the reproach quietly and be obedient.

"Where is the money?" she asked him.

It was divided among the ten of us that night."

She laughed mockingly. "Among ten, indeed. Honour among thieves, is it? Listen! I intend that the owner of the money gets it back, every mite."

Wil's face fell when he heard that and he started to make excuses but she was having none if it.

"Have it back he must, so go at once to your hiding place and bring me forty guineas, in the squire's own leather wallet. Tomorrow you can visit your obedient lads and see how much honour remains in them. We'll see if your partner in crime Robin 'y Pandy' is willing to renounce his share for your sake."

Wil's face took on an ugly look but he had to go and do as he was told. He left for his cottage, swearing dreadfully.

When Morys was making his way to his own bedchamber by candlelight the following night, he saw, or thought he saw, fleetingly, a beautiful girl, dressed in white from head to toe. On his pillow was the leather wallet, complete with his rent money, down to the last penny.

Chapter 5 *Secret Trade*

Weeks passed during which Morys heard no news of Einir. His love towards her was great and he vowed that, if he could, he would assist her in her quest. He questioned his servants about the appearance of the girl in white on the night that his money was returned, but they denied any knowledge of her and he began to think she had been a figment of his imagination.

One afternoon he asked Siôn Ifan to tell him who owned the blue ship he had seen that afternoon on Cymyran river. The innkeeper knew full well that it was Madam Wen's ship but repeated his usual story that it belonged to 'a gentleman from Bristol' who brought cargoes of wheat, oats, barley or potatoes.

The following evening, when it was dark and Morys, as usual, was wandering, he came to the village of Crigyll, on the edge of the sea, and his way home from there was a rough and inaccessible one. After fording the river, instead of taking the direct route home, he headed for Cymyran River, where the ship lay some two miles further west.

He rode in a leisurely fashion without thinking that anyone except himself was sufficiently idle to be in such a place at close to midnight. But on the outskirts of Llanfair Triffwll,[*5a] *where the path was wildest, he had a rapid awakening from his comfortable dream. He came, unawares, upon the hiding place of others. By the faint light light of the moon in a cloudy sky, he saw two or three men jumping from the place where they had been lurking in the shelter of a grove.*

They were lying in a hollow, and Lewys Ddu was going down the slope before Morys saw the men. They rushed to meet him, leaping to the bridle without a word of greeting or warning. Nearby, tied to a gorse bush, stood three horses. Morys dismounted hastily, ready to fight for his freedom if necessary, and thinking at first that it was Wil Llanfihangel's subjects who were there, feeling glad of the meeting. He placed a heavy hand on the shoulder of one of the men who felt like a child receiving a rebuke.

"Who is here and what do you want with me?" asked Morys.

They turned out to be the King's Men, lying in wait for smugglers. They told him that it was Madam Wen who was held responsible for the smuggling trade in those parts as well as much pillaging and ransacking in the surrounding countryside. Morys offered them his assistance.

Before long a small band of men with ponies laden with wine and spirits, crept up the beach. The Revenue Men managed to ambush the group of smugglers, quickly unloading half the ponies, who took fright and galloped away. Then a fight broke out in which Morys took on Wil Llanfihangel, Robin 'y Pandy' and the innkeeper's three sons. He felled Wil, thus avenging the injury to his horse, Lewys. He was embroiled with Robin when Madam Wen appeared on a white horse. She placed a cloth under the noses of the excisemen which made them cough and sneeze, thus enabling her henchmen to escape. She then issued a challenge to Morys to catch her –

"If Morys Williams wants to break up the band, then he must catch their leader!" she said, moving away. "By God!, I will!" he answered, jumping into the saddle.

"Lewys Ddu moved with fervour, and Morys was determined to run Madam Wen down. But the white horse faded in front of him like an illusion. Through heather, barely touching the ground, through thick bushes and over banks, like birds soaring. But the white horse remained in the lead always. To Maelog's boundaries, and back through the marshes of Crigyll and the lowlands of Traffwll, Lewys Ddu dripping with sweat and Morys on the brink of losing his temper."

Morys pursued her for miles before, frustratingly, after jumping over a stone wall, she mysteriously disappeared.

*5a. The imaginary village of Llanfair Triffwll (St Mary's Church of the Three Pools) is cleverly named by Owen, as there are three fairly large lakes in the area – Traffwll, Penrhyn and Dinam.

Chapter 6 *Trouble at Pant y Gwehydd*

One morning two messengers arrived at the Cymunod Estate bearing letters. One was from Hywel Rhisiart, of Pant y Gwehydd *[Weaver's Hollow]*, requesting Morys's presence at his home as he had been threatened with a visit from Madam Wen, who had accused him of not being the rightful owner of the land which was in his possession. The other was a letter from Einir, asking him to give her his opinion on two farms she was thinking of buying. Desperate to see her again, Morys set off for the house where she was lodging outside Caernarfon.

Einir had gone out walking and Morys went to meet her. He told her how much he had missed her and reproached her for having left Penrhyn so suddenly, leaving him lovesick. In his direct way, he asked her to marry him and, although she said she was not yet ready to lose her freedom, she gave him room to hope that she might, one day, become his wife. Morys naively told her about the unexpected return of his rent money and the night of the smugglers and about Madam Wen's threat to Hywel Rhisiart and his intention of supporting him.

Preparations were well in hand for the defence of Pant y Gwehydd. For three sleepless nights the household waited but the threatened attack did not materialise. Morys went there, as promised, for the first three nights but was prevented from going on the fourth night when a storm was brewing. The youngest servant at Pant y Gwehydd was hastening about his evening duties when he saw that the rickyard of a poor neighbour, Robin Ellis, was on fire. The entire household, except for old Hywel Rhisiart and his wife and the soldier who was guarding them, rushed to help Robin Ellis. After the helpers had returned to Pant y Gwehydd, the Ellis family discovered a purse full of money. It had been left by Madam Wen as compensation for their loss of hay. Meanwhile the cattle, the oxen and the best horses had all been taken from Hywel Rhisiart's stables!

The storm raged all that night and two ships were wrecked on the rocks. Three men, who had been miraculously thrown up on Cymyran beach in a small boat, spent the night in the Boat Tavern. One of them carried a package, which Catrin Parri, the innkeeper's wife took, and opened, while he slept, finding only papers inside. While she was thus engaged, there was a light touch on the door catch and Madam Wen walked in. It was obvious that she was a frequent visitor to the inn.

Chapter 7 *The Man from Bristol*

Two days after the storm, two of the three survivors left the Boat Tavern, leaving only the third, Colonel Sprigg. He was a self-important man of uncertain temper, who had no respect for anyone he deemed to be his social inferior. One morning he returned from a walk to the beach in an even worse temper than usual. Despite having little English, Siôn Ifan was able to work out that he was cursing and swearing. He had tried to attract the attention of the crew of the one-masted ship which the innkeeper told him belonged to 'some man from Bristol' but had been ignored.

That afternoon a handsome, softly-spoken, self-possessed young man arrived at the Boat Tavern and introduced himself as 'Captain White, of Bristol'. Even Siôn Ifan couldn't help but show his surprise. The Colonel told Captain White that he was in the service of King James, who planned to raise armies in France and Ireland in order to help him regain his throne. Colonel Sprigg needed to take messages and money to the Jacobites across the water and the young man assured him that the ship would be at his service, for a price.

Captain White had just told the Colonel that he had heard of his prowess as a swordsman, when they were joined by Morys Williams. Half drunk and resenting the intrusion, the Colonel became abusive and demanded a duel with Morys, which was scheduled for the following morning. While they were awaiting Morys's arrival the following day, and fearing for the squire's safety as he was not an experienced swordsman, Captain White suggested a walk and deliberately picked a quarrel with the Colonel, who drew his sword. The young Captain proceeded to give the older man a lesson in swordsmanship, cutting the buttons from his green silk breeches one by one and finally wounding him superficially above the elbow. The young man walked away saying he was going to fetch help and Morys, who was just approaching, heard a whistle. A white horse leaped over the hedge, greeted the Captain lovingly and away they went like the wind. Morys realised the 'young man' was, in fact, Madam Wen.

Before long Siôn Ifan and Catrin Parri arrived to dress the Colonel's wounds. That evening, in the tavern, a profitable deal was struck between the Colonel and Wil Llanfihangel, now claiming to be the owner of the ship and dismissing 'Captain White' as an imposter!

Chapter 8 *The Sheriff's Misfortune*

Within two months of the trouble at Pant y Gwehydd, two or three other important houses in different parts of the county had also been plundered and the authorities had made up their minds that the miscreants and their bold leader must be caught and brought to justice.

Morys Williams realised that Madam Wen had taken on Colonel Sprigg in order to save him and he remembered that this was not the first favour she had done him. Consequently, when the Sheriff of Anglesey, Sheriff Sparrow {310}, was sent to catch Madam Wen and her associates, Morys resolved to help her if he could.

Since Morys had rescued him from the fight on the night of the feast, Twm 'Pen y Bont' had become his faithful friend. Having established that Twm had once been one of Madam Wen's men, Morys sent him to the cave to warn her of the Sheriff's mission and to offer her refuge at Cymunod. Madam Wen enlisted Twm's help to clear the cave and hide all her possessions.

... she beckoned him to follow her along the crooked path to the farthest cave ... The cave opened out and it was the sparseness of its furnishings which struck the visitor with amazement when he found himself for the first time under its bare roof. There were two long boards resting on shelves of rock and, on them, a strange mixture of clothes and small items. There were one or two wooden stools, and, to Twm's amazement, a spinning wheel in the middle of the floor. The place was lit by two lamps, the like of which could not be seen in the houses of ordinary folk, but their light penetrated to the far corners of the cell, particularly the corner where the roof lowered and the cave narrowed until it was lost in the dark shadows of a narrow entrance on the one side.

She set a lamp to light up the darkest corner of the cell and, by its light, Twm saw that there was a kind of passageway which led somewhere further through the rock. In a gap in the side of that passage, there was plenty of room to hide the spinning wheel, the stools and every one of the packages, and, under her instructions, everything was carried to the hiding place until the main cave was empty. The boards were pushed far into the passageway until they were out of sight.

She asked him to thank the young squire for his kind offer and to tell him that, in view of the early warning she had received, she would probably be able to fend for herself, although, if it became necessary, she might take up his offer of shelter for an elderly relative of hers who was hard of hearing.

The Sheriff, who had set up his headquarters at Cymunod, tried to find out more about Madam Wen by talking to the locals and was beginning to come to the conclusion that she did not really exist, when Siôn Ifan offered to send one of his sons, Ifan, to show him her cave. Ifan led the Sheriff by a circuitous route through the fen to the cave and lit a candle to light the way to the inner chamber, where, of course, they found no sign of habitation. Clumsily, Ifan dropped the candle, which went out, and left the Sheriff alone while he went to retrieve the kindling box, which he had left at the cave entrance, so that he could relight it. Alone in the darkness, the frightened Sheriff's hair stood on end when he heard a strange sound. He felt himself snatched up as if in the jaws of a great beast and swept away, then dropped like a log onto the surface of the lake. Ifan heard a shout, ran to the edge of the water and pulled the dripping and terrified Sheriff to safety, asking him with feigned innocence what had happened. [*8a]

After being provided with dry clothes by Catrin Parri back in the Boat Tavern, Sheriff Sparrow sat stupefied in a corner by the fire, whispering now and again, "God save us!" He remained there for three hours before he felt strong enough to return to Cymunod. In the meantime, another visitor had arrived there, none other than the old man who had been mentioned by Madam Wen to Twm 'Pen y Bont'.

*8a. The author never makes it clear as to how Madam Wen pulls off this 'trick'.

Chapter 9 *The Old Man from the Fields*

Within half an hour of making the acquaintance of his new visitor, Morys had come to realise that the old man was very frail and so hard of hearing that conversation was extremely difficult. The visitor seemed happy, however, to sit in peace while they both awaited the Sheriff's return, which was much later than Morys expected.

When the Sheriff arrived, it was obvious that he had suffered a terrible shock and it was some time before he was able to collect himself sufficiently to relate his experiences. Assured by Morys that the old man would hear nothing of the conversation, he eventually began, and the tale increased in horror with each retelling, the roar of the beast becoming louder and its jaws more enormous. The old man in the corner could scarcely keep a straight face when the Sheriff embarked on the story for the third time! He was convinced he had been set upon by demoniacal powers and that it would be foolish to interfere further with such malicious 'spirits'. He proposed to send a report to the authorities saying that all was quiet in the district of the lakes and that there were no longer any thieves to catch!

Morys realised immediately that the Sheriff had been a victim of one of Madam Wen's tricks and his admiration for her grew. He and the Sheriff spent many hours in conversation, and, to the latter's amazement, Morys found himself praising her abilities, her faithfulness to her followers and her kindness. Had Morys known how attentively the old man listened to the conversation, despite his apparent 'deafness' or the tumult within his breast, he would have been surprised, but the old man kept his counsel.

The Sheriff knew everyone of importance in Gwynedd so, inevitably, the conversation turned to Einir Wyn. The Sheriff asked where she was and Morys assured him that, next time he saw her, he would keep tight hold of her and not let her out of his sight again.

After the Sheriff's departure, Morys accompanied the old man on the first part of his return journey. Morys asked him to tell Madam Wen that she would not have any more trouble from the Sheriff and, that if she were to change her lawless ways, he would welcome her as a neighbour, and that he hoped there would soon be someone else in Cymunod, his future wife, who would welcome her too.

Madam Wen spent sad, sleepless hours in her cave that night. Love, Shame and Jealousy were the giants who took up arms against her. She had gone to Morys's home disguised as the old man, only to satisfy a foolish curiosity and this was her punishment. She had heard her lifestyle condemned by the one she loved and she felt envy for the security that other girls in love were able to enjoy.

Chapter 10 *The Swallow's Voyage*

Madam Wen decided that the best cure for her hurt pride was to get completely away from Anglesey. Consequently she was on board her sloop [*10a], the *Swallow,* when it made its next voyage, to the port of Brest. The ship was crewed by ten good men, whose mistress rewarded them generously for their work, and its captain was Huw Bifan, who was skilled, experienced and shrewd. He spoke to Madam Wen :

"There's talk that Abel is about," said Huw casually, after they'd planned the voyage to their satisfaction. "But we haven't seen any sign of him."

"Is he on his own two feet now?"

"Yes, he escaped in a quarrel from Captain Kidd and has stolen a ship belonging to Peter of Russia." Huw laughed as he finished the story: "He's carrying ten big guns and forty hands. And the name he's given his ship is 'Certain Death'.

Everyone who knew about the sea knew of Captain Kidd and the other pirates who brought such fear to sailors from the English Channel to the Pacific. There wasn't a Welshman in the country who didn't know about the arch-pirate Sir Henry Morgan and his atrocities. And here was Abel Owen showing every sign of having determined to make a similar name for himself in evil adventure.

Despite this threat, the *Swallow* made one voyage safely to and from Ireland carrying wheat flour for the King's supporters, while Madam Wen remained in France. She decided to join the sloop on its next voyage to Ireland and then to return to Anglesey.

Opposite the mouth of the River Severn, however, Huw Bifan spotted Abel Owen's ship, *Certain Death,* further up the estuary. The Welsh pirate had recently caught two similar sloops. He had received a handsome sum in ransom money for releasing one of them, because it carried important passengers, and had sold the other in Scandinavia. Huw Bifan changed course, squared the sails and headed for Cork. The *Swallow* gave the pirate ship a run for her money, enraging Abel Owen in the process. Twice the cannon of the pirate ship was fired at the sloop but twice it missed. At that point, Madam Wen judged it wise to yield. The sail was lowered and *Certain Death* came alongside the *Swallow.*

"Send the Captain to me at once," ordered Abel Owen, "and the rest of you prepare to go to the bottom of the sea!"

Madam Wen whispered something in Huw's ear as he lowered himself into the boat. When he came face to face with the pirate captain he affected surprise and asked, in Welsh, "Are you Abel Owen?"

With a curse, the the pirate said he would have shot Huw without more ado were he not a Welshman and asked him who he thought he was in his 'pig's trough'. Huw explained that, although he was the captain, he was not the one who made the decisions, and was sent back to the *Swallow* with orders to send Madam Wen aboard *Certain Death* to answer for the trouble she had caused.

When she climbed aboard the pirate vessel, she saw that Abel was a handsome man of about forty, with black hair and tanned skin ... wearing an expensive waistcoat and breeches of brocaded purple silk. His coat was green and he wore a red feather in his green hat. A diamond cross hung from a heavy gold chain around his neck; in his hand was a sword and, from a silken rope hung two pairs of hand-guns, one pair slung across each shoulder.

*10a **Sloop** (Dutch, *sloep ;* French, *chaloupe*).—" A vessel with one mast like a cutter; but having a *jib stay,* which a cutter has not."

Madam Wen greeted Abel Owen with the words, "My countryman, methinks; also, my fellow-pirate!" Like Huw Bifan, she pretended she had not realised whose ship it was and apologised for the trouble she had caused. It did not take her long to realise, however, that Abel Owen intended to get to know her better...

While the pirate captain was having a word with some of the more villainous members of his crew, Madam Wen discovered from one of the others that the intention was to kill the crew of the *Swallow*. Quickly, she formulated a plan. When the opportunity presented itself she whispered in Abel's ear, "There is something valuable in the *Swallow's* cabin which I'd like you to have without anyone else's knowledge." Abel's pride, greed and lust made him agree readily and when Madam Wen and the pirate boarded the *Swallow,* Huw Bifan knew his mistress well enough to guess, from the expression in her eyes, that lives were at stake.

Madam Wen led Abel down to her own cabin and his eyes glistened with greed when she showed him a box full of gold and jewels, which, she said, were to have been sold to further the Jacobite cause. She suggested it would be wiser for him to conceal the jewellery about his person rather than taking the box. While he was doing so, Madam Wen slipped through the door, Huw secured it and it did not take Abel long to realise he was a prisoner in the depths of the blue ship.

The remaining pirates on board the *Certain Death* were slower to realise what had happened and, when they did, they began to pursue the sloop. However, little love was lost between them and their leader and it was not long before they had put the first mate in shackles, chosen a new captain and changed course for the Atlantic. Huw Bifan and two of the sailors managed to persuade Abel that it would be in his best interests to lay down his arms and to return the jewels. The men would have torn him limb from limb but, fortunately for Abel, their mistress was of a gentler disposition and the pirate was put down near Wexford, on the Irish coast. *'Abel was poorer by far than when he first set eyes on the ship from Cymyran Bay'*

Abel Owens was a well documented member of Captain Kidd's crew. He and eight others, were captured in 1699, in Boston (USA) at the same time as Kidd, after several years of "acts of piracy" on the High Seas off India, Africa and the Americas.

The pirates were taken to London and tried at the Old Bailey in May 1701 (not 1711 as written in the foreword - perhaps a simple proofing error). After a hearing lasting only two days, they were found guilty of "piracy and robbery on the high seas" and were sentenced "to be severally hanged by your necks until you be dead".

Owens had consistently requested the benefit of "His Majesty's Proclamation" (for pardon under certain circumstances – notably giving yourself up) but this was not granted.

Two weeks later, on May 23rd, they were hanged at Execution Dock, Wapping "and afterwards hung up in chains, at some distance from each other, down the river, where their bodies hung exposed for many years". Kidd's legendary buried treasure has never been found.

It should also be noted that WDO calls his character Abel Owen, not Abel Owens, but this is a minor piece of Welsh 'linguistic licence' as he clearly intends this to be one and the same person. {304}

Owen, Owens.—Bapt. 'the son of Owen.' Owens is the genitive form; cf. Jones, Jennings, Williams, Simmonds, &c.

Hoel fil. Oeni, Pipe Roll, 7 Hen. II.
Oenus de Porchint', ibid.
Nicholas fil. Oweyn, co. Oxf., 1273. A.
Richard fil. Owen, co. Camb., ibid.
Matthew Owen, co. Wilts, 1316. M.
1742. Married—Cornelius Owen and Eliz. Rowell: St. Geo. Chap. Mayfair, p. 31.
1747. — Rowland Owens and Sarah Narboys: ibid. p. 96.
London, 76, 6; Philadelphia, 43, 56.

Chapter 11 *Twm Pen y Bont and others*

One fine evening, when Morys had not seen Einir for months, he received a letter from her. She apologised for not having written to him sooner; said that she had been working on the task she had set herself; that she had been far away but without telling him where, and that she had been very successful. Primarily, however, it was a love letter, and Morys felt that his hopes were still very much alive. She ended the letter by teasing him about the interest he showed in Madam Wen, so that Morys, too, began to feel that perhaps Madam Wen was more in his thoughts than she should be!

At the same time, things were not going so well for Twm 'Pen y Bont'. He was a first class agricultural worker who had been much in demand on the local farms, but, for some time now, he had been very independent and only a trusted few, including Madam Wen, knew how he actually made his living. He had been having problems with Margiad, the Shoemaker's wife, whose ducks, despite having a mile of river close to their own home at their service, insisted on using the pools above his cottage. On one occasion, much to Margiad's annoyance, he had shut the ducks in the goose pens in front of his house. That afternoon, having lost her ducks again, Margiad suspected that he might have taken them into the house. She peeped through the window and saw him tending something in an enormous brass pan. She realised immediately that he was distilling whisky and, delighted to have caught him breaking the law, she crept away.

On seeing her shadow pass the window, Twm covered up the brass pan and put away his distilling equipment but, shortly afterwards, two strange men knocked on the door. They pretended at first that they wanted to buy a colt, then, in order to gain entry to the house, said that they were thirsty. Once inside, one of them went straight to the hob and removed the cover from the pan. Twm began to argue and might have resorted to his fists but one of the officials told him it would be wise to accompany them quietly. Twm asked if they would allow him first to have a word with the squire of Cymunod and they agreed, taking with them a bottle each of the liquid from the pan. When they met Morys, the officials explained that they were taking Twm into custody for illegally distilling whisky. It was arranged that Morys would look after Twm's livestock while he was away. The squire offered to put up bail money for his release but this was refused.

That same night, a stranger came the Boat Tavern in search of Madam Wen, whom he had known years previously. Siôn Ifan went in person to fetch her and, when they were alone together, the young man told her of an incident which had occurred near the mouth of the River Narbada, in India. One of his comrades had been killed by hostile natives and he and his remaining friends had plundered their temple. His ship was full of treasures which he asked Madam Wen to safeguard for him. As a token of his gratitude he gave her a huge diamond from a collection of priceless gems which he kept in a pocket in his belt.

Madam Wen would have refused his request had she felt able to do so. Both she and the innkeeper had become mistrustful of some of her followers, particularly Wil Llanfihangel and Robin 'y Pandy', who, they felt, were becoming increasingly less dependable and more villainous. Things were changing and the life which she had so loved was beginning to become burdensome to her.

Chapter 12 *On the Shore*

Madam Wen had arranged to meet the stranger on the seashore when the tide was on the ebb, at five o'clock the following morning. She took no-one except Siôn Ifan into her confidence and arranged to knock on his window at four o'clock so that he could accompany her. The innkeeper slept soundly at first but was woken on three separate occasions by knocking. On each occasion, when he arose, he realised that it was earlier than four o'clock and that there was no sign of Madam Wen or of anyone else. Eventually, very shaken, he set off to meet her earlier than the appointed time. She, too, was early and told him that she had dreamt that the two of them were in trouble and were trying to escape from evil spirits.

They rode in an uneasy silence then tied up the horses and made their way on foot towards the appointed meeting place. They saw no sign of the man they were seeking but, eventually, saw a body on the sand. Madam Wen was overcome by a fear she had never felt before and stood shaking like a leaf. In a ray of moonlight, they saw that it was John Ffowc, the stranger from the previous night.

"He had a belt containing valuable jewellery," whispered Madam Wen. The old man searched and found that it was gone.

Glad to get away from the spot, they set off in the direction of Cymyran to rejoin their horses but saw, ahead of them, a faint light. They both knew of the small, half-ruined storehouse which stood amongst the rocks some five hundred yards from the mouth of the strait. Madam Wen led Siôn Ifan to a hiding place in the shelter of a rock and went on alone. She heard voices and, on peering through the gap between the half-rotten door and its frame, espied two familiar faces. They were quarrelling over the division of their spoils while the man they had murdered still lay on his watery bier.

When she thought they were about to depart, she crept back like a shadow to her waiting companion who also heard the voices of Wil Llanfihangel and Robin 'y Pandy' as they drew nearer. Both the girl and the old man were relieved when they reached the place where they had left their mounts and it was only when they came in sight of Llyn Llywelyn, {311} not far from the inn, that Siôn Ifan told her about the ghostly knocking during the early hours. "Dear Father!" he whispered. "Wil and Robin - murderers! What is to become of us?"

Located as close as possible to the beach and the safe harbour of the boating pool, the Storehouse was used for storage of goods and materials offloaded from the merchant vessels which delivered goods to the village before the opening of Rhosneigr railway station in 1907. Most of the construction materials used in the building of Rhosneigr around the turn of the nineteenth century were initially stored here prior to use (except for sand of course, which was principally taken from the surrounding beaches).

Most of the seaside villages built during this period would have had similar structures, and it is this kind of "half ruined storehouse" to which WDO alludes in this chapter.

Chapter 13 *Siôn Ifan's Illness*

In the days after the murder, Catrin Parri became very concerned about her husband's behaviour. He had taken to walking to and fro mumbling to himself in obvious distress and she had heard the names Wil and Robin mentioned. She confided in Morys' maidservant Nanni 'Allwyn Ddu', who tried to comfort her by telling her that there must have been some squabble which would soon blow over.

Meanwhile the captain of John Ffowc's ship came to the Boat Tavern to ask for news of his master and, as the innkeeper was not about, Catrin Parri informed him, truthfully, that she had not seen the stranger since that first night. The ship remained in the area for another three weeks, watched carefully by a pair of guilty eyes, but the sea had removed all trace of the evil deed and one morning Robin 'y Pandy' was relieved to see the vessel head for the open sea.

Siôn Ifan's condition deteriorated; he developed a fever and Madam Wen advised that he should be put to bed. Nanni went to the old lady at Allwyn Goch Farm *[Red Allwyn Farm]* to fetch medicinal herbs and she and Catrin Parri began the work of nursing the innkeeper, supported by their son Dic who had come home to help. Round about dawn, the sick man woke from a disturbed sleep, sat up and began shouting in an unnaturally loud, strong voice. His thoughts were back on the seashore and he was re-living that terrible night. There were times when it took Dic's strong arms to restrain him and, at one point, he broke down and cried like a baby. Little by little, the whole story came out and it became obvious that one of the old man's concerns was that his own sons would be corrupted by the evil influence of their comrades. Dic was shocked into silence and Nanni became as white as chalk. Gradually the medicines did their work, the patient fell into a more natural sleep and Catrin Parri was left to nurse him alone.

The following evening Nanni was on her way to the inn to enquire after the patient's health when she encountered Wil Llanfihangel. She had dreaded such a meeting, as she had not yet worked out how she would behave if she chanced to meet either of the two scoundrels. Wil boasted that he was now so rich that he could build a mansion and asked her to be his wife and share that mansion with him. He reached for her hand and Nanni sprang away as though he had leprosy, immediately regretting her 'weakness'. Wil had seen the movement, however, and was enraged by it.

"I suppose Madam Wen tells you whom to to marry and whom to refuse," he snarled. "But take my word for it, she is heading for a fall if she goes on as she is doing. Some of us have had enough."

Feeling that there was something demonic in the hatred he expressed towards Madam Wen, Nanni was glad when Wil turned away from her and went on his way.

Chapter 14 *In the County Town*

Morys was surprised to receive word from Einir saying that she had heard about Twm's troubles with the excise men, and would do her best to help him when the time was right. Morys couldn't understand how she knew about Twm but was delighted to hear that she was going to be in the county town at the time of the trial and that she wanted to see him.

On the day of the trial Morys sat through a number of cases before Twm was brought into the courtroom. The judge waited ten minutes while messengers were sent in search of those who were to give evidence against the prisoner but they were nowhere to be found, and Twm was freed as there was no case to answer! For the first time, Morys saw Einir in the courtroom, with a mischievous smile on her face.

Twm thanked Morys for organising his release but, when the squire denied any involvement, Twm realised in a flash that it was Madam Wen's work. When Twm insisted that she had been in the courtroom and had winked at him, the guileless squire was sure he must be mistaken.

Later, after Twm had set out on his homeward journey and Morys and Einir were together on the banks of the Menai Straits, he tried to find out from her how she had known about Twm but she answered him in her usual light-hearted, evasive way. There was nothing light-hearted about Morys's tone, however, when he insisted, "I must have your firm promise tonight, Einir, that we shall be wed within the month!"

Einir wept as she assured him that she loved him but wanted to retain her freedom for another year. White-faced and shaking, she asked him *"Has it ever occurred to you that you might change your mind after it's too late? – That something may come to your knowledge after we are married that will cause you to stop loving me ?" but Morys responded "I love you more than earth can discern or heaven know and I cannot wait any longer".* He was adamant that nothing could ever come between them but the only promise he was able to extract from her was that she would visit him in Cymunod before the end of the month.

Einir left Beaumaris that night. She had a month, only a month, in which to decide and, in the light of her love for Morys, how she hated Madam Wen and the life she had led! She had persuaded herself that her desire for wealth stemmed from respect for her father but she felt now that perhaps she had deluded herself. What had she to offer in return for the love of such a good man but deceit? She saw the pale face of the dead man on the sand turned towards her in mute supplication, as if begging her to have no more to do with murderers. She had basked in the adoration of her followers and knew that some of them, like Siôn Ifan, were good and true, but how she regretted her association with people such as Wil Llanfihangel and Robin 'y Pandy' now that it was too late! She decided that she would keep her promise to visit Cymunod before the end of the month. So great was her deceit that it would not be possible for her to go there to marry but she owed Morys the truth. It would not be easy to confess that she had deceived him for so long and in such a way, but confess she must!

Chapter 15 *Leaving the Cave*

Siôn Ifan knew nothing of the revelations he had made while under the influence of the fever and Dic did not show his father that he knew what had happened on that dreadful night. Dic could see, however, that the old man had aged more in a month than he had in the previous ten years, and insisted on coming home to run the Boat Tavern. So well did he perform this task that he made Siôn Ifan proud of him, and, one evening he took Dic into his confidence and begged him to have nothing to do with the two villains. Dic assured him he no longer had any dealings with them.

Wil and Robin had become dissatisfied because the smuggling trade had slowed down and the plundering raids had stopped altogether. The atrocity on the beach had hardened their hearts and they no longer associated with the other members of Madam Wen's band. Gradually, they came to the conclusion that their next step must be to rob their leader herself and they would stop at nothing to attain that end.

On hearing that they had become 'night birds', Dic set himself the task of keeping an eye on them. One night he followed Wil and watched him bury his savings and the gems he had stolen in an earthenware vessel at the foot of an enormous rock concealed by brambles. He guessed that it was because he did not trust his fellow villain. As Dic passed the entrance to the cave on his way home, he was surprised to see Nanni, dressed in Madam Wen's long grey mantle and cloak. She told him she was keeping watch and asked bitterly, "Where is that band of followers which used to be so faithful? Every one of them has turned his back now at the time of greatest need."

Nanni tried several times to warn Madam Wen that she was in danger from Wil and Robin but was told she had no proof. One day, however, Nanni called at Wil's cottage on a pretext and was terrified when she overheard the two villains discussing their exploits and plotting the imminent robbery of their leader. She ran to Cymunod to fetch Morys and, once she had convinced him that Wil and Robin were murderers and thus posed a real threat to Madam Wen, he made haste to saddle his horse.

As soon as Nanni had left the cottage, the robbers lost no time in heading for the cave. Madam Wen was sitting by the lake and quickly realised the danger she was in, especially as she was not even carrying the gun she usually carried for protection. She knew that there was little of value in the cave but was well aware that the miscreants would not believe her if she tried to tell them so. After an altercation, during which Wil blamed the squire of Cymunod for the way in which things had changed, Wil went ahead to search the cave, leaving Robin to guard its occupant. Watching Robin carefully, Madam Wen saw an opportunity to creep into the cave and retrieve her rifle but, just as she reached the doorway, Robin shot her and she fell and lay still. Caring nothing for her welfare and mistrusting his comrade, Robin followed Wil into the cave.

By this time, Morys was within earshot and heard the shot but it did not occur to him at that moment that he might already be too late He left Lewys grazing near the lake and walked towards the cave but broke into a run when he saw a girl lying on the grass, white faced and with her silken gown covered in blood. How cruel, he thought, that fate had decreed that he should come face to face for the first time with his fair neighbour in such tragic circumstances! He lifted her in his strong arms, fearing the worst, his heart full of anger towards her murderers, and carried her carefully to a glade. Only then did he realise how very like Einir the lady of the lake was!

He gazed intently, almost out of his mind with shock and grief. Like someone in a swoon, he laid his burden down. On his knees on the ground he stared in mute helplessness. Einir! She meant all the world to him! Nanni's approach revived him a little. He stood up and she heard his voice, like the voice of one from another world, saying, "Here is the light of my life!" *15a

Nanni took his place, her mind clearer and her hands readier than his. She saw him walk towards the cave and could not help but fear that he sought to avenge blood with blood.

*15a. The author uses the unusual metaphor in Welsh - 'candle of my eye'.

Chapter 16 *An Undug Grave*

Wil and Robin ransacked the cave but found nothing of value. Wil was furious with Robin for shooting the only person who could have told them where she had hidden her booty, and they went outside to see if Madam Wen was able to tell them what they wanted to know. On finding that she was gone, and assuming that she must have revived and escaped, Wil's old fear of the gallows returned and he began to search for her in the vicinity. Before long, he espied the squire and realised that Morys must have been the cause of Madam Wen's disappearance. Leaving Robin to take his chance, he crept away through the thick gorse to make his escape.

Robin, too, saw the squire approaching and began to walk away. It did not occur to him to deny responsibility for the shooting and he was too stubborn to hasten his stride. Thus, when Morys began to gain on him, he turned onto a path through the marsh which was negotiable, in good conditions, by those familiar with it, but a death trap to a stranger at any time. It is possible that he lost his head when he saw the squire gaining on him but, before long, both men found themselves trapped between the precarious pathway and a steep rock face.

The adversaries faced one another, Robin standing with his back to the fen like some enormous beast. Morys uttered not a word but the murderer read the intention in his eyes, drew a gun, and fired at close range. As if disdaining such petty toys, the squire came forward with a leap. Robin flung the gun down and they began to fight. Morys was the taller and more agile while Robin had fists like rock and the stubbornness of a tiger. For some time they swayed back and forth in iron shackles with neither having the obvious advantage. Robin was the first to get a good grip. The muscles of his arms rose in a mighty effort to destroy his opponent and Morys heard two or three of his own ribs crack like withered gorse twigs. With all his remaining strength, he planted his right hand like steel in Robin's neck and tightened his grip. The villain's face began to turn black, his eyes bulged and he staggered.

"Murderer you may be, Robin, but revenge is the Lord's," said Morys, slackening his grip and stepping back. He felt, for the first time, the stabbing pain in his ribs, which distracted him for a moment, then he heard an oath and, when he turned, Robin was up to his armpits in the quagmire. In great pain, Morys made several efforts to save him but, finally, with a terrified shout, Robin disappeared into the murky depths of the swamp.

Stunned, Morys stared at the spot for some time until he began to feel cold and light-headed. A pain in his side reminded him that he had been shot and he realised that he had bled profusely. He tried to rise, to look for his horse, but was unable to do so. Drifting in and out of consciousness, he was tormented by visions of Einir in the clutches of murderers, entreating him to save her.

Lewys waited obediently where his master had left him but, when night fell, he wandered further afield and some sixth sense brought him to where Morys lay. He could not understand why he received neither warm greeting nor gentle rebuke and, after sniffing carefully around his master's head, he posted himself as guardian above the inert body of the person he loved most in the world.

Chapter 17 *Fulfilling an Old Promise*

Left alone with Madam Wen, Nanni remembered how one of the local farmers had come back from the brink of death after his cart had overturned, and she did not despair for a moment. She was rewarded when she saw a glimmer of movement behind the closed eyelids. When Einir began to come round she had no memory of what had happened and Nanni judged it wise, for the moment, not to enlighten her.

As soon as she felt it was safe to leave her patient for a short while, Nanni hastened to the Boat Tavern to seek help. Siôn Ifan wanted to set out immediately in his shirtsleeves but Nanni suggested that Dic would be quicker and the two of them ran to the edge of the lake where the innkeeper kept a boat ready at all times. Dic rowed and, when they landed, he was the first to minister to their wounded leader and to prove the worth, in a crisis, of his father's good brandy.

By this time, some of the shadows had cleared from Einir's memory and she remembered that Wil and Robin had intended to rob her and that it was Robin who had fired the shot. However, she said little as Dic and Nanni carried her to the boat and, once they had landed, willingly allowed herself to be taken, on horseback, to Nanni's home, 'Allwyn Ddu'.

Nanni found that Einir's wound was not as serious as she had feared, but she had been weakened by loss of blood. On sending a careful message of enquiry to Cymunod, however, the maidservant found that the squire had not returned and she feared that he had come to some harm. She was reluctant to admit her fears to Einir but in the end, had no choice. Einir sat up at once from her pillows and it took all Nanni's patience and wisdom to dissuade her from joining in the search. At last it was agreed that Nanni and Dic would enlist the help of Madam Wen's remaining followers to form a search party.

Dic lost no time in gathering a group of volunteers. Some were sent in search of Wil and Robin and others, including Dic and Nanni, went to the area near the cave. Dic asked Nanni if Morys had been riding his horse and they searched for Lewys for some time before hearing a nervous neigh which filled them with both hope and dread. The black horse came towards them but was reluctant to let them approach the spot he guarded so jealously. When Nanni spoke softly to him, however, he allowed them to follow him. The sound of someone moaning in pain is not normally a pleasant one, but, on this occasion it fell on their ears like the sweetest music.

Morys was enough of a burden for six ordinary men but willing hands were soon found to convey him to his bedchamber in Cymunod. For days he was too ill to tell anyone what had happened. Dic found a gun and signs of a struggle on the edge of the fen and neither Wil nor Robin was anywhere to be found. One evening Morys came to his senses sufficiently to ask for Twm 'Pen y Bont', who went to tend him, as Nanni was still in 'Allwyn Ddu' nursing Einir. It was, therefore, Twm, on a brief visit to the Boat Tavern, who was the first to tell the story of Robin's terrible fate. It was then, too, that the story of what had happened that night on the shore came out and the neighbourhood came to know that Wil and Robin were murderers.

One afternoon Twm visited 'Allwyn Ddu' with a message from Morys asking Einir to visit him on the following day. What a stir his visit caused! The poor girl questioned Nanni over and over again about what the squire had said when she went to tell him that Madam Wen was in danger and to ask him to come at once. She then demanded to know what Morys had said when he knelt beside her inert body and hardly dared to believe, when Nanni repeated the words, "Here is the light of my life!" that it could mean that he forgave and still loved her.

Chapter 18 *The Autumn Feast*

After a year of adversity, Siôn Ifan and Catrin Parri were delighted that their son had settled down and was going to marry Nanni, on the day before the Feast of St Michael. Dic's marriage became a kind of symbol, amongst his peers, of the end of the old way of life and the start of the new. Dic had formed a link between the members of Madam Wen's band and the quieter lads of the area and the revelations about Wil and Robin had shocked many of Madam Wen's followers. Thus, when Dic chose to renounce his lawless ways, the band ceased to exist.

It was natural, on the day of their wedding, that people's thoughts turned to Wil, who had been caught and was in the county jail awaiting his execution, but none of those who had worked alongside him and Robin in the old days spared them a moment's sympathy.

On the day of Dic and Nanni's wedding the *Swallow* was at anchor in Cymyran River but Huw Bifan and the crew were in the Boat Tavern, joining in the celebrations. Their fears that the sloop would be sold to a stranger had been unfounded because Einir had given the sloop to Nanni as her dowry and from then onwards, Dic was the *Swallow's* owner.

On the following morning - the day of Morys and Einir's wedding - Twm was up early washing and dressing for what was obviously going to be an important occasion. He and Morys set off at dawn, crossed the Menai Straits and came to Bangor, where Twm attended to the horses while the squire went on ahead. When he was ready, Twm slipped quietly into the cathedral and stared from a distance at the grand company which was beginning to assemble there. Had he known it, the cream of Gwynedd society was gathered there to pay homage to two of their lineage, of whom they were very fond.

Being short of stature, Twm had to stand up when the bride entered on the arm of the baronet of Penrhyn. He was amazed and overjoyed to see that she was none other than Madam Wen, whose beauty outshone that of every other maiden there. He was the proudest of men when, after the wedding breakfast in Penrhyn Castle, the bride came to seek him out. She asked him to go to the Boat Tavern the following night and tell Nanni all about the wedding. Twm agreed readily, but asked her if she was coming back to the district of the lakes. When she teasingly asked if he thought that was wise, Twm responded from the bottom of his heart, "I don't know what would become of us without you." The following evening, Twm was given a hero's welcome when he revealed the secret in the Boat Tavern and and regaled the company with details of the wedding.

One evening shortly afterwards, Cymunod was full of guests. All were local residents who had come to celebrate the marriage and to welcome the squire's wife to her new home. Some of the guests were seeing Einir Wyn for the first time and were amazed by her beauty and charm. There was another group, however, whose unswerving love for her was rooted in a bygone era, who had been with her through good times and bad, and who were now delighted to see her married to one of the gentlest and most honest men in the country.

But now Siôn Ifan is on his feet and silence is asked for. He is going to wish long life and happiness to the squire and his wife and to propose their good health in a cup of wine. From now on it will be futile to yearn for the old time. A lock that will never be undone is placed on every faithful breast. That is not said, for good reason. But the cup is at the lips of the local lads and what has been, has been. Long life to the squire's wife! And from now on Madam Wen will be nothing but a rumour in the wind.

Bangor. The Cathedral.

Reviews & Comments

OGOF MADAM WEN.

Madam Wen's Cave

The above is a photograph of the entrance to Madam Wen's famous cave, with Miss Evelyn Evans, Penrallt, Bryngwran, standing near it. The cave stands on the bank of Llyn Traffwll [Traffwll Lake] in the western part of Anglesey. It is of this lake that the poet Cynan writes in his lyric poem on 'Sending the Goldfinch to the Waterside'.

According to tradition, it was in this cave that Madam Wen spent most of her time before she left it to become the wife of Morys Williams and live in Cymunod. She also lived for part of the time on her famous yacht, which she used for smuggling on a large-scale, receiving a great deal of help to do so from Sion Ifan of the Boat Tavern and his three expert sons.

Folklore mixed with truth are woven together in the Story of Madam Wen. By now it is not easy to say what is fiction and what is fact. Mr. W. D. Owen, Rhosneigr, wrote a pretty fictional tale based on the tradition, with the title 'Madam Wen'. He gives us a charming and courageous portrayal of the heroine of the cave. The book is full of adventure and heroism therefore it appeals to children and young people. Town schools would do well to arrange trips for the children to see Madam Wen's cave. It is worth seeing, since the spirit of Madam Wen is still in the wind.

Lizzie Williams
Ty Croes, Dothan, Anglesey

The above article appeared in
The Children's Treasury, May 1938, pages 140, 141

4. Reviews and Comments

Elin Cadwaladr

Despite a thorough search of the original newspaper 'Y Genedl Gymreig' *[The Welsh Nation]* for several weeks before and after it was serialised, no previews or reviews of 'Elin Cadwaladr', under its original title 'The Return of The Wanderer', have been found. This is disappointing, if not entirely unexpected. However, Madam Wen has proved more fruitful.

Madam Wen – The Newspaper Serial

We should not forget that barely a week before the final instalment of Madam Wen had been published in 'Y Genedl Gymreig', Archduke Franz Ferdinand had been assassinated in Sarajevo and the world was heading inexorably for the First World War. 1914 was not therefore a good time for 'rave reviews' and it is perhaps unsurprising that, just like Elin Cadwaladr, no reviews of the serialised story have been found.

Madam Wen – The Novel

However, when the book was first published in 1925, some 11 years later, it received positive reviews in several newspapers of the day – indeed, perhaps due to the sad and untimely demise of its author, 'The Welsh Nation' wrote about it – and him – on four separate occasions. The relevant paragraphs from these reviews are included in panels 4.1 to 4.5 on the following pages, and all four have been translated from the original Welsh in which they were first written. A review from the Liverpol Mercury has also been found. The book must have been a reasonably good seller in its day, as it was reprinted in 1929, and in 1975. {400}

To keep the book in context, other books first published in 1925 include: The Great Gatsby (F.Scott Fitzgerald), Gentlemen Prefer Blondes (Anita Loos) and Mein Kampf (Adolf Hitler). {401}

These days, the complete novel itself is only available on the second-hand market, and of course only in Welsh. A brief trawl of the internet at the time of writing revealed five copies available across three of the major websites {402} and of course there may be many more tucked away in local second-hand bookshops up and down the land.

The novel has been quoted as an example of an oral tradition which gained considerably more substance after the novel was published {403} and references to it appear in at least one literary dictionary {404}.

A modern critical appraisal of Madam Wen, compared to Elin Cadwaladr also appears at the end of this section. [panel 4.11]

'Madam Wen', the film

Fifty-seven years after the first publication of the novel, the making of the S4C film breathed new life into the Madam Wen story. A long article by William Williams appeared in the Anglesey publication Y Rhwyd *[The Net]* in April of 1982 (see Appendix 5.1) followed by his brother's article the following month (see Appendix 5.5). And as the film was being shot across the island, it also generated more transient stories in the local media. After its showing, film critics of the day included Glyn Evans in 'Y Cymro' *[The Welshman]* and Bedwyr Jones in 'Y Faner' *[The Banner]* (see panels 4.6 – 4.7 following). All of these articles are reprinted by kind permission.

The television programme synopsis described it as : "A Costume Drama based on the novel by W. D. Owen. Who was Madam Wen? A person of flesh and blood or a creature of folk lore? A corrupt thief or a female Robin Hood? Whoever or whatever she was, the inhabitants of the seventeenth century community in Anglesey - both admired and feared her. However all was to change with the arrival of Morus (sic) Williams".

According to the producer of the film, Gwilym Owen, the controversy over the budget was – at least partly – his fault.

Essentially the decision to produce a film that was so big and complicated, so early in the life of S4C was its downfall. However, as he says, hindsight always has perfect vision.

S4C (along with all the public broadcasters) has been subjected to regular scrutiny over many years, and in 1994, in a major publication entitled "Wales and Cinema" {405} the film and its impact on the channel, were again subjected to detailed criticism in several pages of careful analysis. Extracts of this are reproduced by permission in panel 4.8 following.

As Editor of this work however, and despite having only a very limited Welsh vocabulary *a, I have watched the film and from a purely visual perspective found it quite dated and in need of reworking (as might be expected after all this time). However, in an attempt to be as fair as possible to the film, I asked my translator to provide a 21st century critique based on comparing the film to the book and this is shown in panel 4.9 on page 143.

The film was re-shown a number of times during the following year (1983) and then was 'rested'. For interest, a cast list is also included here in panel 4.10. It is pleasing to be able to report that several of the members of the cast, including 'Madam Wen' herself (or at least the actress Marged Esli who played her) still live on Anglesey. *b

Madam Wen – The Legend

Finally, it is time to consider the earliest known written reference to Madam Wen – an article by John Watkin Huws in the pages of 'Cymru' *[Wales]* from November 1897. This article is included in full in Appendix 5.1 and what little is known about Huws, who is described as 'a Historian from Llanfaelog' is given in a footnote at the end of of the article.

Huws writes with authority, but cites no references and some 'facts' are therefore difficult to verify. The reader is invited to judge for himself whether Wil's 'reversal of horseshoes' could work in practice, or whether it is likely that he managed to escape to America with his head still intact. The 'Spirit of the Lake' as Madam Wen's ghost was called, is also easily described as fantasy, but who would wish to decry the hopeful for looking ?

More recently, (in the early 1980s), Maldwyn Thomas M.A. a well-known lecturer at the University of Wales, Bangor, conducted some detailed research into the history behind the Madam Wen legend. The principal article written by Mr Thomas on the subject, has been translated from Welsh, and is included in Appendix 5.6. This was originally published in Y Faner *[The Banner]* shortly after the Madam Wen film aired on S4C.

It provides an interesting and well researched viewpoint on the subject, identifying the most likely role model for the heroine, drawing comparisons between 'Madam Wen' and 'Lorna Doone' and once again, posing more questions about the legend than it answers. It seems that like all great folklore , the truth is hard to pin down.

Nevertheless, the legend of Madam Wen went on to inspire our hero, William David Owen to write a Novel which claimed his place in history as The Rhosneigr Romanticist.

*a It is believed that on first transmission, English subtitles to the film were produced and aired by the ORACLE teletext system. Unfortunately, there are no records available to confirm the veracity of these anecdotal reports.

*b Marged Esli, the Welsh actress who played the title role in the film 'Madam Wen' still lives on Anglesey and has undertaken a substantial body of acting work over a long career. When not fulfilling acting roles, she is also a regular supply teacher at Bodedern secondary school on Anglesey.

By coincidence, through her mother's side of the family (Hughes, Fferam Bach, Bryn Du), she is also distantly related to W.D.Owen and clearly remembers hearing of the Madam Wen legend as a child.

[panel 4.1]

The Welsh Nation,
Monday November 9, 1925

From Day to Day, by Observer
[The Eighth Paragraph]

I have two new books on the table awaiting their turn. One is "The Book of Jonah," by the Rev. D. Tecwyn Evans, B.A. (James Clarke and Co., Price 1s) and the other is "Madam Wen," a romance by Mr. W. D. Owen (Hughes and Son, 3/6 net). More will be said about them at a later date. The purpose of this paragraph is merely to introduce them to the public.

[panel 4.2]

The Welsh Nation,
Monday November 16, 1925

From Day to Day, Death of an Author, by Observer
[First three paragraphs]

Last week I referred to the new novel, "Madam Wen," by Mr. W. D. Owen, and promised a review of it before long. Now word has come from Anglesey to say that Mr. Owen died in Rhosneigr a week last Wednesday – the same day I was writing the note about his book – and was buried in Gwalchmai cemetery on Saturday.

I was very sorry to hear this. Mr. Owen was only 52 years old {*1a} and was a very able man. He was a native of the Bryngwran area, said Mr. O. H. Owen, Caergeiliog, who kindly wrote to inform me, and his home was a smallholding called Ty Franan. He was a school teacher for a period and then he was chosen as the secretary of the Education Committee in Yorkshire {*1b}. He qualified to become a barrister and, after that, a solicitor.

He opened an office in Rhosneigr, and it was as a solicitor there that he worked in his last years. Two of his peers officiated in his funeral, Rev. Richard Thomas, Bontnewydd, and Rev. W. H. Jones, Bryngwran. Mrs. Owen is an Englishwoman, who is also an authoress and who has edited a women's magazine. It is sad to think of the death of such a man almost the same day that his book was published.

{1a} Owen was in fact aged 51 when he died.
{1b} Inconclusive – see biography.

[panel 4.3]

Liverpool Post and Mercury,
Monday, November 16th 1925

An Anglesey Romance

"Madam Wen," by Mr. W. D. Owen (Wrexham: Hughes and Son, 3s 6d net) is a romance of Anglesey in Jacobite days, with smugglers, highway robbers, an elusive and beautiful chieftainess of a mysterious gang, a local squire of enormous bulk and strength, and horses that gallop like the wind. This is highly satisfactory and as it should be. Some of us prefer yarns before psychology any day, and Mr. Owen provides us with a good yarn, for which, in this all too sombre world, we owe him thanks.

I am not sure that he has always made the best use of his material; not always is the wild, natural background, so important in all adventure stories, exploited as it might be. One would like more skin-creeping details about the gorse thickets, for instance, and I think the discovery of the body on the beach and the overhearing of the murderer's (sic) talk in the abandoned hut might have been elaborated. But as they are, they are thrilling, and one reads on "breath in fist," as the expressive Welsh idiom has it, to the last page. This is the kind of Welsh book we want, a breathless tale that insists upon being read; and, happily, we are getting more of them. Some day, when we learn not to grudge paying for a book a half or a quarter of what we readily give for a concert on [or] cinema ticket, we shall get still more.

I am sorry to learn that the author died a fortnight ago, a few days after his book was published. He was an Anglesey solicitor, practically unknown in Welsh literary circles, but "Madam Wen" proves that he had the gift of telling a good tale. He was, I believe, a middle-aged man. One wonders why one has not heard more of him.

[panel 4.4]

The Welsh Nation,
Monday November 30, 1925

IN PASSING

Choking the Welsh Language

Contrast (by E.M.H.) [The whole article]

If the Welsh language is dying, it is we, the Welsh people, who are to blame. It is necessary to say this. When talking about the language we tend to place the blame everywhere except where we should do so, on our laziness, our stupidity and our lack of courage. I have thought a good deal about what I saw in Anglesey, namely a line of Welsh people in the station asking humbly for their tickets in English – and the boy who was selling the tickets was as good a Welsh-speaking Welshman as they were! What in the world is to be done with people like that?

But I'm sure that we complain and grumble too much and create the impression that the state of the language is worse than it is. A Member of Parliament told me he speaks in Welsh in a village which is within seven miles of England and that the leaflets which advertise the meeting are in Welsh. A man who used to live in Oswestry told me that he sometimes still goes there from time to time. And what struck him was that so much more Welsh is heard in the eating places of that town now than there was twenty or thirty years ago. Much Welsh is heard in the lobby of the House of Commons, in the National Liberal Club and such places. No, it is not as dead by a long way as some parsons, ministers and schoolmasters would have us believe.

THE DANGERS

But die it will, nevertheless, unless we talk less about it and do more in it. It's completely worthless merely to talk about a language all the time and even more ineffectual is the ongoing discussion about the orthography and such like. There is no other country which does this, outside of scholarly circles, as far as I know, and it's possible that no other language would have borne such treatment either.

This came to my mind the other day after reading "Madam Wen". I did not think once about the Welsh language or anything similar whilst reading the story. I did not feel I was doing anything virtuous by reading a Welsh book and I had no desire to pat myself on the back for reading "sublime literature". I read the book from cover to cover because it was impossible not to do so after starting, because the story galloped along and made you gallop with it, because I wanted to know what happened to everybody in the end. And it is only by means of things such as this that the language will be kept alive.

EXTENDING THE FIELD

One could enlarge a great deal on the field. We need many more stories like "Madam Wen" and "The Island of Treasure", "Lona" and "Tomi's Autobiography". We can't have too many such things in Wales. The boys and girls will continue to read their language and that will ensure the future.

But I want more. I would like history books in Welsh, biographies of the famous people of the world, light, interesting books about adventures and discoveries and important events. We have been far too 'literary' and have forgotten the large class who care nothing for poetry but enjoy reading a variety of things and who enjoy – as if without knowing it –a clear, no-nonsense style.

It is my experience that the articles which are most popular and acceptable are those which convey knowledge on a particular topic, the history of a poet or politician, chapters of the history of a country or a movement, without too much philosophising on the one or the other. And that is perfectly natural.

TELLING A STORY

And no man of letters should belittle the craft of telling a story. I don't mean devising a story, but telling any story plainly, comprehensibly and readably. There has been far too little of that in Wales and far too much philosophising and inflammatory writing. But it is much easier to philosophise superficially that to say what you have to say clearly and straightforwardly.

In telling any story, be it the story of a country, an event, or a man's life, you first need to select and formulate. You must need to be able to tell it how it was, anyway, totally clearly and comprehensibly, and that requires more creative ability than most people think. And it must be told in a style which is readable because every unnecessary word has been left out. It is no mean task for anybody to master such a style, but it is essential to have that style of writing if the language is to be kept alive.

THE CONTRAST

I read "Madam Wen." And then I thought how rare such books are in comparison with long pieces of free-verse, odes and poems which no-one, as far as I know, reads or thinks about reading. Their composition takes a great deal of time and energy but many of them are very ordinary and of poor quality. Their authors have plenty of ability but are poets by accident.

Is it not a pity that most of this energy and true skill is not turned to other directions and that our periodicals were not a little more objective than they are? People thirst for history, for facts, and, if they are not given to them in Welsh they will search for them in some other language.

Perhaps I should explain that I am not denigrating sublime literature. My appeal is that we should come down from the abstract, leave the philosophising, which is an evil that threatens to surround us, and take hold of something concrete which says something clearly.

[panel 4.5]

The Welsh Nation,
Monday November 30, 1925

MADAM WEN

LADY OF THE CAVE
(By the Rev. R. Thomas, B.A.) .

In a relatively small area on the South-Western side of Anglesey, there have been, throughout the years, many traditions about the heroine of the banks of Lake Traffwll. Her inexplicable exploits and her mystic influence were talked about. An awesome heroism became attached to her name, and when we children approached the old cave our footsteps involuntarily slowed but our imaginations raced – this was the cave of Madam Wen!

From here, Mr. W. D. Owen, Rhosneigr, obtained the material for a splendid romance. The author awaited its publication for a long time and we heard him mention it from time to time. At last it has been published as a handsome volume by Messrs Hughes and Son, Wrexham, but, sad to say, the man who wrote it has been in his grave for a fortnight.

Nothing better than this volume has entered the literature of our country for some time. We expected it to be good, but it has exceeded that expectation and has come as an eye-opener to the talent and skill of the author. Madam Wen is a heroine from start to finish and some strange charm surrounds her throughout her career. We find in this book a vivid imagination and, more than that, it has a structure and a plot which are worthy of a craftsman. It describes life in the district of the lakes in the seventeenth century. One cannot accuse him of using too much paint. His imagination takes a natural path alongside what he had read and heard all over the locality. By the way, this is the area of the 'Crigyll Robbers' who were immortalised by the late Lewis Morus.

VIVID CHARACTERS

There is scarcely a character here who does not depict some aspect of the social life of the period. Siôn Ifan of the Boat Tavern was a teetotaller on the day of the festival of the patron saint of Llanfihangel when everyone else was half drunk. In this peaceful area, under the shelter of the old church, as it were, there is Wil Llanfihangel, his spirit surging like the sea with villainy. The squire of Cymunod is a good model, as exemplified by his faithfulness in supporting his humble neighbour, Wil Penybont, at his trial. The stories of the pirates, and of the massacre on the shore, are exciting. In the middle of it all Madam Wen comes, with her charm, to visit the cave. She is able to control every outbreak of wildness and her word brings an end to every dispute. The craftsmanship of the conclusion of the plot is excellent.

We have heard Mr Owen say many times that a romance should stir the reader's blood and make it flow more quickly. This is a story which is alive from beginning to end and full of excellent descriptions. We are enchanted by Madam Wen's mysterious movements and we are drawn on by a desire to find the key to the bewitching secret of her story. This is a book which is read voraciously and which is not put down until one has read to the end. This is the kind of literature which is needed nowadays in Wales – literature which appeals to the imagination and attracts the young to read it.

We have here the Welsh language in its best attire – it is refined and dignified, yet it reads easily and naturally. The style is totally Welsh and a living spirit walks in the descriptions.

A WORD ABOUT THE AUTHOR

The circumstances require that we say a word about the author. He was brought up in a small farmhouse called Tyfranan in the area of Bryngwran, Anglesey. He served as a pupil teacher and completed his course in Bangor Normal College, gaining a good grade. For years after that he was a teacher in intermediate schools in England. He became intent on becoming qualified as a barrister and he succeeded. He retreated back to Wales and this was of great benefit to his health, of which he had always had to be careful. For some time he served in the Pensions Office in Anglesey, but for a long time now he has been working as a solicitor, and he was rapidly becoming successful in that calling.

Not only was he possessed of sagacity and a keen mind, but he was also clean-living and had strong principles. He hated deceit and hypocrisy and believed that the good was worth living everywhere.

He could appreciate and judge literature and his opinion was sound. He read more than most of the works of modern poets and writers. He praised some of them highly but said clearly that the terrible and pagan tones of the occasional piece indubitably excluded it from the true temple of literature.

This story belongs to the true temple. Although deeply sorry that the author is no longer living, we rejoice in the idea that he has left to the nation a piece of work which is an evident success. 'Madam Wen' has come to stay in the literature of Wales

[This could be the Rev. Richard Thomas who officiated at WDO's funeral].

[panel 4.6]

Y Cymro, *[The Welshman]*, January 4th 1983

A column on S4C by Glyn Evans

Madam Wen: Worth the Price

[The following is a translation of the part of Glyn Evans's column which deals with the film Madam Wen]

S4C's table was very meagre over the holidays and particularly bare on Christmas Day.

This was made up for by the enormous helping of pudding which Madam Wen provided on Christmas Sunday – which, unlike everyone else, was called Boxing Day by "Sbec" [the S4C programme listings magazine]

This is the film which cost £470,000 instead of £335,000 to make and for which Gwilym Owen, the producer, got the sack.

Having seen it on the screen, however, Mr Owen should be a reasonably happy man - under the circumstances. The film was two and a half hours long rather than an hour and a half, so the price wasn't really too much to pay.

It was a gripping film with plenty of movement and excitement, the big chase at the end providing an excellent climax, despite the fact that the men pulled the dogs after the scent rather than the other way around!

John Pierce Jones as Morris (sic) Cymunod was disappointing and one could be forgiven for thinking that, if there were more big Welsh actors available, he would not have been given the part.

There was the occasional laughable scene too, like expecting his horse to gallop carrying his weight and to catch the beautiful feather that was Madam Wen, who was played with the perfect combination of playful femininity and hard sharpness by Marged Esli.

John Ogwen had a television part he could get his teeth into and it was a polished performance. Trefor Selway also had fun playing the part of the half-English Sheriff.

One would hope now that the idea of Madam Wen will be developed into an adventure series, keeping Marged Esli, John Ogwen, Charles Williams and Trefor Selway, for example, in the appropriate parts.

The fear would be, however, that they will repeat the original film ad nauseam in order to get their money's worth, even breaking it up into weekly episodes.

This would be a lazy and unimaginative answer and an attitude one hopes has been buried with the old order of Welsh television, an attitude which is not consistent with the new spirit of S4C.

Things need to be looked at from a more original standpoint and completely new stories and adventures need to be created.

The canvas and the background are there and the ground has been prepared by Gwilym Owen and the rest.

It would be a pity to lose this opportunity to create a hero(ine) of whom there has never been the like before on Welsh television.

Editor's Note:

Glyn Evans was a journalist on 'Y Cymro' [The Welshman] at the time, although he now works for the BBC. He has asked me to point out that he would not be so critical now, knowing what he now does about the project.

[panel 4.7]

Y Faner *[The Banner]*, January 7th 1983

Bedwyr L Jones weighs up

The Great Saga of Madam Wen

We were three generations watching Madam Wen, the youngest twelve and the eldest eighty-five. The film held the attention of us all. We all enjoyed it, but I was the least satisfied. I, however, was the only one who was fully familiar with the book. This was a big disadvantage because Madam Wen, the film, was not W. D. Owen's Madam Wen.

In the opinion of the two youngest, the chase through the bog was 'great': even the reluctance of one of the dogs to follow the scent only added to their enjoyment. And there were some other good scenes – the one of Madam Wen on her horse against the light from the burning haystacks and the dancing and the merriment in Cymunod as Morys Williams brings back the old neighbourly joy to one of Anglesey's minor mansion houses.

Dafydd Huw Williams's dialogue was powerfully gripping and the acting, on the whole, perfectly good. Siôn Ifan, the Boat Tavern, is the most rounded character in W. D. Owen's story. Charles Williams played the part to perfection, with that gift he has to convey that he knows much more than he says. Catrin Dafydd was a gracious, agreeable landlady. John Ogwen took the opportunity to develop the character of Twm Pen-y-Bont well. I liked two others very much, too, Trefor Selway as Sheriff Sparrow and Ian Saynor as Major Price, a part which hardly exists in the book. The portrayal which gave me the most pleasure of all, however, was that of Janet Aethwy. She brought life and mischievousness to the part of Nanni Allwyn Ddu.

These minor characters and some of the crowd scenes were the strengths of the film. But there were weak moments. The start was slow. The tempo was too slow throughout. The whole film would have been better if it had been half an hour shorter. Some of the exciting scenes were not exciting enough. The glimpse we had of the ship was a complete failure. It was too obvious that it was a model in a tub. Why on earth could they not have borrowed a few moments from a film of a proper sailing ship for such a short scene instead of shattering the illusion they were trying to create?

These, however, are small production and editorial errors, things which can be put right as we gain more experience of producing such ambitious films. But something else concerned me and that was in the script. "Who was Madam Wen? A flesh and blood person or a mythical illusion? An unprincipled thief or a saint bent on helping the poor?" Those are the words of the blurb in Sbec. [the S4C programme listings magazine] W. D. Owen was in no doubt about his Madam Wen. She was a flesh and blood woman, a Welsh Robin Hood leading a band of robbers in order to take revenge on the oppressive rich and taking great care that nobody knew who she was. A string of her adventures bubbled out of the story-teller one after the other, juxtaposed with the story of Einir Wyn, the girl from the other side of the Menai Straits, who enchanted Morys Williams, being careful, as far as he could, to keep the two girls apart.

Dafydd Huw Williams wove the material more complexly and closely. He brought Madam Wen herself to Cymunod when the Sheriff was searching the cave. It is the old man from the fields who is the visitor in the story; the mystery is greater and the strain of accepting Morys Williams's stupidity is less. Part of the same complication was showing Madam Wen alone with her thoughts in Cymunod Woods, after the Scot got killed on the beach, and bringing Siôn Ifan to Cymunod, when the Sheriff was leaving, to philosophise about all the trouble. I would have been happier without these scenes. I certainly would have thrown out the frequent and unnecessary references to an old Celtic goddess, a temple, an altar and the dark side of the moon. I am fully aware that this is the exact area of Llyn Cerrig Bach but this has nothing to do with the simple romance of Madam Wen. The reference to "the old tribal right, the right of the goddess of the cave and her altars" to hang Wil was also an unnecessary complication.

I haven't yet mentioned the two main characters – Morys Williams and Einir Wyn. They are, to a large degree, puppets in the story. John Pierce Jones and Marged Esli made a fair attempt at portraying them, although I suspect that John would have been happier as one of the leaders of the gang rather than as a country squire.

Have I been unfair in what I have said? I have, I am sure, because I am fond of the story and had produced the film in my head before I saw it. Almost everyone to whom I have spoken enjoyed the Film Board's Madam Wen. Had it been half an hour shorter, had it been simpler and slightly more exciting, it would have been a complete success. As it was, however, it scored eleven out of twelve, not twelve.

Marged Esli as Madam Wen

John Pierce Jones as Morys Williams

Editor's Note:

Bedwyr Lewis-Jones was professor of Welsh, (specialising in Literature & Linguistics) at the University College of North Wales, Bangor. He died in 1993.

[panel 4.8]

Wales and Cinema (1994) by Dave Berry {405}
(partial extracts from pages 323-326)

[There was a] sense of disappointment felt after the premiere, in 1982, of Madam Wen *[White Lady]*, a film entertaining on its own unambitious level but scarcely original or inspired enough for the vanguard of a channel carrying such high hopes and launched after highly emotive campaigns and a series of political convulsions. It was significant that the two major dramas in S4C's early days were both set in the distant past. They epitomized too much of the channel's dramatic output in the 1980s. ..... Madam Wen did arouse fierce discussions, but its artistic merits and treatment seemed almost incidental during the row that developed around its budget. The film, S4C's first Boxing Day offering, and scripted by Dafydd Huw Williams, was conceived as family entertainment — according to its producer Gwilym Owen who became director of Bwrdd Ffilmiau Cymraeg (The Welsh Film Board) in 1980. Owen had been asked for a 'blockbuster' by Ogwen Williams [the first Director of Programmes for S4C] who was 'anxious that the first dramatic feature should come from independents'.

Owen wanted to make 'Helynt Coed Y Gell' (Trouble at Coed Y Gell), a smuggling tale, based on a story by G. Wynne Griffith and set off Anglesey's north-east coast. That would have involved few locations and a small cast. But the sea scenes were deemed a problem and S4C decided instead to shoot the legend of Madam Wen, the mysterious seventeenth-century robber, a Robin Hood character also reminiscent of sixteenth-century Welsh folk hero Twm Sion Catti. Owen said later that Williams was anxious to have a Welshman based in London to direct 'rather than the Aarons and Claytons' in order to demonstrate S4C's willingness to lure proven professionals back to Wales. Owen thought Williams was right to go for something non-political and 'a period piece adventure with love, romance, beauty . . .' - but he denies there was any negative thinking or fear of embracing a more contentious subject after the flak the channel had already taken from some MPs and critics who feared S4C would be 'a gravy train for Welsh-speakers'.

Owen's first choice as director was Geraint Morris, an experienced TV drama series hand then working in Scotland, but he was unavailable and the assignment went to London-based Pennant Roberts (b. 1940, Weston-super-Mare, of Welsh parents) who had made episodes of Dr Who, The Onedin Line and Juliet Bravo. Roberts brought his own production team down from London and it was apparently accepted that the whole crew would be on standby for six weeks. Above all, the team lacked an experienced accountant on set, and this was to cost S4C and its credibility dear in ensuing weeks as the budget soared out of control, even though Roberts wrapped up shooting within schedule. There were also fundamental miscastings, with John Pierce Jones playing the male lead Morys, scarcely the romantic figure envisaged in the 1930s book of Madam Wen. Owen would have preferred John Ogwen for the lead but Ogwen had just appeared as the hero in BBC's similar Hawkmoor series about Twm Sion Catti. The final choices forced script changes to emphasize the pathos of Morys, forever hankering after an unattainable romance, and his awkwardness and limitations as a potential lover. Marged Esli, though personable and efficient as Madam Wen, rarely suggested the glamorous enigma conveyed in the script.

Originally budgeted at between £240,000 and £270,000, according to Owen, but commissioned officially for £335,000, the film finally cost between £500,000 and £550,000. It also placed at risk the future of its producers, the Welsh Film Board. ..... The 135-minute feature was shot in six weeks and some actors were on location the whole time when needed only briefly, though Roberts claimed he kept a minimum crew, except for the beach and ballroom setpieces. Owen himself, with roots in literature and journalism, had little experience with film or large budgets. There were swift repercussions as the overspending became a cause celebre. With as many as 150 people on set, costs escalated but Owen only 'saw the light' after five weeks: 'I told S4C we were in trouble.' Costs might have been higher if the production team had not skimped on extras - they used only twelve cavalrymen, for example, and completed model shots cheaply at the old Hammer Studios in Bray, Berkshire.

'We were working in absolutely new conditions,' Owen said later. 'Certainly I was to blame for some of the things to happen, but only some. We should have taken on board all the location costs. I should have had an accountant on set and I should have questioned things more - but I was so excited by the possibilities.' Owen was fired from the film during the editing — feeling he had been made a scapegoat — and Dafydd Huw Williams took over as producer, amidst much unfavourable publicity and with S4C attempting 'damage limitation' by issuing statements condemning the overspending and expressing grave concern. Roberts later claimed the channel did not 'sell' the film afterwards — 'having created a bete noire they did not want to publicize it.' In the prevailing atmosphere, it would have been surprising if Madam Wen had been impressive enough to disarm S4C s opponents and forestall further criticism. At least the finished product looked polished enough to reflect the production values, even if the editing of swashbuckling beach scenes at the finale seemed confused.

Madam Wen is established early on as a local aristocrat on Anglesey's west coast, who charms the bluebloods around her - even Englishman George Price (Ian Saynor), a cold-fish military martinet. One of her victims is Morys, a local squire in her social circle, who bemoans the loss of his rent money to highwaymen. Madam Wen in her highwayman's guise is seen as a masked, elusive figure materializing suddenly in a white dress on a white horse, at night or in the shadows, to taunt the gentry with raids for rent money, which she later tosses away to poor tenants. But the bandit leader is troubled by the dissension within her gang's ranks and the criminal forays by a faction led by one follower, Wil. Finally Wen's loyal followers and Wil's renegades clash by the beach but Wen's party escapes. When Morys finally learns the identity of his female scourge, he arranges to help her flee across a lake to her cottage retreat. The film has a pleasing uniformity of colour on interiors and a persuasive wintry feel to exteriors, but it never overcomes the casting flaws, and merely skirts the political issues and national and economic divisions of the day. The feature made little impact with the public or critics after the ballyhoo during its gestation.

Owen stayed on to complete his year's contract with the Film Board but the organization, already suffering budgeting constraints, was severely embarrassed by the incident, and certain of its films, which might have brought in income from TV screenings, were shown free on S4C as a part of a quid pro quo deal after the budget problems.

[panel 4.9]

A 21st Century review of the film by J.W. Hyatt

One suspects that those who watched S4C's much publicised film version of W. D. Owen's 'Madam Wen', on that 'Christmas Sunday' afternoon in 1982, will have fallen into two camps, those who had not read the book and will, therefore have found it reasonably entertaining, and those who had read the book and will, therefore, have been disappointed.

Obviously, the pool of Welsh actors from which to choose the cast would have been limited, but one felt, particularly, that Morys Williams should have been considerably taller, broader and more imposing than the other men in the story, and should have stood out as being 'of a different class'; that Twm Pen y Bont should have been much more thickset; that the villains were not rough enough and that Nanni Allwyn Ddu should have been a little older and more mature. On the whole, though, I felt that the acting was perfectly adequate and I particularly liked the portrayal of Sheriff Sparrow, whose Welsh was spoken with an English accent and was heavily interspersed with English phrases.

Some scenes are well-depicted, for example the burning of Robin Ellis's hayricks, the fight between the smugglers and the lawmen on the beach, and the party at Cymunod.

The biggest disappointment, for me, however, was the number of exciting scenes from the book which had been omitted altogether. For example, the self-important Colonel Sprigg and his sword duel with Madam Wen disguised as 'Captain White' do not figure in the film at all and neither do Madam Wen's voyage on 'The Swallow' and her encounter with Abel Owen, the pirate.

Other scenes are portrayed differently in the film, for example, the fight at the beginning of the story takes place in the Boat Tavern, not outside, and Morys Williams throws Wil Llanfihangel out through the tavern door, not over the hedge. When Madam Wen stays overnight at Cymunod, she is dressed as Madam Wen, not disguised as a deaf old man, which renders Morys Williams's failure to recognise her as his beloved Einir Wyn even more incomprehensible in the film than it is in the book!

In the film, Einir Wyn's father was the old squire of Cymunod, and it was there that Einir spent her childhood, so that, when she marries Morys Williams, she is coming home. In the novel, however, Einir is a member of a family from Gwynedd. The references in the film to an old Celtic goddess who had previously inhabited Madam Wen's cave do not figure in the novel and seem an unnecessary embellishment.

The ending is changed completely. It is only Madam Wen who is wounded, not Morys Williams, and Robin y Pandy is swallowed by the bog when trying to run away, not as the result of a fight with Morys, which would have been much more exciting. In the film the two miscreants are pursued at the end by Madam Wen's faithful followers and their dogs, whose complete inability to follow the scent provides a touch of unintentional comedy!

This was the first film that the newly created S4C had ever attempted and it provides a reasonable outline of the novel and a 'taste' of the real thing. In many ways, it is successful entertainment, but, as Bedwyr L. Jones said in his article in 'Y Faner' on January 7th 1983, "Madam Wen, the film, was not W. D. Owen's Madam Wen".

[panel 4.10]

Cast list from the 1982 film

Madam Wen – Marged Esli

Morus Williams of Cymunod – John Pierce Jones

Sion Ifan – Charles Williams

Twm Pen y Bont – John Ogwen

Wil Llanfihangel – Iestyn Garlick

Nanni – Janet Aethwy

Major Preis – Ian Saynor

Siryf (Sheriff) Sparrow – Trefor Selway

Catrin Parri – Catrin Dafydd

Dic Tafarn y Cwch (Dic from the Boat Tavern) – Gwyn Vaughan

Robin y Pandy (Robin the Miller) – Derek Parry

Syr (Sir) Rhisiart Bwcle – J.O.Roberts

Hywel Rhisiart – Guto Roberts

Eban – J.O.Jones

Ellis – Albert Owen

Jac – Dewi Wyn Evans

Seimon – John Henry Hughes

Now – Grey Evans

Wmffra – Tony Jones

Huw – Robin Huws

Sarsiant (Sargeant) Roberts – Anthony Thomas

Mabel Preis – Sara Tudor

Sgweiar (Squire) Preis – Len Roberts

Syr (Sir) Robert Williams – W.H.Roberts

Gwraig (Woman) – Sian Miarczynska

Gwr (Man) – Gwyn Lloyd

Ficer (Vicar) – Malcolm Llywarch

Crythor (Fiddler) – Huw Roberts

Telynor (Harpist) – Robin James Jones

Baledwr (Balladeer) – Robin Edwards

Houses

The Welsh Film Council wishes to thank the owners of the following Houses :

Ty Fry, Pentraeth

Henblas, Bodorgan

Presaddfed, Bodedern

Bodysgallen, Llandudno

[panel 4.11]

'Elin Cadwaladr' and 'Madam Wen' by W. D. Owen

A Critical Appraisal
by J.W. Hyatt

'Elin Cadwaladr' tells the story of David Charles, a young preacher, the son of the minister of Engedi Chapel, and his sweetheart, the eponymous heroine. At the beginning of the novel, David Charles preaches his first sermon in Engedi. He and Elin, who is deeply religious, drift apart when he goes up to Oxford and becomes involved with Socialism. He serves as the minister of a prestigious chapel in a London suburb for a year but loses his religious conviction and begins to practise law. He is chosen as a parliamentary candidate but, shortly before the General Election, Elin Cadwaladr becomes seriously ill. Informed of her illness by his mother, David returns to Anglesey at once, giving up the parliamentary campaign, and marries Elin while she lies in her sickbed. The young bride recovers, David regains his faith, gives up his high-income career and begins to preach once again.

Elin Cadwaladr is, largely, a novel of social change, loosely strung together by the love story of Elin and David. Religion and politics are central themes and the novel has a strong moral and didactic bias. It is a novel of contrasts. In addition to the antithesis between religion and politics, the differences between young and old, traditional and new ideas, village and city life are all explored. The novel provides an excellent historical record of changing social conditions in Anglesey during the early part of the twentieth century. Issues such as the growth of the tourist industry, living conditions and the fight against tuberculosis are explored in some depth.

The novel clearly portrays the centrality of the chapel in village life in Wales a century ago and the importance of chapel values. The chapel goers' heroes are not film stars and sports personalities but the well-known preachers of the day, and the main topic of conversation in the village shop is often the previous Sunday's sermon. We see how, in the absence of modern forms of entertainment, harvest services, music festivals and chapel concerts are extremely well attended, yet already concerns are being expressed that secular interests are beginning to tempt young people away from the chapels.

Elin, however, is devoted to the chapel and is idealistically portrayed as a paragon among women, beautiful, intelligent, musical, caring, practical and possessed of a social conscience and an excellent business acumen. David is depicted as an excellent orator, intelligent and talented, but confused by the conflict which, he feels, exists between the 'old' and the 'new' ideologies. His character is never very fully developed, however, whereas some of the minor characters such as Parry, the Shopkeeper and Price, the Schoolmaster are skilfully drawn.

The author's strengths are also demonstrated in satirical touches and comic scenes which are are a very accurate reflection of village life. For example, Parry is said to be considered 'musical' because he once knew a famous tenor and follows the careers of well-known singers. There is a piano and an American organ in one of the village houses, Gwynfryn, and a copy of the 'piano tutor' is frequently seen in the drawing room. *Who then, could say, in the face of facts like that, that Miss Jennie Evans, Gwynfryn, is not an authority on all things musical?*

Village characters and attitudes are delightfully delineated, as in the following two examples. After it is rumoured that Price the Schoolmaster has received a sizeable bequest, Dick Griffith, the rabbit catcher and William Pirs the carrier, start tugging their forelocks to him in the street *in case there was something in the story of his inheritance*. When David's name is splashed all over the daily papers after he has spoken in the miners' meeting in Bakewell Heath, the postman at Bryn Siriol, 'Thomas Hughes y Post', shows the titbit of news to everyone he meets in the village and the author comments: *Nothing of this level of interest had happened in Bryn Siriol since the son of 'Y Llecyn' shot himself after his father married the maid.*

There is a tellingly satirical passage about the attempts of the shallow and obsequious Rev Deubwll Williams's attempts to be invited to be minister of Engedi: *There was pluck to be admired in Deubwll and, in many ways he'd have made a perfectly good minister in an area like Bryn Siriol. He was exceptionally faithful for months in his visits to the most influential families amongst his supporters, thus gaining much ground.*

W. D Owen's skill as a comic writer is illustrated when Dr. Tom Evans visits Ty Hen in order to ask Elin's father, John Cadwaladr's permission to pay his attentions to Elin, but is embarrassed when he finds both father and daughter at home. Elin tactfully withdraws to the kitchen while Tom, sweating profusely and half in Welsh, which he has largely forgotten during his time in medical college in England, and half in English, of which John Cadwaladr understands barely a word, tries to get his message across. When John Cadwaladr finally understands what Tom wants, after telling him that Elin is spoken for, he mischievously suggests that Tom should tell Elin himself and calls her, leaving the room and leaving Tom yet more discomfited.

The writing of dialogue such as this is one of W. D. Owen's strengths and is again illustrated in an amusing scene towards the end of the novel, when Johnnie, Y Pant, interrupts an animated conversation in Parry's shop about where Dr Tom Evans and his new bride are going to live. Johnnie is talking about an important cricket match. Parry, who is trying to hold two conversations at once, becomes very confused and, when asked if he would like to be there, says, *"Where? The cricket ground or the piece of land near the parsonage?"* The comedy continues when Johnnie then reads out the announcement of David and Elin's secret marriage from the newspaper and none of the assembled company will believe him because he has a reputation as a joker.

In his article 'Tad Madam Wen' (The Father of Madam Wen), Tomos Roberts says, "Elin Cadwaladr is neither a romance nor a historical novel," {406} and this uncertainty of purpose is, perhaps the novel's weakness. The love story is the vehicle through which W. D. Owen explores his more serious subject matter. However, the constancy of Elin's love for David, despite years of being ignored by him, and the alacrity with which both Dr Tom Evans and Price the Schoolmaster, find new loves after her rejection of them, detract from the credibility of the story.

The last chapter of *Dychweliad y Crwydryn (Return of the Wanderer)* [Elin Cadwaladr] was published in Y Genedl Gymreig on January 6th 1914. In the same issue, the foreword of W. D Owen's new serialised novel, Madam Wen Arwres yr Ogof (White Madam Heroine of the Cave) was published. Madam Wen then appeared weekly until July 7th 1914 and was published in book form, with very few amendments, by Hughes and Son of Wrexham, shortly before the author's untimely death in 1925.

W. D. Owen's second novel is less complex and ambitious and is consequently, a more assured work, described by Sir Thomas Parry as the 'best of its period' {407}. Madam Wen is based on an Anglesey legend of the same name and tells the story of the love of an honest, guileless country squire for his beautiful and intelligent kinswoman, who, unbeknown to him, leads a double life as the leader of a band of robbers and smugglers.

The daring exploits of the mysterious Madam Wen and her followers, including an encounter with a pirate ship and culminating in an attempt on her life, make it primarily an adventure story. Reminiscent of the Dorset-based novel 'Moonfleet', by W. Meade Faulkner, published in 1898, Madam Wen was intended for children but could be enjoyed either by older children or by adults.

In this work, the author is confident of his genre and his racy style is eminently suited to it. There are several colourful and exciting scenes including the confrontation between the smugglers and the King's Men; the encounter with the pirate, Abel Owen; the discovery of the body on the beach and the horrifying death of Robin y Pandy. The action of the novel takes place between Michaelmas 1690 and Michaelmas 1691 at the time of the Jacobite uprising in Ireland, and W. D. Owen succeeds in conjuring up the atmosphere of the period convincingly. The feeling of historical accuracy is enhanced by the author's use of old or archaic words and the novel is enriched throughout by his extensive vocabulary and use of synonyms. The author uses colour and detail to bring his descriptions to life, as in the portrait of Abel Owen, the pirate:

When (Madam Wen) climbed aboard the pirate vessel, she saw that Abel was a handsome man of about forty, with black hair and tanned skin, wearing an expensive waistcoat and breeches of brocaded purple silk. His coat was green and he wore a red feather in his green hat. A diamond cross hung from a heavy gold chain around his neck; in his hand was a sword and, from a silken rope hung two pairs of hand-guns, one pair slung across each shoulder.

The author's use of colour is seen again in the description of John Ffowc's jewels, which is further enhanced by his use of compound words such as heirddwyrddion ('beautifulgreen') to describe emeralds and claerwynion ('clearwhite') in relation to pearls.

Like Elin Cadwaladr, the novel is one of intense contrasts, such as those between rustic folk and gentry, faithfulness and treachery, honesty and deceit. The contrasts between the two young people at the centre of the story are, perhaps, the most striking of all. Morys is described as *almost seven feet tall, making a dwarf even of Robin y Pandy and causing the ceiling of the Boat Tavern to look low. He was well-built, too, amazingly so, creating the effect of a giant amongst men.* Einir is described as beautiful, lithe and graceful, with huge eyes and a hint of sadness behind her ready smile. Morys is immensely strong but gentle, kind, serious and ingenuous. He lacks Einir's sharp intellect, quickness of thought and teasing nature.

"It is not known with complete certainty whether the legend has any historical basis," according to Cydymaith i Lenyddiaeth Cymru, (Companion to Welsh Literature) edited by Meic Stephens, "but recent research confirms the traditional belief that it is on Margaret Wynne, the wife of Robert Williams, the squire of Chwaen Wen towards the middle of the eighteenth century, that Einir Wyn, alias Madam Wen, is based." {408}

Some of the the names chosen by the author for the characters in Madam Wen are clearly taken from this tradition, but W. D. Owen maximises their symbolic significance. Einir Wyn and her alter ego, Madam Wen, share the same surname, since Wyn and Wen in Welsh both mean 'white'. When Einir disguises herself as the young ship's captain, she calls herself 'Captain White'. Madam Wen dresses in white and rides a white horse. The constant use of white symbolises good rather than evil and suggests that, despite her dual identity and wild lifestyle, she is essentially honourable and virtuous. 'Einir' itself means 'honesty' or 'respect'. The name 'Morys Williams' seems to convey the hero's solidity and strength as well as his honesty.

Sheriff Sparrow's name was probably taken from the Sparrow family of Red Hill, Beaumaris, who were Sheriffs of Anglesey in the late eighteenth and early nineteenth centuries, and the name Colonel Sprigg may be similarly derived. {310} These characters, however, are portrayed in a belittling manner in the novel and (with due respect to present readers bearing these names) it is undeniable that the names Sparrow and Sprigg have a certain levity, reflecting the author's wry sense of humour.

This humour is also expressed in Einir's use of disguises, particularly when she sits in the corner of Morys's home, Cymunod, disguised as a frail, deaf old man, and hears every word of the sheriff's conversation with the young squire about the fright he received at the hands of the evil and powerful 'Madam Wen'!

The setting for this second novel is the 'district of the lakes' in the south west corner of Anglesey. It is the area where the Crigyll Wreckers used to hide their spoils after luring unsuspecting sailors to the treacherous rocks near the estuary in Rhosneigr. In this area there are three lakes, the largest being Llyn Traffwll. In the foreword to the novel, we are told: *To the south side of the lake and half encircling it, are the fields of Traffwll. Here, years ago, the gorse grew tall and thick, forming a dense forest, and, in the shadows of that dark forest lurked Madam Wen's cave at the edge of the water.*

This area around the cave plays an important part in the novel. The paths through the gorse, known only to the initiated, enable Madam Wen's followers to reach her more quickly than those taking more conventional routes, thus giving her time, for example, to organise the trick on Sheriff Sparrow. The danger of the swamp is, of course, illustrated by the death of Robin y Pandy. This remote and untamed landscape also seems to symbolise the wild side of Madam Wen's nature, which is free, unfettered and not subject to man's control, rather like the moor in Bronte's Wuthering Heights.

The Liverpool Post of the day {409} described Madam Wen as "a romance of Anglesey in Jacobite days, with smugglers, highway robbers, an elusive and beautiful chieftainess of a mysterious gang, a local squire of enormous bulk and strength and horses that gallop like the wind ... a breathless tale that insists upon being read." Like that of Elin Cadwaladr, the plot has weaknesses. The hero's naivety in not realising that Einir and Madam Wen are one and the same stretches the credibility of a modern reader, yet, in this world of make-believe set in a bygone age, the suspension of disbelief is less unwilling.

Tafarn y Cwch (The Boat Tavern) at the entrance to the village of Llanfihangel yn Nhowyn is now a private house.

George Cockram was a well known Landscape painter and Watercolourist. He was born in Birkenhead in 1861, but moved to Rhosneigr in 1895 when he married Lucy Cole, the elder sister of Henry Cole, the owner of the Bay Hotel. They lived at 'The Dunes' and later at 'Noddfa' until his death, in tragic circumstances, in 1950. His work is in the collections of several Art Galleries across the U.K. and he exhibited at the Royal Academy for many years.

Appendices

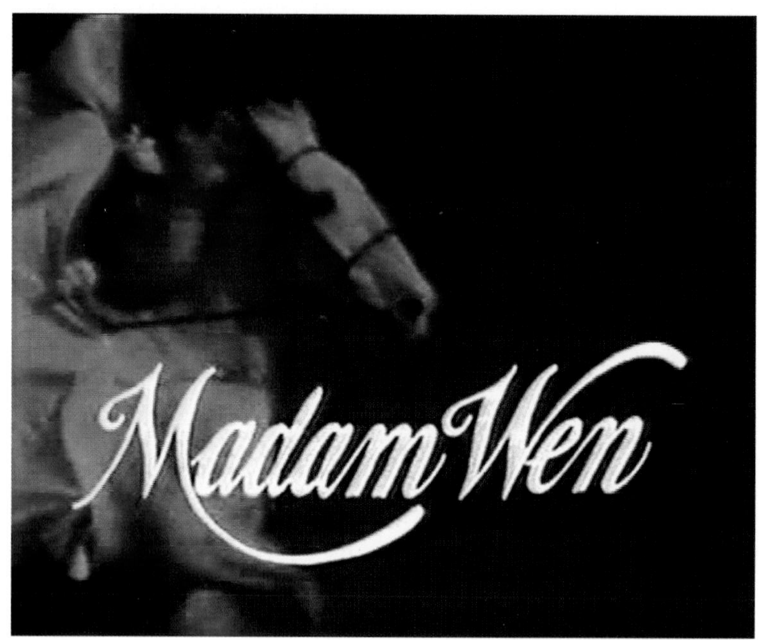

Screen grab from the title sequence of the 1982 film.

5 *Appendices*

5.1: Madam Wen' by J W Huws,

Published in 'Cymru' ('Wales'), Editor O. M. Edwards, November 1897

Madam Wen was a native of Anglesey living towards the beginning of the 18th century. The family surname was Wyn but because of the characteristics of the Welsh language, and in the style of the ordinary folk of the period, she was called 'Madam Wen' rather than 'Madam Wyn'.

It can be can seen from the title 'Madam' that she moved in higher social circles than the ordinary folk of the country but she had also, in some ways, a more remarkable character, and, as often happens with such characters, many baseless fables were created which often make it difficult to draw a line between truth and falsehood and between fiction and fact. So it was with Madam Wen. However, it can be said, and this is a fact, that she was a heroine of whom many in the country were afraid. She had a large number of relations and also many manservants and maidservants, such that it could be said of her that she had a sort of small army, of which she herself was the sort of captain, -

"Cast off the demands of a myriad cares
On your long, bold and lively journey through Anglesey."

She rode one of the best steeds of the period and it is said that she rode around in the daytime, sometimes to the far regions of the country, to see what she could find here and there, so that she could, when it became dark, return with her band and take what she considered good – and there was not much that she did not consider good. A few frail men did not dare to stand up to her and her band, if they happened to see her, because of their fear of her, so it was just:

"Hilter, halter,
Skilter, skelter,
And away they would go."

At that time her name was as well known in Anglesey and Gwynedd, if not throughout Wales, as the Red Bandits of Mawddwy were in their time. [*a]

The authorities made many attempts to catch and punish her and her followers for their arrogance, but every attempt was in vain until the end of her life, as she and her band were too clever for them and they always managed to escape justice.

In the Western part of Anglesey there was a lake, - and it is still there come to that, - which was not far from Madam Wen's home; and near the lake there is a 'cave', if it can be called a cave, where, it is said, she had a secluded hiding place, in case she met with anything she preferred to avoid. The 'cave' is still pointed out as Madam Wen's place of refuge but, if the cave existed in the 18th century in the *same form* as it does today, it would have been a sorry place for anyone to hide from the avenger. One thing which is known that would have helped to conceal it, is that there were gorse bushes, an abundance of them in that period, as high as the tops of houses, closing around the hidden place. In the shelter of those gorse bushes, the horses etc. could easily have been concealed, as they were sufficiently high and dense. As for the 'cave' itself, no more than four or five people, six at the most, could push or squeeze into it for the slightest bit of security

It is said that, on one occasion, she went on an expedition when there happened to be a covering of snow on the ground and she had been more than usually presumptuous. The authorities were certain that they could catch her this time without fail, by following the horses' tracks. But, God help them, this time again, like all the times before, the old witch was far cleverer than the authorities. There was one named Wil, - a son or a grandson or at least, one of the band, - who was very able and skilful as well as being wickedly cunning, like Madam herself. As well as being crafty, Wil was also a good and able blacksmith. On the above occasion Wil had shoed the horses the wrong way around, that is, the shoes were placed with the front end under the horse's heel and the heel of the horsehoe under the front of the animal's foot; therefore, when the authorities thought that they were correctly following the trail in the snow, the poor things were going in totally the wrong direction. Instead of quickly overtaking as they were sure they would, they were going further and further backwards, and they still haven't succeeded in catching Madam Wen. [*b]

As Madam Wen was a remarkable character who instilled fear and pain wherever she went, she soon became the subject of superstitious stories and the empty, foolish imaginings of the impressionable people of that age. After playing the most unpleasant tricks throughout her life,

And causing much,
Pain and trouble,
And much uneasiness,

through the whole country, she moved away, and gathered her family about her, and the land had peace.

After,
Madam Wen was dead and gone
From a position of high influence to the land of the sod

many people still feared her for a long time. Some people made her a sort of half apparition when she was alive, but after her death a thousand more stories grew up about her, which are considered unfounded now but were believed by the superstitious people of that period.

One of the strange things that happened after her death was her swimming, in the lake which was mentioned. It was said that she was occasionally seen, sometimes squatting, sometimes sitting; moving on the surface of the lake, and perhaps disappearing from sight, or sinking to the depths, as impossible to pin down in death as she had been in life, had any of the credulous been brave enough to embark on such an adventure. It was said that for years she was seen on Easter Sunday morning, swimming in a sitting position, amusing herself by moving backwards and forwards; after reaching the centre of the lake, she would sink from sight and would not be seen again until the next Easter Sunday morning. It is said that many were credulous enough to go to the lake on Easter morning, thinking and expecting that they would see her, but I have never heard that anyone was fortunate enough to get a look at the Spirit of the Lake despite going there, several times in some cases.

Madam Wen succeeded in escaping punishment under the law of Great Britain, as did her followers, all except Wil, [who was caught] a few years later. Madam Wen's band lost heart after losing its leader. Wil happened to go to Porthaethwy *[Menai Bridge]* Fair on the back of his

Brisk, lively, light steed

as usual. When he was preparing to turn for home, in some haste, he happened to take someone else's saddle in genuine error, it is said, instead of his own saddle. But poor Wil was caught, and once they'd got hold of him, even though the offence on that occasion was dubious, and bore no comparison to some of the earlier crimes, poor Wil was punished extremely severely, so that, from necessity and shame, he had to leave the land of his birth. It is said that many years later someone saw him in America and asked him, "William?" "Yes", he answered. "Well, what drove you to this place?" Wil replied, "Well, not my righteousness, you can be sure."

Madam Wen originally had some inheritance but now there is very little of her estate left. She herself,

"Went from the world to the extremity of the grave;
She lies in the earth."

It is said that some of her descendants are still living but that they are scattered here and there in the different countries of the world.

*a The Red Bandits were a 16th century band of robbers from Mawddwy in Mid-Wales.

*b This story about the reversal of horseshoes is also given prominence in the short section about Madam Wen in Dafydd Meirion's book 'Walking Adventures on Anglesey' but does not appear in Owen's 'Madam Wen'. {301}

At the bottom of the original article there is a note by the editor, Owen M. Edwards:

LOCAL TRADITIONS, - it is expected that the pages of 'Cymru' *['Wales']* will be full of these. The romance has started to develop in Wales and it is based on traditions. The romantic writer can breathe life into the dry bones of tradition.
A suggestion is enough for him.

Editor's Notes:

(i) John Watkin Huws was a Farmer, Historian and staunch Methodist. He was born in 1836 and lived at 'BrynTeg' Llanfaelog. He wrote a book on the history of Methodism in the area {501} and he was also known as a musician and local historian. His particular significance to this work, is that this article in 'Cymru' *['Wales']* is the first known written reference to 'Madam Wen'.

(ii) The rationale for including 'verses' (shown in italics) is not obvious and may have been included by the author to somehow enliven the text, or, as the Madam Wen tradition is oral, may have been verses in common use at the time. There is also no explanation of why some verses were printed between quotation marks and some not.

5.2: W. D. Owen (died 1925) – romance author by R. Maldwyn Thomas

in Gwŷr Môn, *[Men of Anglesey]* ed. Bedwyr Lewis Jones, First Impression, 1979, Cyngor Gwlad Gwynedd, pages 145 – 147

William David Owen is included in this volume because he is the author of Madam Wen, one of the best romances written in Welsh.

The story is set in the 'district of the lakes' namely the area which includes the parishes of Llanfihangel-yn-Nhywyn, Llanfair-yn-Neubwll and Llechylched in the west of Anglesey. It is an area of marshes and gorse groves and a number of lakes, - between the sea in Cymyran Bay and the main Holyhead road. One of the lakes, Llyn Traffwll, is quite large, and, according to local tradition, the secret cave of Madam Wen, W. D. Owen's heroine, was in a crevasse which can be seen at the side of this lake.

W. D. Owen knew this area well. He was born in Tyn-franan (sic) – a smallholding at the bottom of Bodedern Parish, within a stone's throw of the district of the lakes, and he was a pupil in Bryngwran Board School. By the college year 1894-95 he was a very successful student in Bangor Normal College. He was a schoolteacher in Clay Cross where he met his wife, Gwendoline Empsell (sic), who was, in her time, also an authoress and the editor of a women's magazine. But then W. D. Owen turned his back on the world of schools and studied law, qualifying as a lawyer. He was not a strong man and one of the reasons why he returned to the area of his youth in the west of Anglesey was in the hope of improving his health. It was in the village of Rhosneigr, on the edge of the district of the lakes, that he spent the rest of his life. He worked for a while in the office for soldiers' pensions in Llangefni [*a] and had also started a solicitor's business in Rhosneigr. Here, in the area which he knew, there was hope for good health and a successful career.

W. D. Owen soon became prominent in public circles in Rhosneigr. The village was very active at that time. Rhosneigr had already started selling itself as a holiday centre – the Rhosneigr of the large, dark golf hotels on the sand-dunes, the

Rhosneigr of 'Maelog Villa' and 'Môrawel Apartments', the Rhosneigr which was convenient for the L.M.S. railway and the romantic Rhosneigr near the cave of Madam Wen, "the famous Lady Robin Hood of North Wales" as WDO himself described her in an official book of welcome to visitors *b. It was in Rhosneigr that W. D. Owen set about writing Madam Wen.

But it was not long before his Indian Summer came to an end. His wife was ill and her condition constantly deteriorated, to WDO's great grief. They had to move to live with his mother and sisters. He himself wasn't getting better either. He probably wrote about all Madam Wen's exciting and galloping adventures when he himself was sinking ever more deeply into the prison of ill-health. *c The last months were exceptionally depressing but he did manage to see copies of Madam Wen in print shortly before his death from TB, a man little over fifty years old, on 4th November 1925.

A summary of the events of the romance is unlikely to explain the popularity of W. D. Owen's work. It is the story of Einir Wyn, namely 'Madam Wen', a beautiful young gentlewoman who lost her inheritance in the turmoil after the Civil War, and the way in which she led a band of robbers until she fell in love with and married the man who is almost the hero of the book, Morys Williams, the squire of the large farmhouse Cymunod in the area. Courtships and murders, a faithful maidservant and manservant, the guile of robbers, fighting on the Saint's Day and a dance in a mansion house, smugglers and a judge, a robbers' cave and the squire's farmhouse, - they are all here as they are to be found in many other romances of the period. But that which is interesting about Madam Wen is that W. D. Owen has set it all, with historical detail, primarily in a small area in the west of Anglesey, and during a relatively brief period in the 1680s.

This achievement ensured the book a special unity and he ensured something else too, in connection with Madam Wen herself. Morys Williams, the squire of Cymunod, is a stranger in the district at the beginning of the story but, gradually, he comes to know the area and its people. Through the eyes of the squire the reader too comes to know the district of the lakes and its people. Morys Williams loves Einir Wyn and all her mystery and W. D. Owen ensures that Morys is the medium through which the reader loves Madam Wen and all her secrecy too.

Editor's Note:

R. Maldwyn Thomas M.A. was born in 1939 and brought up near Caernarfon. For most of his working life he has been a lecturer in Education at the University of Wales, Bangor. He has also broadcasted for BBC Cymru for many years on various topics including the Welsh newspaper and periodical press, and on religious issues. His research on Madam Wen still continues. (See also Appendix 5.6)

*a See biography section, Panel 1.1 on page 13.

*b No evidence has come to light in support of this statement, although several of the Guides to Rhosneigr do mention the Madam Wen / Robin Hood legend.

*c This is unlikely, as Madam Wen was written no later than 1914. This is well over a decade before Owen began to suffer from the effects of T.B. although he may of course have carried the disease for years without showing any significant symptoms (Latent tuberculosis).

5.3: 'The Father of Madam Wen' by Tomos Roberts,

'Y Casglwr' *[The Collector]*, Volume 10, (March 1980) page 6

William David Owen, Rhosneigr, the author of the romance Madam Wen, remains almost as chimerical as the heroine of the romance itself. An essay on him can be found in the appendix to the *Bywgraffiadur Cymreig [Welsh Biographical Dictionary]* and another was published by Mr R Maldwyn Thomas in *Gwŷr Môn [Men of Anglesey]*. An obituary, too, appeared in *Y Cloriannydd [The Evaluator]* on November 11th 1925. Despite all this, little is known about him, his background or his literature.

He was born in Tynfranen, Bodedern, Anglesey, in 1874. For a period he was a pupil teacher with L. D. Jones (Llew Tegid) *[a] in Garth School, Bangor, and then a student in Bangor Normal College. After that he became a teacher in England. Later he studied law and became a barrister.

Then, for the sake of his health, he returned to Anglesey and set up a solicitor's business in Rhosneigr and Llangefni. But his health deteriorated, particularly during the summer of 1925, and he died in November of that year aged 51. He is chiefly remembered for his romance *Madam Wen,* - the best of its period according to Sir Thomas Parry *[b]. It was published by Hughes and Son, Wrexham, shortly before his death.

Some time ago the Library of the College of the North, Bangor [Bangor University] received two documents which once belonged to W D Owen, as a gift from the Rev Huw Llywelyn Williams, Valley *[c]. One is a serialised novel and the other is W D Owen's 1925 diary. These documents shed fresh light on W D Owen and his method of publication.

ELIN CADWALADR is the title of the novel. It was cut out from a newspaper and pasted onto sheets of paper. It has been much amended and it seems that the author had tried to adapt it to be published as a complete book. The name W D Owen, Seaforth, Rhosneigr, appears on the first page and, on the same page, in another hand, the name John E. Roberts, Cheadle Hulme, Cheshire.

The novel first appeared in *Y Genedl Gymreig [The Welsh Nation]* between June 6th 1913 and January 6th 1914 under the title *Dychweliad y Crwydryn,* or *Taro Tant a Newid Cywair [The Return of the Wanderer* or *Strike a Chord and Change Key]*. The name of the author is not given in the paper but it's fairly obvious that it's W D Owen. *Elin Cadwaladr* is neither a romance nor an historical novel but it is set in the same area as Madam Wen. In it one is told the story of the people who live in the village and parish of Bryn Siriol, in the hundred of Hirfon in Anglesey. The village of Bryn Siriol stands on the borders of 'The Big Beach'. The beach became a seaside resort for strangers from the towns of England and a small town was built for the visitors on the sandbanks. Immediately after that the price of butter rose in Bryn Siriol.

The residents of Bryn Siriol are people who live and work hard: They laugh when they see the Englishmen of the Big Beach walking miles in all weathers through the heather and ferns after a small white ball. They laugh just as heartily when they hear the English talking about health rules and the relationship between sick cattle and consumption.

These are obvious references to Llechylched Parish, the villages of Bryngwran and Rhosneigr, and the area around Trwan Beach. {502} There is a touch of satire too. W D Owen was a member of Rhosneigr Golf Club and he suffered from TB.

After introducing the residents of Bryn Siriol, the author goes on to tell the story of David Charles, a young preacher, the son of the minister of Engedi, Bryn Siriol, and his sweetheart, Elin Cadwaladr. At the beginning of the novel, David Charles preaches his first sermon in Engedi. Then, after a year at Oxford, he gives up preaching and goes to London to study law. He becomes a Socialist and is chosen as the parliamentary candidate for Newlea Marsh. But, shortly before the General Election, Elin Cadwaladr is taken ill. David returns home in haste, giving up the parliamentary campaign, and marries Elin Cadwaladr while she lies sick in bed. Elin gets better and David Charles begins to preach in Engedi once again.

The last chapter of 'Dychweliad y Crwydryn' *['Return of the Wanderer']* appeared in *Y Genedl Gymreig* on January 6th 1914. In the same issue, W D Owen published the foreword of his new serialised novel, *Madam Wen Arwres yr Ogof [White Madam Heroine of the Cave]*. *Madam Wen* then appeared weekly in *Y Genedl Gymreig* until July 7th 1914.

There is no basic difference between the version of Madam Wen which appeared in Y Genedl Gymreig and the one which was published by Hughes and Son in 1925. The author tidied up the orthography, changed the occasional paragraph and heading and combined some of the chapters. He added paragraphs at the beginning or end of some of the chapters and changed the name of Abel Owen's ship from 'Sudden Death' to 'Certain Death'. There are more alterations in the foreword than in the romance itself. In the foreword to the 1925 version a 'man from the area' sits on a hillock near Madam Wen's cave then digs in the cave and discovers the underground hiding place and Madam Wen's diary but in the 1914 version it is the author himself who discovers the hiding place.

In the foreword to Madam Wen the author says that he obtained a lot of information about Madam Wen from her diary. Similarly, much information about W D Owen himself can be found in his diary for 1925. It appears that his main reason for keeping a diary was to record the legal work that he did.

There are, however, a host of other references apart from those about drawing up deeds and wills and journeys to his office in Llangefni. The diary is written in English but one finds in it the occasional Welsh word or expression. It shows that W D Owen was a member of the Anglesey Monthly Meeting (Calvinistic Methodists). He was also a member of the Secret Society of Freemasons in Llangefni and attended a meeting there every month. As I said before, he was a member of Rhosneigr Golf Club and he had walked after a 'little white ball' with Dr R Alun Roberts more than once during the summer of 1925.

Between January and March 1925 he had read the novel by Galsworthy in the Forsyte Saga series. In July he looked over the essays and stories of W J Griffith, Henllys Fawr, Aberffraw, including 'Eos y Pentan' *[Nightingale of the Chimney Corner]*. He also promised he would let W J Griffith see the proofs of Madam Wen.

There are also a number of other references to Madam Wen in the diary. He proof-read it between May and July. In July he discussed the presentation and the binding with the publishers. He received the first copies on October 22nd, exactly a fortnight before he died.

In July he started to have a new house built in Rhosneigr and he went to see it almost every day. Ironically, as the new house progressed so his own health deteriorated. There are more and more references to the state of his health during August and September. This is what he wrote on September 30th: A lovely day and I feel rotten.

It's very likely that there are more of W D Owen's stories to be found in papers and magazines. It said in the obituary in *Y Cloriannydd* that he had written many Welsh sonnets. I have never yet seen one of them. It would also be interesting to find out more about the historical background to Madam Wen and I understand that Maldwyn Thomas is currently working on this aspect of W D Owen's work.

Editor's Note:

Tomos Roberts was the archivist at Bangor University between 1983 and 1999 and is a committee member of the Anglesey Antiquarian Society.

*a Llew Tegid was the Bardic name of L.D.Jones. See note d on page 25.

*b Sir Thomas Parry (1904-1985) was a distinguished academic, holding posts which included Professor in Welsh at Bangor University, Principal of the University of Wales, Aberystwyth and President of the Court of the National Library of Wales. In his reference work "Welsh Literature 1900-1945" he writes on Novels : 'There is one class of stories that are based on historical background and some of them feature real characters. ...... The best story of this type is Madam Wen by W.D.Owen.'

*c Originally misprinted as 'Holyhead' and here corrected to 'Valley' on the instruction of Mr Roberts..

5.4: Welsh Herald, Tuesday, April 13th, 1982

William Williams claims that ... 'The legend of Madam Wen is fantasy not history'

The novel *Madam Wen* has had a great deal of attention recently because of the intention to film it for S4C. I remember reading it avidly as a boy and thinking, at that time, that every word was true!

When I saw a picture of MW's cave in *Trysorfa'r Plant [The Children's Treasury]* May 1938, {503} with Miss Evelyn Evans, Penrallt, Bryngwran, standing near it, I was possessed by a desire to go there without delay, to examine it if not to excavate, but I have never done so.

Under the picture in The Treasury these words had been written by Mrs Jenkins, Ty Croes, Llanbeulan (who now lives in Llangefni): "W. D. Owen's book is full of adventure and heroism and therefore it appeals greatly to children and young people. Town schools would do well to arrange trips for the children to see Madam Wen's cave. It is worth seeing since Madam Wen's spirit is still in the wind".

Her Spirit

In truth, a spirit in the wind is what the story is, in other words, sheer fable. It is an old legend. It is not the fruit of W D Owen's imagination since the fable existed before he turned it into a romance. [*a]

What he did, very cleverly, was to take a story he knew well, setting the exciting parts of the story in the area of his youth and naming places such as Tywyn Trewan *[Beach by Owain's homestead]*, Alltwen Ddu *[Black White Wooded Hillside]* [*b], Bro Maelog *[the region of St. Maelog]* and so on, and produced a gripping romance. By introducing the names of local places, he immortalised the area of which he thought so highly and put it on the map.

As everything about Madam Wen is fictitious, the Morrises of Anglesey [*c] don't mention the name any more than they mention the myths which exist about the Hwntw Mawr *[the Big South-Walian]* or Lleidr Llandyfrydog *[the Llandyfrydog Robber]*. Her name is not mentioned, either, by Thomas Lloyd, Llywenau, in his booklet 'The History of Caergeiliog and its Surroundings'. It is an old story which has been passed down by word of mouth from generation to generation without any basis in fact. I heard the story from my family just as they had heard it from their ancestors.

Illusion

To prove that the title of W D Owen's story is not the fruit of imagination, there is an article on 'Madam Wen' by John Watkin Huws, the historian from Llanfaelog, in O.M. Edwards' 'Cymru' *[Wales]* November 1897 [Reproduced in Appendix 5.1]. We can tell from the tone of his article that it is all an illusion. He was writing with his tongue in his cheek!

Huws says that Madam Wen was a native of Anglesey living towards the beginning of the 18th century. The family surname was Wyn but because of the characteristics if the Welsh language she was called 'Madam Wen' rather than 'Madam Wyn'. We can glean from the title 'Madam' that she was of a higher social standing than most people and, as often happens with people like that, many baseless fables grew up about her.

She was a heroine who instilled fear in the bosoms of many.

Well-known

J W Huws goes on to say that she rode one of the best steeds in the country, riding around in the daytime, sometimes to the farthest reaches of the country, to see what she and her band could take when night fell. At that time her name was as well-known in Anglesey and Gwynedd, if not throughout Wales, says Huws, as the Red Bandits of Mawddwy were in the 16th century.

He goes on to say that the authorities made many attempts to catch her and to bring her and her followers to justice but that every attempt was in vain until the end of her life, as she and her band were too clever at evading the hand of justice. He afterwards mentioned the lake "in the western part of Anglesey" and, near the lake, the "cave", if it could be called a cave, where her "special hiding place" was reputed to be.

To emphasise the mythical nature of the story, I like what J W Huws says next: "But if the cave existed in the 18th century in the same form as it is now it would have been a poor place for anyone to hide from the avenger!"

"It could be said that no more than four or five, at the most six people could squeeze into it for the slightest bit of security." He talks about the gorse bushes which were "as high as the tops of houses closing around the hidden place".

He talks about an expedition which the Lady took on one occasion in the snow. The authorities were sure they could catch her by following the horses' tracks but Wil, one of the band, confused them by putting on the horses' shoes the wrong way round. As Madam Wen was a remarkable character in her age, who instilled fear throughout all the regions, she soon became the subject of superstitious fears and foolish stories.

Her Death

After playing the most unbelievable tricks throughout her life, Madam Wen died, but her reputation lived on. More and more stories grew up about her, which were believed by the superstitious people of that period.

One of the remarkable things that happened after her death was that her ghost was believed to appear at the lake in the west of Anglesey. It was said that she was sometimes squatting, sometimes sitting; the image constantly moving, as impossible to pin down in death as she had been in life. For years she was seen on Easter Sunday morning, floating in a sitting position on the lake, eventually sinking from sight not to reappear until the following Easter Sunday.

The Lady succeeded in escaping from the law of Great Britain as did her followers, all except Wil. He was caught stealing in Borth Fair and had to flee from the country. Some years later someone saw him in America and asked him what had brought him there. Wil replied, "Well, not my righteousness, you can be sure!"

Madam Wen originally had some inheritance but now her estate has been broken up and there is very little of it left.

It is said that she has descendants still living but that they are scattered all over the world.

In the article J W Huws quotes some verse about Madam Wen:

"After
Madam Wen was dead and gone
From a position of high influence to the land of the sod ..."

Who was the poet? How did he know about the tradition?

I have used these quotations from the article to prove that the legend of Madam Wen was in existence in this area before W D Owen wrote his romance and that the title he chose for his book is not the fruit of his imagination. He knew the old story well.

Romance

At the bottom of the article in *Cymru [Wales]*, the editor, O. M. Edwards, has written: "Local Traditions – it is expected that the pages of 'Cymru' will be full of these. The romance has begun to develop in Wales ... The romantic writer can breathe life into the dry bones of tradition. A suggestion is enough for him."

And that's what W D Owen did – he gathered together the dry bones and created a living story.

We will hear about the author in the next article [*d].

Editor's Note:

William Williams has lived in the village of Bryn Du, within the parish of Llanfaelog, since 1923. He has served his community as preacher, journalist and clerk for over 70 years, his activities mainly centred on the Welsh Presbyterian chapel at Bryn Du. The author of many articles on local history, he has also published a book entitled 'Cipdrem ar Hanes Plwyf Maelog' *[A glimpse at the history of the parish of Llanfaelog]* {504}.

*a In fairness to Owen, it must be remembered that he never claimed the story was his own invention.

*b The name 'Allwyn Ddu' is inadvertantly mis-spelled 'Alltwen Ddu' which gives it a completetly different meaning. This is most probably a simple typing error and should be discounted.

*c By 'The Morrises' Mr Williams is referring to the 'Morrisiad Mon' (The Morrises of Anglesey) a celebrated family who are remembered for their many and varied literary and scholarly interests. They included Lewis Morris and his brothers Richard, William and John.

*d The second article (as listed in the Bibliography) tells us little more about WDO than we already know, and is not included for that reason.

5.5: More about Madam Wen,

Y Rhwyd *[The Net]*, May 1982 by Huw Williams, Bangor.

It says again in the April edition of *The Net* that Madam Wen was "the fruit of pure imagination". If this observation refers to **Madam Wen** (or Einir Wyn), the heroine of W D Owen's novel, I agree 100% with the statement. But if it is Madam Wen, the romance, which is meant, I must disagree emphatically with the statement and emphasise once again that what W D Owen did in his book was to take advantage of a tradition that he had heard in Maelog Parish and weave a very skilful story around that tradition.

The tradition referred to is, without doubt, oral rather than written; it is a sure and certain tradition, nonetheless, and one which can be traced back to a period before J W Huws, Llanfaelog, referred to it in black and white on the pages of *Cymru [Wales]* (1897) (O M Edwards).

It was from Jane Owen, his mother, and from Margaret Evans, the grandmother of Mr Hywel Roberts *a, 1 Bryn Teg, Bangor (and one of the descendants of the poet 'Hywel Eryri' / *Hywel Snowdonia*) that W D Owen heard first of all about the tradition of Madam Wen. Margaret Evans (Thomas after marriage) was born in 'Cerrig Bach' *[Small Stones]* near Lake Traffwll, in 1849, and, after marriage, lived in 'Harlech' *b, a smallholding on Tywyn Trewan *[Trewan Dunes]* which has now fallen into complete ruin.

Mr Hywel Roberts, Bangor, has no doubts at all about his mother's assertion that his grandmother was immersed in the story of Madam Wen and that the tradition was very much alive in the 'district of the lakes' in Anglesey over a century ago. It should also be noted that Mr Hywel Roberts's mother and W D Owen were bosom friends, both having been born in 1874, and that they had been courting for a brief period when they were young *c. We remember also that Jane Owen, W D Owen's mother, was one of the children of 'Cerrig Cynrig' *[Cynrig's Stones]* and that 'Cerrig Cynrig' and 'Harlech' were not far apart in the last century, when the Madam Wen tradition in the area was alive and real.

Another of the children of Margaret Evans (Thomas) and an uncle to Mr Hywel Roberts (his mother's brother) was Rev. Richard Thomas, Bontnewydd (1871 – 1950). It was he who tidied up the orthography of Madam Wen for W D Owen before the romance was published in book form in 1925, [*d] and we cannot ignore what he said in the pages of *Y Cloriannydd [The Evaluator]* about a fortnight after W. D. Owen was buried in 1925:

"....... in a fairly small area, on the south-western side of Anglesey, there were, throughout the years, many traditions about the heroine of the banks of Traffwll Lake. Her inexplicable exploits and her mysterious influence were recounted. A fearsome homage was paid to her name, and when we children approached the old cave, without our being aware of it, our steps slowed, but our imaginations quickened – this was the cave of Madam Wen. From here W. D. Owen, Rhosneigr, obtained splendid material for a romance .... He cannot be accused of using too much paint .... His imagination walked a natural path alongside that which he had seen and heard all over the locality ...."

Perhaps it is significant that Rev. Richard Thomas uses the words "in a fairly small area" in referring to the tradition of Madam Wen. I admit that the Morrises [*e] do not mention the name Madam Wen.

Editor's Note:

Huw Williams (1922-2002) was a native of Anglesey, having been born in Bryngwran, but became a schoolteacher in Flintshire for most of his working life. He was renowned as an authority on the history of Welsh Music, and wrote copiously on the subject. Published works include 'Tonau a'u Hawduron' *[Tunes and their Authors]* in 1967 and 'Taro Tant' *[Strike a Chord]* in 1994.

He was an occasional broadcaster on radio and television and also published several volumes on Flintshire local history. {505}

*a Hywel Roberts was a schoolfriend of Huw Williams

*b Harlech was another cottage on Towyn Trewan *(Trewan Dunes)* at the time, but has now been subsumed under the buildings at RAF Valley.

*c According to William Williams, (Huw's brother), he has no recollection as to the veracity of this statement but considers it 'possible'.

*d This is the only source proposing this supposition. It is known that Owen spent days working on the proofs of Madam Wen (his diary tells us so) but it is of course quite possible that he took opinion from other members of his extended family.

*e By 'The Morrises' Mr Williams is referring to the 'Morrisiad Mon' (The Morrises of Anglesey) a celebrated family who are remembered for their many and varied literary and scholarly interests. They included Lewis Morris and his brothers Richard, William and John.

5.6: Wanton Madam Wen?

The Banner, January 14, 1983

In this revealing article, MALDWYN THOMAS discloses, for the first time, detailed evidence that Madam Wen was not such a romantic figure as was supposed.

One of a number of good things in Dafydd Huw Williams's script in the film Madam Wen was the scene where Einir Wyn was standing outside the walls of Cymunod looking at the fun going on in the farmyard. Einir Wyn the exile. This represented what the author described as 'sad hours' *(Madam Wen, Foreword, viii)*. The novel is, of course, an adventure story, - "the best of plenty" in the opinion of Dafydd Jenkins in 'Y Nofel' *[The Novel]* – but there is another craft here too. Through the eyes of Morys Williams, the clumsy squire, a man who is almost the hero of the novel, we come to know about the area of Traffwll, about the robbers and about Einir Wyn; and is not the portrayal of Einir Wyn hating her other half – Madam Wen – to whom she is in thrall, one of the excellent features of the novel?

The romance was published in 'Y Genedl Gymreig' *[The Welsh Nation]* in 1914 and then as a book in 1925. But it is a romance which is based on a wealth of local traditions about its subject.

The Traditions of the Llanfaelog area

According to J. W. Huws (*Wales,* Nov. 1897), [see appendix 5.1] M.W. was a gentlewoman called Wyn, except that in the oral tradition her name had become Wen, who lived in the early years of the 18th century and who had a relative or accomplice named Wil. He referred to a cave on the banks of a lake and, after her death, it was believed that she used to appear on the surface of the water.

The notes of John Owen, Plas, Llanfair yn Neubwll, - W. D. Owen's cousin [*a] – refer to the period before the publication of the romance. They are notes from an oral tradition, which I obtained through the kindness of Mr and Mrs John Owen, Henblas, who are well-versed in the oral tradition of the Traffwll area and who gave a talk on the subject to the BBC in 1947.

According to these notes, M.W. was the daughter of Chwaen Wen, *[White Windy Place]*, Llantrisant, who stole the property of the arrogant rich and divided it among the poor, who hid in a cave and in the Chwaen Wen haystack and who could turn herself into a swan on Traffwll Lake in order to escape the law. She married "one of the country's gentry".

Wil Llanfihangel, the vice captain of the robbers, is dated at about 1730 – 1780. Morys Williams is referred to as a flesh and blood person, but there is a strong similarity between him and Huw Cymunod, the strong man who lived in the area in the 19th century, according to Dafydd Wyn Williams in 'Môn' *[Anglesey]*, 1964. The location of M.W.'s cave is pinpointed and the Crigyll robbers are mentioned clearly enough.

In the Bodedern area, on the other hand, it is thought that Madam Wen did not marry, but that she had a number of illegitimate children by Wil Llanfihangel; the local people rose up against her and she was drowned in Llyn Traffwll. It is also suggested that Mrs W. D. Owen, who wrote for English magazines, helped her husband to write the book [*b].

In the Aberffraw area, there is an old tradition about M.W. appearing in the village foretelling death. I collected a number of other traditions about her in Anglesey. But, of course, a romance about a female robber is not limited to Anglesey, nor to Wales either, as will be seen.

Lorna Doone

This "romance"was published by R. D. Blackmore in 1869 and W. D. Owen describes his novel as a "romance" too. L. D. is set in Exmoor in the 80s of the 17th century – compare M.W. in the marshlands and gorse woods of western Anglesey in the same period. John Ridd, the hero of L. D., is a fairly well-to-do farmer, a giant of a man, rather slow in his responses – like Morys Williams Cymunod. Lorna Doone, a girl who has lost her inheritance, is the heroine of the book – compare her with Einir Wyn. The Doones are the robbers in Blackmore's novel; a gang of thieves hiding in a wild area – like M.W.'s gang in the area round Traffwll Lake; the law, namely the magistrate De Whichehalse, seeks out the Doones – in the same way Sheriff Sparrow comes on the trail of M.W. Lorna Doone has a cave – her hiding place from the Doones. So, according to the novel, does M. W; both heroines are also close to nature.

Carver Doone is the cruel, gigantic scoundrel in L. D., and the bloodthirsty, corporal Robin 'y Pandy' *[Robin the Miller]* is the murderer in M.W. Carver shoots Lorna and Robin shoots Einir; John Ridd fights Carver Doone on the edge of a muck-heap; Doone is drowned, and the fate of Robin 'y Pandy' is exactly the same when he fights with Morys Williams in Traffwll Bog. There are two worlds in L. D., the world of Plover's Barrows farm and the world of the Doones; similarly in M.W., the reader is hurled from Cymunod into the arms of the Llanfihangel robbers.

The Madam Wen of history?

Was there a woman of the squire stratum of society living as an outlaw in Anglesey around the period of the novel? Acccording to the pattern of the traditions and the novel, I cast the net in the parish registers of Llanfihangel-yn-Nhywyn, Bodedern and Llantrisant, and the court papers, and searched from the period of the romance until the end of the 18th century. There was no reference to Einir Wyn or Morys or M.W. in the history of Cymunod Farm. There was no sign, as far as I could see, in the area of Llanfihangel. Yes, there was an occasional woman wandering around Anglesey in the 18th century but these were yeoman women, poor vagrants. It is true that vagrants stole at times in the 17th century – as Trefor Owen reveals in 'Llên a Llafar Môn' *[Literature and Speech of Anglesey]* – but there was nothing else here which bore any resemblance to the story of M.W. A public whipping in 1737, transportation for stealing property worth 10d in 1773 – such was the fate of petty thieves amongst the women of Anglesey in the 18th century, as Nesta Evans said in discussing the records of the Anglesey Quarter Sessions [*c].

But Margaret Williams from Llantrisant parish was the wife of a squire and she was on the run in Anglesey in the middle of the 18th century. In May 1747, Judge Rogers Holland (Justice of Anglesey 1737 - 1761) sent a summons to Sheriff William Thomas asking him to arrest "Margaret, the wife of Robert Williams of Chwaen Ddu *[Black Windy Place]* ... gentleman." The charge against her was much worse than the "petty larceny" which was punished so cruelly by the courts of the island because the judge summoned Margaret Williams "to be answer us of Certain Ffolony *[felony]* and other offences whereof she stood indicted..." But "not to be found within my county" was the Sheriff's answer. Felony "created prejudice against the accused" as D. Jenkins said in 'Cyfraith Trosedd' *[Criminal Law]*.

Margaret Williams – Madam Wen?

Margaret Williams was the daughter of Rhyd Angharad *[Angharad's Ford]* farm, Llanrhuddlad. Her first marriage was to William Wynne the second, the heir of Chwaen Ddu estate, Llantrisant – a barrister who was educated in Gray's Inn, the son of William Wynne the squire. During his time in the law schools, the son received considerable property from his father. Margaret Williams had married well, - from the point of view of worldly wealth, at least.

But then the shadow of Lewis Morris fell across Margaret Wynne's story. It was just a spiteful noise at the beginning, perhaps – Lewis Morris, writing on 4th August 1733, under the title "Speculation", prophesied, "... ye seed of Mrs. Wynne my daughter shall Flourish & Blossom in Chwaen Ddu to ye Admiration of ye Beholders. Rhyd Angharad."

Richard Morris wrote to [his brother] Lewis in September 1740 to thank him "... for the poem Rhyd Anghariad." It appears that Rhyd Angharad and Margaret Wynne were perhaps a talking point in the area during these years, sufficiently prominent to attract the full attention of Lewis Morris.

Information about Margaret Wynne and her strange nature are given in Lewis Morris's ribald poem "The Lament of the Man from Anghariad's Ford", or "Angharad's Ford" according to his daughter on the Big Medley." {506}

The passionate widow

Robert Williams, the plunderer and stabber, was her second husband. It seems that he and the passionate widow had married by 1737 and that they lived in Chwaen Ddu. The name "Robert Williams, of Chwaen Ddu, Gent." was one of fifteen Anglesey men who were the jurors in the Great Sessions of August 1737 – the first visit of Judge Holland to Anglesey, as we read in the diary of squire Bulkeley of Brynddu *[Blackhill]*. He, it is likely, is the "Robert Williams" who was one of the wardens of Llantrisant in 1740. Children were born of this marriage – Margaret, Elizabeth / Margaret Elizabeth and William (according to the record of the *Pedigrees*). There are plenty of names in the parish records which could be relevant. When was Margaret Williams breaking the law? Did the Sheriff invite her as the wife of the squire in 1747 / 8?

Was she a romantic figure?

So was Margaret Williams, who was once Madam Wynne, the passionate subject of a lascivious poem in the west of Anglesey, with its obvious allusions, who was a thief on the run from the law, and who was the wife of two squires including Robert Williams "Llanfihangel", - the origin of the story of "Madam Wen"? Was the 19th century busy scouring this story clean, as it scoured the 'noson lawen' *[soirée]*, the interlude and the folk-singing, to give us Einir Wyn, the good thief who was a friend to the poor? Did unknown elements of the story of Margaret of Chwaen Ddu, woven together with more recent traditions, and with parts of Lorna Doone, form the creative embroidery of W. D. Owen when he wrote Madam Wen, the Heroine of the Cave?

Editor's Notes:

(i) Refer to the bottom of Appendix 5.2 for a biographical note about the author of this article, Maldwyn Thomas.

(ii) The author is an acknowledged expert on the historic aspects of the Madam Wen legend. No attempt has been made to verify the research in this essay on the origins of Madam Wen, as this is beyond the scope of this book.

*a The name 'John Owen' does appear as a 'cousin' in the list of mourners at Owen's funeral, but there is no listed address which could be verified. The John Owen to whom Mr Thomas spoke in the late 1970s was the son of WD's cousin.

*b This is the only written source proposing this hypothesis. there is no proof one way or the other, but Gwen may not have been able to speak Welsh well enough to offer much assistance to her husband on the matter.

*c 'Social Life In Mid-Eighteenth Century Anglesey' by Nesta Evans (Cardiff, 1936)

5.7: Article entitled W. D., by Edgar Jones,

from 'Y Rhwyd' ('The Net'), May 1986, p 3

The other day I was in Ty Frannan, in Bodedern parish. I was very pleased to see two people as young as Mr and Mrs John Griffith, the owners, taking the utmost care to ensure that the character of this Welsh cottage was not destroyed by their renovation. The modern part has been built in the back, without disturbing the original cottage. They intend to erect a slate to show that it was there that W. D. Owen, Queen's Counsel, [*a] author of the novel 'Madam Wen', was born in 1874.

After leaving Bangor Normal College, W. D. Owen was a teacher in Clay Cross, Derbyshire. There he met Gwendoline Empsell, (sic) whom he married. He wasn't very happy as a teacher and decided to study law. He was accepted as a barrister. Unfortunately he lost his health and returned to Anglesey, making his home in Rhosneigr.

The 1914 – 18 war left its mark on the young men of Anglesey. An office was opened in Llangefni [*b] so that the wounded could claim their pensions. W. D. obtained a post there and, at the same time, dealt with legal matters in [from] his home in Rhosneigr.

W. D. enjoyed the company of his fellow men and happily joined in the social life of the village. There was plenty going on in the early years following the war. It was a time to spend and to forget about the horrors. Factory workers earned enough to go on holiday for the first time in their history. Rhosneigr was a very pleasant place for visitors. The village grew like a mushroom. The hotels, villas and apartments were built. W. D. was asked to write a booklet to extol the area [*c] and in it he says that Rhosneigr is in the area of 'the famous Lady Robin Hood of North Wales'.

These were certainly happy days for W. D., but his Indian summer came to an end when he was told that he was suffering from tuberculosis and could no longer work but, though his body was frail, his mind was as active as ever. He began writing about 'the Lady Robin Hood'. [*d]

When he was a boy he had seen a cleft in a rock beside Llyn Traffwll. In his imagination he turned it into a cave. At one time, Jane Wyn was the owner of Cymunod. There is a memorial to her in Bodedern Church. Jane Wyn was a spinster, and like all spinsters had been exceptionally beautiful in her youth. W. D. called her Einir Wyn. At one time Huw Roberts was the tenant of Cymunod and he is remembered as 'Huw Cymunod', the exceptionally strong man. In the novel, 'Morys Williams', the squire of Cymunod, is able to lift Wil Llanfihangel, like lifting a cat, and throw him over the hedge. But the Robbers of Crigyll were assuredly the starting point of it all; no fruits of the imagination, these, but the servants of the devil in the district of the lakes. In his book, 'Llwynogod Môn' *[Foxes of Anglesey]*, the editor of Y Rhwyd *[The Net]* has written two chapters about them. Reading about their savage acts is enough to make your hair stand on end. The mouth of the River Crigyll is in Rhosneigr and, in the bay, there are jagged rocks. Sailing ships used to get hurled against these. The robbers would appear after a shipwreck making out that they wanted to help the travellers and crew but they used to kill and steal. The names of the robbers are known, like Samuel Roberts, Ceirchiog; Thomas Roberts, Llanfaelog; John Ambrose, Llanfihangel and John Parry, Rhoscolyn. These men were brought before the judge in Beaumaris. One was hanged and others exiled but the majority escaped.

W. D. died in 1925, with 'Madam Wen' newly published. His widow went to Caergeiliog to lodge. In the last years of her life she thought she could talk to the birds and the poor thing would go along the sides of the hedgerows twittering. She had to go to hospital but she was not forgotten. Mrs Mary Griffith, Post, Caergeiliog, told me that she remembered her mother-in-law, Mrs Catherine Griffith, visiting Mrs Owen. W. D.'s sisters were not forgotten either. Every autumn Miss Grace Hughes, Cymunod, went to the hillocks near Tyn (sic) Frannan to pick blackberries. Having filled her basket, away she would go on her bicycle to Rhosneigr. There were saints as well as robbers in the district of the lakes.

P.S. The old name for Ty Frannan was Cynddel's Garden. A man named Richard Brannan (who died in 1582) came to live there and the house started to be called Brannan Mansion. Cynddel's Garden or Brannan Mansion was in the field across the way from the present cottage. I saw the name Ty Frannan [mentioned] for the first time in 1789. The place was an inn from 1630 – 90. Ed. [of y Rhwyd]

Editor's Note:

Rev Edgar Jones graduated from Bangor University and started his clerical career in Holyhead. He later became a primary school teacher and worked for many years at Ysgol Gynradd in Cemaes Bay. After retirement, he continued to help out at many parishes on Anglesey. He never married, and sadly, Edgar died in February 2009 at the age of 76. He had drowned in lake Llywenan, near Bodedern. No suspicious circumstances were found. {507}

*a There is no evidence that Owen ever became a Q.C. (Queen's Counsel) although he did become a barrister, furthermore if Owen had been appointed to 'Silk' he would have been a K.C. (King's Counsel) as the monarch on the throne at the time was King George V. [Surprisingly, according to the Bar Council and the Ministry of Justice, there are no official records of appointees dating back before the 1980s].

*b See Biography section, Panel 1.1 on page 13.

*c There is no evidence to indicate that WD actually did this, although several of the 'Guides to Rhosneigr' do mention the Madam Wen, 'Robin Hood'. legend.

*d Madam Wen was actually written several years before this time.

References, Bibliography & Index

6 References & Bibliography

Unless specifically noted, all the photographs, maps, postcards, ephemera and illustrations are taken from the Editor's own collection and other relevant information has been provided in the caption. The Editor is grateful for permission to use additional illustrations and extracts from publications as noted in the text, or below.

Section 1 – Biography.

Principal Summary

101 (Adoption of middle names)
(i) A fascinating topic all of its own. Broadly speaking, it was done to demonstrate individuality in a society where the population was growing quickly and the practical necessity of doing so, particularly in the professions, was becoming ever more important. See several titles by the authors John & Sheila Rowlands. eg 'The Surnames of Wales' (Genealogical Pub Co, 1996. ISBN 0806315164)
(ii) www.bbc.co.uk/wales/history (History of Welsh Names).

102 Allegedly the Robin Hood description was penned by Owen himself, although the nature of Gwen's journalistic career (see section 1.7) suggests that it may have been her who wrote the piece, not him – if indeed either of them wrote it.

103 'Morlais' information extracted from several Rhosneigr Guides dating back as early as 1920, as well as Owen's diary.

104 'Laneton' information from the deeds, courtesy Mr & Mrs Jim & Carol Walker.

105 Soldiers Pensions Office (War Pensions Committees)
Service Personnel & Veterans Agency - www.veterans-uk.info/wpcomits/index.html.
Hansard, 28th May 1918 vol 106 cc687-790.
SSAFA (Anglesey branch) Sir Richard Williams-Bulkley, Lorna Wood, Mrs Pat Ade.
Ministry of Defence Archives "Accounts of Area Offices".
Royal Welch Fusiliers Museum, Caernarfon. (Brian Owen, Curator. Anne Pedley, Archivist)

106 National Probate calendar, 1926 (The National Archives, London).
Revaluation - www.measuringworth.com

Picture References

p8 (& back cover) photo of WDO, author's scan, courtesy Sara Richards collection.

p9 Owen family photo, author's scan, courtesy Robert Owen collection.

p9 Ty Franan, 2815.tif

p10 Clay Cross school, 4016.tif

p10 Newry Street Holyhead, 2736.tif

p11 Seaforth, 1899.jpg

p11 Ashton, undated postcard, ref 1663 no publisher listed, c1912.

p12 Valentine's postcard No.65292, undated, c1912.

p13 Close-up of masonic detail on gravestone, 2063.jpg

p14 Undated Real Photograph postcard probably by S.Feather of Rhosneigr. c1920.

p14 Jerusalem chapel, 2075.jpg

p15 Owen gravestone, Gwalchmai graveyard, 2068.jpg

General References & Acknowledgements

Bennett's Business Directory of North Wales (1910 & 1917) (Llangefni Archives)

The Law Society (Records & Statistical Office) London, www.lawsociety.org.uk (Theresa Thurston)

Bryngwran

107 Royal Society for the Prevention of Cruelty to Animals (RSPCA) Horsham, Sussex.
Mr Chris Reed, (Information & Records Manager)
Mrs Pam Rowe (Caernarfon & Anglesey Branch)
Mair Eluned (North Wales Co-ordinator)
Kate Jones (Regional Office, Cardiff)

Picture References

p18 Admission register, author's photo, courtesy Bryngwran school collection. 3518.jpg

p18 Bryngwran postcard c1910, author's scan, courtesy Vaughan Evans collection.

p19 Old schoolroom, 2590.tif

p19 Logbook, author's photo, courtesy Bryngwran school collection. p57.tif

p20 Class photo, author's scan, courtesy Vaughan Evans collection, c1900.

p21 Logbook, author's photo, courtesy Bryngwran school collection. p176.tif

p22 Logbook entries, author's photos, courtesy Bryngwran school collection. p195.tif & p196.tif

p23 Plaque, 2594.tif

General References & Acknowledgements

Bryngwran Community Council (Iorweth Roberts & Ceri Thomas).

Bryngwran Community School (Henry Jones & Mrs Dwynwen Powell)

Mr & Mrs Vaughan & Anne Evans

Mr Eric Hughes

Mr William R. Owen

Mr J. Richard Williams

Garth

108 Gwynedd Archives & Museums Service (Caernarfon) (D. Whiteside Thomas)

109 British School information from Derbyshire Record Office, Matlock.

110 Llew Tegid information from www.archivesnetworkwales.info (Bangor University archives – papers of Llew Tegid) ref GB 0222 BMSS TEG.

Picture References

p25 Garth school buildings, 2906.jpg & 2918.jpg

General References & Acknowledgements

CADW (The Historic Environment Service of the Welsh Assembly Government). Mr Mike Bennett – Listed buildings Section, CADW, Cardiff. ['CADW' (pronounced cad-oo), is a Welsh word meaning 'to keep'.]

Gwynedd Council - Bangor Planning & Conservation Dept. (Gareth Roberts)

Bangor Normal College

University of Wales, Bangor, Archives Dept. (Einion Thomas, Ellen Simpson & Ann Hughes)

Picture References

p26 Undated postcard produced for Sydney V. Galloway & Co, Bookseller, Upper Bangor. c1917.

p27 College yearbook, 1894.

Joys Green

111 Gloucestershire Archives. www.gloucestershire.gov.uk/archives (logbooks 1896-1923. S208/1), (Katrina Keir)

Picture References

p28 Kelly's directory extract, 1897.

p29 Joy's Green school class photo courtesy Rita James collection

p29 Joy's Green school buildings photo courtesy Peggy Kear collection

General References & Acknowledgements

A Brief Account of the History of Lydbrook by Father Michael, November 1991.

A History of the County of Gloucester, Vol.5

Archive-images.co.uk (Neil Parkhouse)

Cinderford Library (Janet Barker)

Forestofdeanhistory.org.uk

Forestofdean.net (David Watkins)

Historical Online Directories (Kelly's Gloucestershire 1897) : www.historicaldirectories.org

Joy's Green County Primary School Reunion booklet, 1993

Mrs Rita James

Mrs Peggy Kear (nee Douglas)

Mrs Margaret Miles

Mrs Sue Stafford (family history researcher)

Clay Cross/Clay Lane

112 Many School log books were examined and proved unhelpful. the list below should provide a starting point for anyone wishing to research this aspect of Owen & Gwen's life further. (CCUDSB = Clay Cross United District School Board.) (*nearby schools, but not part of CCUDSB)

113 Entries in various school log books note these visits – see also list below.

The following school log books were examined :

(References beginning 'D' are at the Derbyshire Record office, Matlock.)

Clay Cross Senior Boys (D6194/1/3 & D6194/1/4)

Clay Cross Senior Girls (D2867/5/1)

Clay Cross Junior Girls (D2867/5/1)

Clay Cross Infants (D2867/3/1);

*Danesmoor Infants (D7084/1/3)

*Grassmoor Primary School 1886-1904 (D4199/1/2)

Parkhouse Boys 1889-1912 (D2867/1/1)

Parkhouse Centenary Booklet 1889-1989 (L372PIL at Chesterfield Library)

Parkhouse (Lower Pilsley) Girls 1889-1902 (still at the school)

Parkhouse Evening school 1901-1911 (D2567/2/1)

Pilsley Evening School 1891-1910 (D236/6)

Pilsley Infants School 1900-1928 (still at the school)

Pilsley Boys School (D236/1/2)

Pilsley Girls' School 1876-1902 & 1902-1935 (still at the school)

The following school log books were not available, or not available for the dates in question:

Clay Cross Science School (missing)
Clay Cross Juniors (mixed) 1892-1900 (wrong dates)
*Danesmoor 1869-1892 (D6193/1/1) (wrong dates)
*Deerleap Charity School 1790-1853 (wrong dates)
Egstow (no school listed)
Parkhouse Girls 1902-1920 (missing)
Parkhouse primary (Junior, mixed & Infants) (wrong dates)
Pilsley Infants School 1876-1900 (wrong dates) (D236)
North Wingfield Junior (wrong dates)
North Wingfield Boys (missing)
North Wingfield Girls 1926-1930 (wrong dates)
*St Bartholomew's National School (D6196) (wrong dates)
Stretton Handley School (missing)
Tupton Primary School (wrong dates)
Tupton Hall School (D4393/1/1) 1930+ (wrong dates)
Woodthorpe (no school listed)

Picture References

p30 Clay Cross. Valentine's postcard, undated, c1910.
p31 Derbyshire Courier, author's photo, courtesy Derbyshire Libraries' collection. 3804.tif
p31 Elm Walk, 3668.tif
p32 Board schools, Valentine's postcard No.29615, card dated 1906.
p32 Inset photo, 4028.tif
p33 Board schools plaque, 3877.tif
p33 Coldwell Farm, 2853.tif

General References & Acknowledgements

192.com & ThomsonLocal.com (house names search)
British Library, Humanities section, London. Social-sciences@bl.uk (Michael Chambers)
Clay Cross Adult Education Centre (Norman Leah)
Clay Cross Chronicle (Derbyshire Libraries Collection)
Clay Cross Post Office & Royal Mail Delivery Offices (Chesterfield & Clay Cross)
Derbyshire Libraries – Chesterfield Local Studies (Lesley Phillips – Local Studies Librarian)
Derbyshire Libraries – Matlock Archives (Karen Millhouse – Archivist)
Derbyshire Times Newspapers (Mike Wilson & Ian Dempsey)
"Handbook of the Education Committee" (Yorkshire County Council) British Library, Social Sciences Dept, London (Phil Ruston) and Boston Spa, Yorkshire. (Sue Walker)
Kelly's Directory of Derbyshire, 1899, 1900, 1904, 1908. (Kellys not published in 1901, 1902, 1903, 1905, 1906 or 1907)
Kelly's Online Directories (Clay Cross 1899) : www.historicaldirectories.org
Mr Chris Goodlad, (Chesterfield)
Mr Trevor Nurse (Pilsley)
Mr Cliff Willliams, Clay Cross (who has also published several books on the area)
Mrs Joan Measham, (Family History Researcher), Matlock.
North Wingfield Primary School (Ruth Starsbrook, School secretary)
Parkhouse Primary School (Annette Cooper, School Secretary)
Pilsley Methodist Church (Betty Thompson) also Sandra Shaw.
Pilsley Primary School (Julie, School Secretary)
Sharley Park School (Karen Sewell)
Tupton Primary School (Christina Proctor, Headmistress)
www.claycross.org.uk (Neil Wilson)

Muswell Hill & Law

114 University of London Student Records Index 1836-1926. Senate House Library online at www.shl.lon.ac.uk. (Richard Temple, Archivist & Ruth MacLeod, Assistant Archivist).
115 (Gorsuch) The Database of 19th Century Photographers and Allied Trades in London. www.photolondon.org.uk
116 British Library – 'The Law Lists' 1841-1976 (system No. 011120411)
117 (i) The Bar Council, London and Cardiff. (www.barcouncil.org.uk)
(ii) Court of the King's Bench, Barristers Rolls (1868-1986)
The National Archives, London. Nationalarchives.gov.uk/catalogue (reference KB4)
(iii) Institute of Advanced Legal Studies, London. (Elizabeth Dawson) http://www.ials.sas.ac.uk/
Bar Exams : Vol CLE/11/7
Solicitor's Exams : Vol LSOC 10/046
(iv) The Law Society (Records & Statistical Office) London. (Theresa Thurston) www.lawsociety.org.uk
(v) Lexis Nexis (incorporating the legal directories from Butterworth's, Tolley's and Halsbury's.) www.lexisnexis.co.uk
(vi) Ministry of justice - www.justice.gov.uk

Picture References

p34 Raphael Tuck postcard (artist Charles E. Flower). dated 1904.
p35 Muswell Hill postcard courtesy Hugh Garnsworthy collection.

General References & Acknowledgements

Law

3 Serjeants Inn Chambers, London
Central Law College Library, Guildford. (Laura Sutton)

Chester Archives – www.cheshire.gov.uk/recoff/home.htm

Chester Assizes Records - recordoffice@cheshirewest.gov.uk

College of Law, Christleton, Chester. (David Battersby, Information Officer)

Court of King's Bench, Crown Side, and Supreme Court of Judicature, High Court of Justice,

Honourable Society of Gray's Inn (Andrew Mussell, archivist)

London University - www.london.ac.uk/history

Middle Temple Archives Dept (archivists - Lesley Whitelaw & Hannah Baker) 0207-427-4800

Middle Temple – Register of Admissions. pub 1949 (H.A.C.Sturgess)

Nicholas Street Chambers, Chester.

Queen's Counsel Appointments Office, London. (0207-831-0020)

Stanley Place Chambers, Chester

Whitefriars Chambers, Chester.

Muswell Hill

Hornsey Historical Society (Hugh Garnsworthy & Janet Owen)

JHK Estates, Muswell Hill (Felix Felix)

Methodist Archives – John Rylands Library, Manchester University. (Peter Nockles)

Middle Lane Methodist Church, Hornsey, (Emma Aidoo)

Mountview Estates plc

Mr Ken Gay

Muswell Hill Methodist Church (Gill Simpson)

Gwen's Publishing Career

104 (Laneton) see above

112 (Clay cross school research) see above

118 Pentre Traeth literally means 'Beach Home on the Headland' but here it roughly translates as 'home beach'. In WD's obituary, 'Pentretraeth' is given as the address of "Richard Roberts (cousins)".

Picture References

p37 Laneton photo RSR184. Reproduced from an original Francis Frith postcard, c1930s.

p38 Water tower from Rhosneigr Water report c1931.

p38 Park Mount, 2811.jpg

p39-40 Magazines in the author's collection.

General References & Acknowledgements

Mrs P. Gasson

Mrs I. Owen

The British Library (newspapers section), Colindale, London. (Stewart Gillies).

Bolton Local History Archives (regional office for the magazine 'Holiday Mail')

archives@bolton.gov.uk (Teri Booth)

Viv Burgess (independent newspaper researcher) vivburgess@yahoo.co.uk

Owen's Diary

University of Wales, Bangor, Archives Dept. (Einion Thomas, Ellen Simpson & Ann Hughes)

Picture References

p42 Bay Hotel 'Peacock' postcard No.MC2258, c1908.

p42 Pencarnisiog. Valentine's postcard, c1906.

p43-46 Author's photos, courtesy Bangor University collection.

Obituary

Y Cloriannydd *(The Evaluator)* – National Library of Wales, Aberystwyth.

Florence Nightingale Connection

119 Letters to Nelly Owen in Anglesey Archives dept. Llangefni. (See detailed LA refs below).

120 Interview with Nelly Owen, from Bryngwran school collection. Original source & author unknown.

121 Claydon House Trust Archives, Buckinghamshire (Mrs Sue Baxter-archivist) (Other major collections include the British Library, the Wellcome Trust and the Florence Nightingale Museum.)

122 - 126

Florence Nightingale 1820-1910 by C.Woodham-Smith. (Constable 1951) extracts used bypermission A.M.Heath & Co Ltd, London. (Literary Agents) (text of earlier edition available online at www.archive.org). [There had been other biographies of Florence Nightingale, but the 1950 biography, by (Mrs) Cecil Woodham-Smith was the first to make use of the enormous resource of letters and notes which had been gathered together in various archives. Despite the enormous quantity of material available, it is interesting and a little surprising that Ellen Owen, whom Florence calls 'Nelly', is actually mentioned by name (on p.578) in the 594-page book.]

122 Ibid p.433

123 Ibid p.578

124 Ibid p.577

125 Ibid p.577

126 Ibid p.577/8

127 'Bronant' advert from 1938 'Guide to Rhosneigr' by the [Rhosneigr] Advertising Association.

128 (Burial of Ellen Owen & Sarah Owen). Paran Chapel records provide brief obituaries, and Ellen's grave is not in doubt. However, despite extensive investigations, the burial place of Sarah Owen, who died on 24th July 1960, (there were other Sarah Owens who died on Anglesey at about the same time) has not been found.

129 (Verney/Pleasley)
Alumni Oxonienses : The Members of the University of Oxford 1715-1886 by Joseph Foster (1888) (Lambeth Palace)
Borthwick Institute, York University Library & Archives, (Emma Dobson)
Claydon House Trust (Sue Baxter, Archivist)
Crockford's Clerical Directory 1870-1876 & 1885 (Borthwick Institute)
Derbyshire Record office, Matlock (Dr. Margaret O'Sullivan)
Kelly's Directory of Derbyshire 1899
Lambeth Palace Library, London, www.lambethpalacelibrary.org (Rachel Corgrave, Deputy Archivist)
Norfolk County Council Record office (Edwin King - Duty Archivist, Jenny Watts, Victoria Horth)
Pleasley 'museum' (John Wilmot)
The Lodge, Old Lakenham, Norwich (Julia Leach, Ben Smith)
White's Directory of Derbyshire 1857 (Derbyshire Record Office)
York Diocesan Calendar 1873 (Borthwick Institute)

Letters To and About Nelly Owen - references

H = HM private collection
H1 WM 545/10
H3 WM 545/8 & WM 545/12
H4 Claydon, Sept 12th 1890 (not in Llangefni)
H5 WM 545/9
H6 WM 545/11
LA = Llangefni Archives collection,
LA1 WM 545/1
LA2 WM 545/2
LA4 WM 545/3
LA6 WM 545/5
LA7 WM 545/6
LA8 WM 545/7
V = Verney collection, (Claydon House Trust Archives)
V1,V2, V3 ex bundle N173, letters 1886
V4, V5, V6 ex bundle N174, letters 1887
V7, V8 ex bundle N175, letters 1887
V9, V10, V11, V12, V13 ex bundle N356, letters 1890
V14 ex bundle N358, letters 1892

Picture References

p48 Nightingale postcard by LS&Co, No.123, dated 1910.
p49 Lea Hurst postcard, Midland Railway 'official'.
p49 Claydon House, 3693.tif
p50 Plas Rhoscolyn, (13/31) courtesy Claydon Claydon House Trust Archives, Buckinghamshire.
p50 Inset photo of Plas Rhoscolyn, photo courtesy Emily Hale.
p51 (ref V2) author's photo, courtesy Claydon House Trust Archives.
p52 (ref H3) author's photo, courtesy HM collection.
p54 Plas Rhianfa from Bangor. 2902.jpg
p55 (ref LA8) courtesy Llangefni Archives collection.
p56 Owen sisters photo courtesy H.Morgan collection.
p57 Owen sisters & mother, photo courtesy Bryngwran school collection.

General References & Acknowledgements

David J.Wright (Sheffield University Dept. of Nursing & Midwifery)
Williams & Goodwin, Bangor (Rhianfa) (Mr Tim Goodwin)
The Florence Nightingale Musuem, St Thomas's Hospital, London. (Kirsteen Nixon, collections manager) www.florence-nightingale.co.uk
The Claydon Estate, Buckinghamshire (Sir Edmund Verney)
Dr Lynn McDonald PhD, University of Guelph, Ontario, Canada.
Shore family of Norton Hall (courtesy P. Paskiewicz) www.geocities.com/layedwyer/smith.htm
The Life of Florence Nightingale by Sarah A. Tooley, Cassell & Co, 1914. (full text available online at www.archive.org
www.1911census.co.uk
www.ancestry.com
www.archivesnetworkwales.info
www.countryjoe.com (Nightingale family tree)
www.florence-nightingale-avenging-angel.co.uk
www.jstor.org (Frances Parthenope, Lady Verney)
www.maximiliangenealogy.co.uk
www.rootsweb.com
www.telegraph.co.uk/news/obituaries (Sir Ralph Verney)
www.thepeerage.com

Rhosneigr & Anglesey (general)

Mr Dave Buckland
Mr & Mrs Michael & Carolyn Clark (Seaforth)

Mr J.B. Cowell
Mr John Donovan (Anglesey Golf Club)
Mrs Pauline Gasson
Mr & Mrs John & Audrey Griffiths (Ty Franan)
Mrs Ann Eastman
Dr Maredudd Ap Huw
Mr Iolo Jenkins
Mrs Eleanor King
Mrs Dilys Moore
Mr Anthony S. Moore
Mrs Haulwen Morgan (nee Owen) & Gareth Morgan
Mr Charles 'Tiffy' Owen
Mrs Beryl Owen & the late Arthur G. Owen
Mrs Ida Owen (Carna)
Mr Gordon Owen (Caergeiliog)
Mr John Owen (Altrincham)
Mr Robert Owen (Carna)
Mrs Eflyn Owen-Jones
Mr Martyn Rees
Mrs Marion Reeve
Mrs Sara Richards (Bronant)
Mr Arthur Roberts (Y Rhwyd)
Mr Tomos Roberts
Mrs Sheila Rowlands (Welsh Names)
Mr Charles Stephenson
Mr Maldwyn Thomas
Dr Dafydd Wyn Williams
Mrs Olwen Williams (widow of Mr Huw Williams)
Mr William Williams
Mr Stewart Wood
Anglesey County Record Office, Llangefni. (Anne Venables, Gaynor Nice, Amanda Sweet)
archives@anglesey.gov.uk
Guide to Rhosneigr (c1914) Llangefni Archives ref 3569 (and other editions in the editor's collection)
Llanfihangel yn Nhowyn - http://www.tywyn.anglesey.sch.uk/school.htm
National Library of Wales, Aberystwyth. (Mark Strong, Reader Services)
Towyn Trewan & District Community Group (Roger Foreman)

Churches & Chapels

English Presbyterian Church, Newry St., Holyhead (Selwyn Rees, Treasurer)
Gwalchmai Uchaf (Jerusalem) Chapel (Lewis R. Jones, Evan Evans, Dewi Parry)
New Park English Baptist Chapel, Newry St., Holyhead (Clive Alder, Minister)
Paran Chapel (Mrs Enid Jones)
St Maelog's Church, Llanfaelog (Rev. Madeline Brady)
Christ Church, Morristown, Rhosneigr (now converted to a private house) (Mr & Mrs K. Dunbar, Mr D. Armstrong)
Horeb Chapel, Rhosneigr (Tony Golder)
Other Graveyards inspected include : Bryngwran (Eglwys y Drindod, Salem, Hebron), Llanfihangel yn Nhowyn, Caergeiliog (Siloth), Bryndu MC, Bodedern (Gilgal, Cemetery, Eglwys y Plwyf), Llechyched, Rhosneigr (English Church)
The Church in Wales (Diocese of Bangor) – Bishop's Office. www.churchinwales.org.uk
Gwynedd Family History Society, Caernarfon. www.gwyneddfhs.org (Gwyndaf Williams) whose information on many Anglesey churches, chapels & memorial inscriptions proved interesting but in the end, nothing of relevance to this research was found. These included – Llanfihangel Yn Nhowyn (St Mihangel) and Llechylched Old Church.

Section 2 - Elin Cadwaladr

201 Little has been written on nineteenth-century and early twentieth century Welsh fiction, but the following reference contains a wealth of information on serialised novels in Welsh :- Huw Walters, 'The Welsh periodical press: a survey' in "A Bibliography of Welsh Periodicals, 1851-1900", Aberystwyth: National Library of Wales, 1994, xix-lxxvii. (Dr Huw Walters BLib PhD FSA)

202 E. G. Millward, 'Ffugchwedlau'r bedwaredd ganrif ar bymtheg', Llen Cymru, XII (Ionor/Gorffennaf 1972), 244-64; *('Novels of the nineteenth century', Literature of Wales, XII (January/July 1972).*

203 Chapter One author's amendments in Elin Cadwaladr

Page 1: In the sentence *But let no-one jump to the conclusion that the people of Bryn Siriol lack sense,* the word used for 'people' was 'teulu', literally 'family'. This has been amended to 'trigolion' – 'residents' followed by a question mark.

Page 3: Originally, *The day had come when it was necessary to be serious* (i.e. David was no longer playing at preaching, he was doing it for real.) This has been altered to *The day had come for him to be serious.*

David is thinking about how ready was his wit when he had no audience – the word for 'wit' ('ffraethineb') has been changed to 'ymadrodd' – 'speech' or 'expression'.

...he doubted his own skill to utter his sermon has been changed to *he doubted his own ability to deliver his sermon.*

The word 'oherwydd' – 'because' has been inserted.

Mary Charles, his mother, was there also – the words 'his mother' have been crossed out.

In describing Mary Charles, the words 'incomparable good sense and true godliness' have been replaced with 'incomparable good sense, discretion and godliness'.

204 (John E Roberts & Mellor Rd.searches)
1911.census.co.uk
Stockport Library – localheritagelibrary@stockport.gov.uk (Andrew Lucas)
Cheshire Record Office –
www.cheshirewestandchester.gov.uk (Jennie Hood)
http://www.cheshirewestandchester.gov.uk/leisure_culture_and_tourism.aspx

205 E. G. Millward, 'Rhagor o nofelau'r bedwaredd ganrif ar bymtheg', Llen Cymru, XXIV (Ionor/Gorffennaf 2001), 131-48. *('More Nineteenth Century Novels in The Literature of Wales', January/July 2001).*

206 (TB shelter)
Photo : Cambridgeshire Archives, J476 Open Air Shelter, ref 1140/25/1/299

Cambridgeshire Archives - cambridgeshire.gov.uk (Sue Martin)

The Varrier Jones papers

Cambridgeshire Tuberculosis Colony – Papworth & Bourn.

Picture References

p62 Original 1905 raffle ticket.

p63 Newspaper Masthead 'Y Genedl Gymraeg', from 1913 edition.

p63-64 Author's photos. Scrapbook courtesy University of Bangor collection.

p66 'Davies' series postcard by Peacock (MC2446) undated, c1908.

p68 Paran Chapel, 2686.jpg

p69 Postcard of 'Y Bonc' by 'JRW' dated 1910.

p70 Golf Club, 3399.jpg

p71 Henry Farmer's Piano Tutor, 1910 edition, 3048.jpg

P72 Tonypandy postcard by Evans & Short. Postmarked 1908.

p75 Wm Walker & Co, Manchester – single page advertising leaflet.

p77 Comic Billiards postcard by Bamforths, postmarked 1914.

p78 Alexandra Palace postcard by NLPP Co, c1950s.

p79 Harmonium from small French trade card - Paul Ulmann, Clermont-Ferrand. Undated.

p80 Welsh Cottage Rhosneigr by S.Feather. Undated, c1920.

p83 Cattle postcard. Unidentified publisher, dating from late 1930s.

p84 TB shelter photograph. Courtesy Cambridgeshire Archives. See ref 206 above.

p86 Pavilion Rhosneigr, author's scan, courtesy Pauline Gasson Collection.

p87 T.B. postcard. Commercial Colortype Co. Chicago, 1920.

p88 Hymnbook cover, author's collection, courtesy Paran Chapel (Enid Jones).

p89 Mill postcard, Wickens series, undated c1910.

p90 Track to Traffwll. 1904.jpg

p91 Hall's Distemper label, by Sissons Bros. of Hull. Undated, c1920.

p92 Rhosneigr station postcard (spc354, RTAN p104)

p94 Valentine's postcrad No.315, undated, c1905.

p97 Kent postcard 1906 by Mockford of Tonbridge, Yorkshire postcard 1908 by E.Hawkins. (It proved completely impossible to find a photo of ANY Kent Vs Yorkshire match from the period. If you have one, please let the YCC or KCC archivists (or me) have a copy!)

p99 Valentine's Real Photo postcard, c1919.

General References & Acknowledgements

Kent County Cricket Club – David Robertson, archives curator.

Mr & Mrs D. Miller (Maen Hir)

Mr S.O'Connell (Minstrel Lodge)

Piano magazines – rec.music.makers.piano

'Piano' magazine, Witney, Oxfordshire. (Jeremy Siepmann, editor)

Yorkshire County Cricket club – Ron Deaton, archivist.

Section 3 – Madam Wen

301 A very brief interpretation of a small part of the 'Madam Wen' legend was published in 2004. Dafydd Meirion – Walking Adventures on Anglesey (p34-37). The short extract contained a number of story elements which, although they may have been orally associated with the legend of Madam Wen, were not in W.D.Owen's book.

302 S4C = Sianel Pedwar Cymru = Channel Four Wales.
The television channel was set up in response to sustained demand for a dedicated Welsh language channel throughout the 1970s and before. In response, the Conservative government of Margaret Thatcher made a manifesto commitment to provide a Welsh language channel and (after some civil unrest when the newly elected government of 1979 proved reticent to do so) eventually set up S4C under the 1981 Broadcasting Act. The channel's first broadcast was on November 1st 1982, just 24 hours before the English version, Channel 4, began broadcasting. [source: S4C & The Select Committee on BBC Charter Review, 2005]

303 The VHS video tape of the S4C broadcast film of Madam Wen (title No. 1671) is now also available in DVD format from : The National Screen and Sound Archive of Wales, at the National Library of Wales, Aberystwyth, Ceredigion, SY23 3BU. (Elen T. Jones)

304 Pirate Abel Owen – see panel on page 119 . Sources :

(i) The Pirates Own Book – Authentic Narratives of the most Celebrated Sea Robbers by Charles Ellms. 1837. (available to read online on free licence by project Gutenberg).

(ii) The Trial of Captain Kidd - edited by Graham Brooks, 1930.

(iii) Owen name image from - 'A Dictionary of English and Welsh Surnames' by Charles Wareing Bardsley (London, 1901)

305 National Fairground Archive, The University of Sheffield. www.nfa.dept.sheff.ac.uk www.nfa.dept.shef.ac.uk/history/shows/menageries.html

306 www.measuringworth.com

307 The 'Boat Tavern' at Llanfihangel-yn-Nhowyn has long since been converted to a private house. It still stands at the entrance to the village, at the junction of Minfordd Rd and the (unnamed) back road to Caergeiliog – and barely a mile from Owen's boyhood home. A photograph of the house is shown on page 148 and the oldest deeds are said to go back to 1725.

There was some doubt as to whether the name of the building should be translated as the 'Boat Tavern' or the 'Ship Inn'. 'Boat Tavern' is the literal meaning, preferred by most people I consulted, but 'Ship Inn' flows more naturally to 21st Century readers, The reader will see that I decided to go with the literal translation for authenticity.

308 Cymunod was, and still is, the name of a farm virtually "next door" to the cottage where W.D.Owen was born. Cymuned means 'community' but the precise meaning of Cymunod is not clear. (principal source : Tomos Roberts, co-author of 'The Place Names of Anglesey', ISBN 0-904567-71-0)

309 "The orphaned daughter of the noble Wyn family of Gwynedd". The author of the Companion to Welsh Literature, Meic Stephens states that Madam Wen was based on Margaret Wynne, the wife of Robert Williams, the squire of Chwaen Wen, *[White Windy Place]* [Anglesey]; Maldwyn Thomas has a more detailed view (see appendix 5.6). Also suggested, by the late Edgar Jones, was Jane Wyn, "The owner of Cymunod" but other writers skirt the issue. The legend that Owen embellished was undoubtedly based on something, but like all legends, it was probably a combination of factors, rather than one single event. Does it detract from the story? Not one jot.

310 (i) It is likely that Sherriff Sparrow's name was lifted directly from the Sparrow family of Red Hill, Beaumaris, several of whom were High Sherriffs of Anglesey in the late 18th and early 19th centuries. (source – Burke's Peerage, various dates).

(ii) 'Annals and Antiquities of the counties and families of Wales' (1872) by Thomas Nicholas. (available online at www.archive.org).

(iii) Constructing 16th century Welsh Names - www.heraldry.sca.org/laurel/welsh16.html

311 Llyn (Lake) Llywelyn was clearly intended to be what we now call Llyn Penrhyn, as in chapter eight, (in a short paragraph not included) a farm worker describes the lakes to the Sheriff - *"Llyn Traffwll is the nearest, Llyn Llywelyn the next one to it, and Llyn Dinam the other side"*. I am told by local informants that there are maps in existence which show the name of the Island in Penrhyn lake as Llywelyn Island. Tomos Roberts, in 'The Place Names of Anglesey' (ISBN 0-904567-71-0 p.148) notes that 'Ynys Llywelyn' relates to a 'peninsula on the lakeshore' but so far neither the National Library of Wales or Llangefni Archives have been able to produce tangible evidence for verification.

Picture References

- p102 Map of Anglesey engraved by Robert Baugh (1748-1832) and 'published according to Act of Parliament by J.Evans'. Undated, c1795-1797.
- p103 Book photo 3417.jpg
- p104 Cave photos, 1959.jpg & 1961.jpg
- p106 Rhosneigr Fair photo, Author's scan, courtesy Pauline Gasson collection, undated, c1890s.
- p110 Meissner & Busch postcard, undivided back, undated, pre-1902.
- p114 Rough sea photo, Rhosneigr beach, 0785.jpg
- p117 Pirate flag photo, Rhosneigr beach, 1556.jpg
- p118 Sloop graphic from 'A Dictionary of Sea Terms' by A.Ansted, pub. Brown & Son, 1919.
- p121 Storehouse photo, author's scan, courtesy Vicky Clancy collection. Undated, c1890s.
- p122 Real photographic postcard of Sloop off Irish Coast. Postmarked Belfast, 1906.
- p125 Madam Wen lying injured – original illustration comissioned for this book by Anna Brown, Sheffield. www.anna-brown.co.uk
- p128 Rhosneigr beach real photo postcard by Wickens & Co. Undated, c1920.
- p129 Bangor Cathedral, 'Peacock' postcard No.266. Undated, undivided back, pre-1902.

General References & Acknowledgements

Ann Corkett, Alice Whalley & Llyr Lewis (preliminary translations)

BBC Bangor (Gwilym Owen & Glyn Evans)

Miss Marged Esli

William Henry James (Tafarn y Cwch information)

Mr John Pierce Jones

National Screen & Sound Archive (Elen T. Jones)
rootsweb.com
S4C Cardiff (Gwydion Lyn - Communications Officer)
Tafarn y Cwch (Mrs Poole)
Wales Screen Commission (Mike Wallwork)
Y Cymro (William Owen, editor)
Llanfihangel yn Nhowyn information from :
A find of the Early iron age from llyn Cerrig Bach, Anglesey by Sir Cyril Fox. (National Museum of Wales, Cardiff, 1946)
www.tywyn.anglesey.sch.uk/school.htm
www.genuki.org.uk

Section 4 – Reviews & Comments

400 Madam Wen by W.D.Owen, published by Hughes a'i Fab, (Hughes & Son) Wrexham. 1925, 1929, 1975.

Hughes and Son were printers in Wrexham from 1820 to 1971, at which time they were bought by Llyfrau Drwy Llandybie. This company is now Christopher Davies Publishers Ltd of Swansea. In 1975, Madam Wen was reprinted for the third time, and sometime in the early 1980s, Hughes & Son was sold to S4C – presumably in preparation for producing the film, as at that time, copyright in the book would not yet have expired.

Source: Wrexham Local Studies Library (Joy Thomas) and Christopher Davies Publishers (Christopher Davies)

401 Other books published in 1925 from : (i) The People's Chronology edited by James Trager. Aurum Press (1992) ISBN 1 85410 234 6 (ii) www.nationmaster.com 1925 encyclopaedia.

402 Major websites consulted included Ebay, Amazon & Abebooks.

403 "A local tradition about Madam Wen, the lady smuggler, became far more detailed after the publication of W.D.Owen's novel of that name in 1925".
'Owen of Wales: The End of the House of Gwynedd' by Anthony D. Carr, 1991, p97

404 'The Oxford Companion to the Literature of Wales' by Meic Stephens, 1986, p454

405 (panel 4.8) (i) Wales and Cinema : The First Hundred Years by David Berry. 567 pages inc 100 b/w ills. 1996 paperback ISBN 0-7083-1370-1 (ii) Also : 'Channel Four in Wales' by Gwynfor Evans. 1982. (included in 'What's This Channel Four?' by Simon Blanchard, 1982).

406 Tomos Roberts, in *Tad Madam Wen (The Father of Madam Wen), Y Casglwr, (The Collector),* Volume 10, page 6, 1980. [Reproduced in full in Appendix 5.3].

407 Sir Thomas Parry – see note b to appendix 5.3.

408 Cydymaith i Lenyddiaeth Cymru (Companion to Welsh Literature) ed. Meic Stephens, 1997, p 561. See also Maldwyn Thomas's article in Appendix 5.6.

409 *Liverpool Daily Post and Mercury,* Monday, November 16, 1925, p14. [Reproduced in full in panel 4.3]

Picture References

p132 'Ogof Madam Wen' (and article) from 'The Children's Treasury' *(Trysorfa'r y Plant)* May 1938 p140/141.

p140 & 142 Screen-Grabs from the film, courtesy S4C.

p148 Tafarn y Cwch photo, 2805.jpg

p149 George Cockram Watercolour, 1208.tif

Section 5 – Appendices

501 'Hanes Methodistiaeth, Bryn Du, Mon', (The History of Methodism in Bryn Du, Anglesey). by John Watkin Hughes. Published 1912.

502 Trwan Beach – Before RAF valley was built in 1940/41, the area of Sand Dunes between Cymyran Bay and Traffwll lake was known as Towyn Trewan (or Trwan) and indeed this area of designated common land is still so named. The original meaning of the words are :
Towyn – Duneland
Tyn – Smallholding.
Trwan/Trewan – derived from 'Tref Owain' (Owain's House) according to the Anglesey Historian Tomos Roberts in his book 'The Place Names of Anglesey' pub.1996 Anglesey County Council. ISBN 0-904567-71-0

503 The complete article is shown on p132. The Children's Treasury' *(Trysorfa'r y Plant)* May 1938 p140/141.

504 'Cipdrem ar Hanes Plwyf Maelog' *(A glimpse at the history of the parish of Llanfaelog)* by William Williams (Llanrwst: Gwasg Carreg Gwalch, 2003).'

505 Distilled from a long Obituary in 'Y Glannau' (The Shores) in 2002.

506 Information about Margaret Wynne and her strange nature are given in Lewis Morris's ribald poem "The Lament of the Man from Rhyd Anghariad, or Rhyd Angharad according to his daughter on the *Great Medley,* a folk dance". (Cwrtmawr Manuscripts, National Library of Wales, Aberystwyth, [vol] 125).

507 'Tributes to Anglesey Lake Death Vicar' - Daily Post North Wales, Feb 14th 2009.

Picture References

p152 Screen Grab from Madam Wen film, courtesy S4C.

p155 Huws photo from 'The History of Methodism in Bryn Du' (see ref 501 above)

General References & Acknowledgements

Morrises of Anglesey – National Library of Wales – www.llgc.org.uk

Appendix 5.1 Cymru *[Wales]* November 1897

Appendix 5.2 Gwyr Mon *[Men of Anglesey]* ed Bedwyr lewis Jones. 1st impression 1979, Cyngor Gwlad, Gwynedd, pp145-147

Appendix 5.3 Y Casglwr *[The Collector]* vol 10, March 1980, p.6

Appendix 5.4 Yr Herald Gymraeg *[the Welsh Herald]*, April 13 1982

Appendix 5.5 Y Rhwyd *[The Net]* May 1982

Appendix 5.6 Y Faner *[The Banner]* Jan 14th 1983

Appendix 5.7 Y Rhwyd *[The Net]* May 1986.

Additional Bibliography

Dyfrig, Rhodri ap - 'The Welsh Language in the Media' by Rhodri ap Dyfrig (et al) – Mercator Media Monographs, 2006.

Hughes, Gwynn - *'Dewiniaid Difyr',* ('Amusing Magicians') by Mairwen & Gwynn Hughes, Gomer 1983

'James, W.H. - Tafarn Y Cwch' ('The Boat Tavern'), Y Rhwyd, August 1982.

Jenkins, Prof. R.T. - Dictionary of Welsh Biography (National Library of Wales)

(available online at http://wbo.llgc.org.uk/en/index.html)

OWEN, WILLIAM DAVID (1874-1925; D.W.B., 1145) lawyer and journalist; b. 21 Oct. 1874 in Ty Franan, Bodedern, Anglesey, son of William and Jane Owen. He was a pupil teacher in the village school and later in the Garth, Bangor (under L. D. Jones, Bywg., 464). He was also a student in Bangor Normal College. After spending a period as a school teacher he turned to journalism. After that he became a barrister and lastly he returned to Anglesey as a solicitor in Rhosneigr and Llangefni. He died in Rhosneigr 4 Nov. 1925, and was buried 7 Nov. in Gwalchmai. He married Gwendoline Empsell (sic) who was the editor of a women's magazine.

Owen is given a place in this volume as the author of the exceptionally lively and popular romance Madam Wen (Wrexham, 1925).

Bibliography - Information given by his sister, Miss Sarah Owen, Rhosneigr, to Mr. Hugh Jenkins, Rhos.

Author - Emeritus Professor Robert Thomas Jenkins, C.B.E., D.Litt., Ll.D., F.S.A., (1881-1969), Bangor.

Jones, Edgar - 'White Lady'. Anglesey Tales (Helfa'r Rhwyd) 2001 p99-100

Owen, William R. - Bryngwran yn 1871 *[Bryngwran in 1871]*. Y Rhwyd *[The Net]* April 1987, p6.

Owen, Hugh. - Hanes M.C.Mon 1880-1935 (the History of Calvinistic Methodism in Anglesey 1880-1935) edited by Hugh Owen. Published on behalf of the Anglesey Monthly Meeting by Hugh Evans & Sons Ltd., Liverpool, 1937. page 178. *"The same year that R.E.Jones* [one of the Deacons] *died, another prominent member of this church passed away – W.D.Owen, solicitor, and author of the popular novel "Madam Wen".*

Roberts, Tomos - The Place Names of Anglesey by Tomos Roberts & Gwilym T. Jones, 1996, ISBN 0-904567-71-0

Sturgess, H. A. C., *Register of Admissions to the Honourable Society of the Middle Temple (from the Fifteenth Century to 1944),* Butterworth & Co., 1949

Thomas, Maldwyn – 'Hanes Madam Mon' *[The story of Anglesey's Madam]* Golwyg, *(Sight)* March 28th 2002, p18/19. In which Maldwyn Thomas continues with his theme, as detailed in Appendix 5.6, that Madam Wen had a more sexual theme than the Methodist Revival and non-conformist traditions of the Church would allow. A topic which is beyond the scope of this volume, but which might surely be the subject for future study?

Williams, Huw - 'Madam Wen Eto', ('Madam Wen Again'). Y Rhwyd, April 1982.

Williams, William – Introducing William David Owen, the author of Madam Wen. The Welsh Herald *(Yr Herald Gymraeg)* April 27th 1982.

Unknown - *North Wales Chronicle,* November 13th 1925, page 5, writer unknown, funeral report under the heading Rhosneigr

Unknown - 'Madam Wen' by an un-named author, Y Rhwyd, March 1982.

Unknown - 'Madam Wen ac Ardal Y Llynnoedd' ('Madam Wen and the District of the Lakes') by an un-named author. Undated & with page 3 missing. Bryngwran School Collection.

Unknown - 'Myth Madam Wen,' Pais, Rhagfyr 1982 t12 ('The Myth of Madam Wen', Petticoat Magazine, December 1982, p12).

Unknown - 'Swn y Seliwlod', Pais, Rhagfyr 1982, t13 ('The Charm of the Celluloid', Petticoat Magazine, December 1982, p13.)

Other Documents Examined

Obituary 'Gwr cryf ei ben a thirion ei galon' [A man strong of head and tender of heart] Y Brython *[The Briton]* November 19th 1925.

The 1904 marriage certificate of William Owen and Edith Gwendolen Empsall.

The 1925 Death Certificate of William David Owen

The 1960 Death Certificate of Sarah Owen

The Owen gravestones, Upper Gwalchmai Chapel Graveyard

Government Register Office indexes of births, marriages and deaths

Census returns for 1871, 1881, 1891, 1901 and 1911

Register of Electors, Anglesey, 1915, 1919, 1921, 1924, 1929,

Index

Produced with the help of Textract.
www.texyz.com

7 Index

About the Author

Tim Hale was born in Sheffield in 1953 and still lives in the 'Steel City'. He first visited Rhosneigr with his parents and grandparents when he was about five years old, and from that time there hasn't been a year when he has not stayed in the village - for many years on Beach Terrace, and latterly on Harrison Drive. Half Welsh on his father's side he has always had a keen interest in the area's Local History and his first book, 'Rhosneigr Then and Now' (pub. 1990) provided the first published insight into the development of the village.

Tim has been married to his immensely tolerant wife Jane for over 30 years and they have 3 daughters, all Rhosneigr devotees.

About the Translator

Jenni Wyn Hyatt, (née Williams), was born, and, for the most part, brought up, in Maesteg, South Wales, although her paternal grandparents came, originally, from the south-west of Anglesey. She studied English and Welsh at Aberystwyth but then spent most of her adult life teaching and bringing up her children in Worcestershire. She has a son and two daughters, two stepdaughters and four grandchildren. She retired from teaching and returned to Wales in 1997. She currently works as a freelance translator and family history researcher and lives in Aberystwyth with husband Pete and cat, Mabon.